SCREENING AMERICA

United States History Through Film Since 1900

* * *

JAMES J. LORENCE
Gainesville College

PEARSON
Longman

New York   San Francisco   Boston
London   Toronto   Sydney   Tokyo   Singapore   Madrid
Mexico City   Munich   Paris   Cape Town   Hong Kong   Montreal

Executive Editor: Michael Boezi
Executive Marketing Manager: Sue Westmoreland
Supplements Editor: Kristi Olson
Production Manager: Joseph Vella
Project Coordination, Text Design,
    and Electronic Page Makeup: Thompson Steele, Inc.
Senior Cover Design Manager/Designer: Nancy Danahy
Cover Images: © Getty Images, Inc.
Manufacturing Manager: Mary Fischer
Manufacturing Buyer: Dennis J. Para
Printer and Binder: Hamilton Printing Company
Cover Printer: Phoenix Color Corp.

For permission to use copyrighted material, grateful acknowledgment is made to the copyright holders on pp. 207–208, which are hereby made part of this copyright page.

Library of Congress Cataloging-in-Publication Data
Lorence, James J.
    Screening America : United States history through film since 1900 / James J. Lorence.
        p.   cm.
    Includes filmography.
    Includes bibliographical references.
    ISBN 0-321-14316-7
    1. United States—In motion pictures   2. Motion pictures and history   I. Title.
PN1995.9.U64L67   2005
791.43'63273—dc22

                                                                    2004022544

Please visit our website at http://www.ablongman.com

ISBN 0-321-14316-7

1 2 3 4 5 6 7 8 9 10—HT—08 07 06 05

Contents

Preface

Of all the twentieth-century innovations in the communications media, none was more influential than the technological breakthrough that brought moving images to the silver screen. Before long, the entrepreneurs who had developed this new medium and the aggressive businessmen who saw the potential of the mass market found ways to tap the interests, hopes, and desires of first a working-class audience and then a broader middle-class clientele, both of whom embraced the movies as the democratic art they became. The result was the motion picture industry's emergence as the purveyor of a product that, like none other, touched the innermost thoughts and dreams of an immense moviegoing public. Hence, any student or scholar seeking a complete understanding of popular culture in the twentieth century cannot afford to ignore the feature film as a primary source that reveals much about the concerns, attitudes, and beliefs of the American people at the historical moment in which those celluloid documents were produced and consumed.

Film as Historical Document

This volume is based on the fundamental premise that students may be introduced to the nature of the historical discipline through exposure to these most accessible of primary sources, the motion pictures produced for the domestic market in the United States. Its primary objective is to promote a critical approach to the employment of moving image materials and to encourage their use within the structure of standard historical method. By treating visual materials as documentary evidence, students may expand their definition of source material and think in new and creative ways about the process by which history is written, learned, and understood. By combining critical analysis of the celluloid evidence with a careful examination of the print sources that support the visual images, students will participate in an important exercise in historical thinking while gaining a sophisticated and complete understanding of the cultural history of the United States in a period of breathtaking social, economic, and technological change.

As users of this text proceed with this analysis, it will quickly become apparent that film study is a complex and multifaceted undertaking requiring the same analytical rigor as would any other academic exercise. Students will not only examine the motion picture as historical document, but also gain an understanding of the filmmaker's techniques, tools, and procedures. Film is a unique form of mass communication with its own rules, a separate language, and a distinct set of artistic techniques. By devoting attention to the production process and the artists' approaches, the careful analyst will come to understand the film medium as an important creative field. This appreciation of the motion picture as an art form will be enhanced by exposure to textual criticism as well as the independent study of film history itself. In short, the movies have a history of their own and filmmakers bring independent creative talents to the production process.

Analysis of Primary Sources

Fully aware of these considerations, the history student must return to the sources for insight into the society in which the movies were first screened. This text is grounded on the primacy of historical context in a serious analysis of motion picture content and meaning. Hence, students and instructors will want to begin their analyses of each film with a thorough examination of the dominant themes of the historical era in which the movie appeared. At the simplest, most basic level, a film may be studied for its visual re-creation of the styles, conventions, assumptions, and values of the society of which it is an extension. More to the central point of critical analysis, however, historical context immediately becomes important. Each chapter includes a brief historical sketch providing background on the period under consideration and placing a particular film within that social milieu. Instructors may deepen this contextual knowledge with introductory lectures stressing the central themes of the era in which the moving picture first appeared. As they undertake the task of analysis, students must therefore begin by asking which theme or themes from that historical period the film is addressing. Armed with background reading and classroom lecture-discussion on historical context, students may proceed to the critical analysis of the motion picture that is the centerpiece of the chapter under review.

The critical process may be advanced in a variety of ways. When time permits, complete films may be screened in a classroom environment, so that exposure to the celluloid evidence can be a collaborative experience. Much is to be said for this approach, as it recalls the communal setting in which the films were originally viewed by American consumers. These sessions may occur during or outside of class time, but a group experience will best enhance student appreciation of the original community reception of the images projected.

If scheduling limitations inhibit this approach, it is possible that judicious employment of selected film clips will capture the essence of a particular film. In this situation, the instructor will surely want to provide full historical background as well as plot summaries that place the selections in an understandable context, so that students may extract historical meanings from the visual materials. The use of clipped extracts will also enable students and instructors to pursue comparative analyses of the focal film and other pictures released during the same historical period. These exercises in comparison may also be completed through the use of out-of-class assignments that enable students to make their own judgments concerning the relationships among contemporary films, which may then be brought to class for discussion. Indeed, one of the most effective approaches to the study of the film as social history involves independent out-of-class critical analysis of those films whose length may limit their classroom usefulness.

Whichever format is pursued, the text is designed to promote thoughtful analysis of the motion picture as primary source. Each chapter contains a series of analytical questions that should be considered before students are exposed to the visual images. The most effective use of the textbook begins with a thorough reading of the historical backgrounds, analytical material, and historical perspective sections of the text prior to film viewing sessions. After reading the background text, students should proceed to the print source sections of the chapters, which provide fuller historical context for an understanding of the immediate historical situation, production process, and contemporary reaction for each film. These documents will deepen the student's awareness of the social, economic, and political environment in which the picture was created. For each chapter, analytical questions are provided to guide students through both the print sources and the subject film. For best results, these thought questions should be reviewed prior to film screenings. Systematic use of the study questions will not only assist students in dealing with the documents but will also deepen understanding of the historical issues raised by the motion pictures viewed. Moreover, these questions will stimulate productive classroom discussion following exposure to the celluloid documents.

As students explore the subject matter, it will become clear that every chapter addresses one or more prominent issues and themes peculiar to the distinct historical era in which the featured motion picture was first viewed. Hence, films of the Progressive era will reflect the spirit of social and economic reform, while those of the 1920s will mirror the profound social changes of that period. Likewise, class relationships will dominate the movies first screened during the Great Depression, just as race and gender are addressed by the films of post-1960s America. It is the student's task to use the Hollywood product to illuminate the dominant themes of American social, cultural, and political life at various points in the history of the twentieth century.

The Impact of Film

Throughout this analytical process, it will be important to remember that the movies were a business operation—big business at that. As a consequence, students should at all times be aware of box office trends, critical responses, and other evidence of popular reception. In a capitalist society, the business decisions made by the entertainment industry speak volumes about the entrepreneur's best judgment concerning the preferences and interests of the target audience. Therefore, students may make judgments about the underlying cultural trends of a given historical era based at least in part on the popular response to the product of Hollywood. At all points, instructors and students must take into consideration the success or failure of a particular film as they make judgments on the dominant themes of an era.

Themes

As students explore the issue of public response, it is essential that they confront the problem of the motion picture's importance as a signifier of influence or reflective meaning. From the birth of the movies on, social critics have debated the issue of influence and scorned the motion picture as purveyor of allegedly corrosive social values. For reasons to be explored in this text, these forces were to result in the negative critique of the 1920s and the institutionalization of self-censorship by the early Depression years. The external attack on the motion picture industry has not abated as we move into the twenty-first century. Given the widespread assumption that the movies exerted a damaging influence on the American value system, students must themselves weigh the question of Hollywood's influence on social behavior and consensus values at various points in twentieth-century history. Each film should be studied with an eye to its impact on the mass audience and the social beliefs of the American public. Hard questions must be posed, beginning with the search for evidence to support an argument for Hollywood's influence.

As students grapple with the issue of Hollywood's influence, they must also consider the motion picture's significance as a mirror for widely accepted values and audience preferences. If the movies were essentially business operations, and as market research became more sophisticated, is it possible that films were designed to reinforce or reconfirm widely held beliefs and values? In this context, the box office response trumps the critical reaction as an analytical tool. Bearing in mind the meaning of audience response, students should think about the importance of a particular film's track record. In turn, this analysis should inform the student's formation of generalizations about the film's historical significance. At all times, the student must stay focused on historical context.

As students pursue their analysis of the film as historical document, several themes in this text will become evident. The central theme addressed in *Screening America* involves the importance of issues related to the intersection of race, class, and gender in twentieth-century American life. By examining the films included in this text, it will be possible to trace the development and evolution of American attitudes concerning the way in which twentieth century Americans have dealt with (and sometimes struggled with) the issue of multicultural diversity in United States history. Through careful analysis of selected films, it will be possible to track the changes in American thought, action, and policy on the problem of race in modern American society. Likewise, several films included in the text explore a variety of social responses to the changing role of women throughout the twentieth century. Students should watch for differences of opinion expressed at various historical moments and account for the changes observed. Finally, a critical theme explored in several films is the significance of class as a feature in the history of the United States. It will be important for students to compare attitudes expressed concerning social responsibility, upward mobility, and the character of class relations across the many historical periods addressed in this volume, with an analytical eye to the explanation for variations, depending on historical context. Any analysis of class relations according to Hollywood must, of course, consider the commitment of Hollywood to the preservation of the capitalist system of which the movies were a part and the way in which motion picture outcomes mirrored that economic reality. Reflection upon the links among race, class, and gender as addressed in the films explored in *Screening America* will reveal key interpretive strands in the fabric of American social and economic life.

Beyond race, class, and gender as organizing principles, this text also encourages the student to give careful thought to the place of the United States among the nations of the world in the twentieth century. From World War I onward, there has been an ongoing debate within the American public over American foreign and military policy, particularly on the question of American intervention in foreign conflicts. Students should note that the question of the United States as a responsible actor on the world stage, including the consequences flowing from the acceptance of that role, is addressed in several of the films chosen for analysis. The student should reflect upon the diverse attitudes expressed in the celluloid evidence concerning the position of the United States in world affairs, American diplomatic goals, and the sometimes unanticipated results of foreign-policy decisions.

A third theme that threads its way through this volume is the assumption that the motion picture is a visual record of American social history at the time of production. As previously noted, the Hollywood feature film can serve as a barometer of popular opinion or public concern at a given historical moment. In this connection, it is essential to consider box office performance as an indicator of the national state of mind at the time of a film's release. There is no better index of public sentiment on a public issue or social topic than audience response to a Hollywood product addressing that concern. Thus, students must be prepared to subject these social documents to painstaking historical analysis.

While penetrating cultural issues and the sweep of social change dominate the narrative line in *Screening America*, readers should never lose sight of the basic function of the Hollywood feature film—to entertain while exploring questions of social and cultural relevance to a mass audience. As Hollywood offered popular amusement and satisfied the needs and aspirations of the public, it provided Americans with images of themselves and the narrative of a national story that, in the final analysis, addressed the question of class amelioration and racial accommodation. It is the student's responsibility as a scholar to dissect the moving images produced in earlier generations to determine whether the American dream intersected with the reality of American life.

Acknowledgments

During the course of writing *Screening America*, I have benefited from insights and assistance provided by many gifted and dedicated people. I wish to thank my former colleagues Professors Blake McNulty of he University of Wisconsin–Waukesha and David Huehner of the University of Wisconsin–Washington County, both of whom provided ideas that found their way into this book. Equally valuable was the guidance offered by Harry Miller and Maxine Ducey, both skilled professionals at the Wisconsin Historical Society, in accessing the invaluable resources of the Wisconsin Center for Film and Theater Research. Their work eased the task of researching and preparing materials for inclusion in this volume.

Of course, no enterprise of this sort can succeed without the support of progressive academic institutions that recognize that time is the most important resource for any scholar seeking to complete a major writing project. I therefore express my appreciation to the Gainesville College Social Sciences Division for providing me with the opportunity to complete the manuscript. Dr. Charles Karcher and President Martha Nesbitt were helpful in understanding the important link between teaching and scholarship, so that work on this book could be considered an important extension of my duties as Eminent Scholar of History. Both Julia Davies and Suzanne Polk eased the process of manuscript preparation.

I also owe a debt of gratitude to the dedicated editors and staff at Longman Publishers and Thompson Steele, without whom this book could not have been completed. Special thanks are due to Priscilla McGeehon for shepherding the project through its final phases under difficult circumstances, Teresa Minnaugh for bringing the concept of the publisher's attention, and Ashley Dodge for her encouragement when the volume was only an idea. I am also grateful to the many scholars and readers who provided useful criticism and helpful suggestions for the book's improvement at various stages of its development. Finally, Jacob Drill handled many of the crucial details of manuscript preparation that have contributed to a successful outcome.

I'd like to thank the following reviewers for their insight and advice: Allan W. Austin, College Misericordia; Alan Bloom, Valparaiso University; Herbert Ershkowitz,

Temple University; David R. Huehner, University of Wisconsin—Washington County; Juli Jones, St. Charles Community College; John H. Lenihan, Texas A&M University; Chris H. Lewis, University of Colorado at Boulder; Joanne Maypole, Front Range Community College; Anne Paulet, Humboldt State University; David Richards, SUNY Oneonta; Cornelia F. Sexauer, University of Wisconsin—Marathon County; Bryant Simon, Temple University; and Paddy Swiney, Tulsa Community College.

In a larger sense, I am obligated to those scholars who have in recent years taken the motion picture seriously as a primary source and thereby prepared the ground for a text that advances our ability to employ film in a classroom setting. I have been fortunate to have learned from many historians, film studies scholars, and other students of film about the problems and opportunities presented by the motion picture as a teaching resource. Among those who have provided inspiration are John O'Connor, David Culbert, Robert Toplin, Stephen Vaughn, Thomas Doherty, and Paul Buhle, all of whose work has taught me much about film as historical document. It is my hope that this volume will contribute to the serious study of the motion picture as a central feature of twentieth-century cultural history.

JAMES J. LORENCE

Introduction

The Analysis of Primary Sources

Primary Sources and Critical Thinking

The study and interpretation of history takes place on hotly contested terrain. It is not at all unusual for two competent historians to arrive at strikingly different conclusions while examining the same historical evidence. The process of arriving at those conclusions through disciplined interrogation of the available sources lies at the heart of the historian's work. Effective historical analysis therefore requires the student to use available evidence to arrive at independent conclusions and shape an understanding of the past. As a critical analyst, you are expected to question the sources as you develop your arguments about issues and problems faced by the men and women of previous generations. While you strive to be objective in your examination of the sources, it is important to recognize that other readings of the evidence may lead some history students to arrive at conflicting interpretations. The reasoned development of these differences is the heart of the analytical process we call "historical thinking." You will become more comfortable with uncertainty as you work to support your view of the past with a combination of logic and evidence.

The raw material used in framing the historian's arguments is to be found in documents known as *primary sources*. A primary source is some form of direct record original to the historical period you are studying. These records are the materials that survive from the past; they provide the body of evidence that may be used as students make their own sense out of history. The sources may be found in many forms: written, visual, or material. What they have in common is their origin in a particular time frame subject to historical examination.

In order to employ the sources as historical evidence, students must work to think historically. In so doing, there must be a conscious effort to analyze the available records in order to find meaning in these raw materials of historical scholarship. This process begins with the development of the habit of skepticism. The critical exercise is rooted in an awareness of the full historical context in which a document was created, including the social, economic, political, and cultural environment that prevailed when the item first appeared. Equally important is knowledge of the witness's personal background, assumptions, motivations, biases, and purposes at the time a document was created. The key feature of the critical process now set in motion involves the framing of good questions. Always look beyond the literal meaning of the document and inquire into the objectives

1

of its author. Remember that the analysis of evidence is a questioning exercise. The questions to be raised include the following:

1. To whom or to what audience was the document addressed?
2. What was the witness's objective?
3. When did the document appear?
4. What content in the document helps you to know why it was created?
5. How are words used to convey meaning?
6. How does the document compare with other sources from the same era?
7. Was the witness in a position to know that this account was accurate?
8. How much time elapsed between the actual event and the creation of the document describing it?
9. What are your own biases and assumptions?

After questioning the text, you are ready for the crucial critical act—the exercise of historical imagination. Once you have screened the source for motives and bias, you are prepared to make a historical judgment. What do your own critical powers tell you about the document's reliability and meaning? What conclusions may be drawn about the source as a reflection of the society in which it was created? Recognize the limits of historical interpretation on the basis of the surviving evidence, and accept the resulting uncertainty as you explore other sources related to the subject of your analysis.

The Motion Picture as Primary Source

While historians have usually focused on written evidence as they frame their discussion of the past, this volume invites students to broaden the definition of historical documentation to include the motion picture as primary source. In recent years, historians have recognized that movies are celluloid documents that record the values, attitudes, concerns, and issues that prevailed in the society and culture in which they were produced and viewed. The primary assumption on which *Screening America* is based is the idea that motion pictures may be studied as primary sources from which students may derive important knowledge and frame conclusions about the historical period in which the films first appeared. Studied in combination with print sources, films can open a door that enable us to better understand the people and problems of the past.

While not exclusively focused on Hollywood, this book stresses feature films produced and marketed in the twentieth-century United States. This approach makes sense because in a capitalistic society, the product of the film industry is a consumer item that must meet the needs of the public for which movies are made. Movies must be relevant to the audience, speak its language, and address issues of wide interest. In 1929, MGM producer Irving Thalberg argued that movies were the most effective medium for showing future generations how Americans lived because they had to sell and therefore address themes familiar to moviegoers. Similarly, modern film scholar I. C. Jarvie asserts that "there is nothing comparable from the point of view of getting under the skin of a . . . society as viewing the films made for the home market."[1] By the 1920s the movie business ranked among the ten most profitable industries in the United States; to remain successful, it was essential that its product appeal to the interests and tastes of the mass audience. The topical material addressed in motion pictures therefore reflected the preferences of consumers in the age of mass culture.

Because they are valid documents, films must be studied with the same critical rigor students apply to other forms of historical evidence. Many of the questions applied to other primary sources are equally useful as analytical tools in the examination of celluloid evidence. The critical exercise thus begins with thoughtful consideration of the social, economic, and cultural context in which a film is produced and viewed. Careful attention should be paid to the circumstances and conditions under which a motion picture came into existence. Students must raise rigorous analytical questions.

1. In what way does the movie reflect the society in which it appeared, and what does it tell us as historians of that historical moment?
2. Is there evidence that the motion picture influenced contemporary viewers? In what way, if any, did the film play a role in shaping history?
3. What evidence does the film offer of the styles, patterns, designs, and language of the historical period in which it appeared?
4. How was the film part of the experience of Americans in the audience at a given time and place? What did it mean to the original viewers?
5. How does the movie clarify or illuminate the most important historical themes of the period in which it was first screened?[2]

Beyond the study of historical context, film content and directorial/technical approach must also be subject to close examination, with attention to visual images, the use of light and shadow, film editing, sound track, and the ways in which these elements are combined to create the final product. Finally, no analysis is complete without attention to audience and critical response,[3] since box office performance may be understood as one measure of the producers' success in tapping public interest.

Of course, not every film was intended for the mass audience. The study of documentary film raises additional analytical questions. The study of documentaries presents problems that are related to, but different from, those relevant to feature films. Of particular importance are the purposes of production and the target audience. The goals of the filmmaker are especially significant because documentary film is openly intended to make an argument. Among the other questions to be considered when studying documentaries are the following:

1. To what extent did such films serve a propaganda purpose?
2. Which footage was incorporated into the document and what was discarded? Why were these choices made?
3. How did the film's narrative and visual language support the central themes of the picture?

Always be aware of the motion picture's limits as a historical source that must be screened for bias. Remember that the visual image, including documentary footage, does not "speak for itself" without further critical examination.

Reading Film: The Analytical Process

In order to study the motion picture as historical document, it is very important to consider the elements of film production and language. While this book focuses on the social and cultural context in which films are created, the analytic process will improve with careful attention to the fundamentals of film construction and visual language. In order to subject a film to close analysis, you must become familiar with the language of visual communication. The key feature of film construction is the basic shot, a single, uninterrupted piece of footage. Scenes are created by linking a series of shots in an orderly way. Through editing, shots are logically connected to one another. In turn, scenes are linked together to produce sequences that express a theme. The basic elements in film production include shot length, lighting, color, field (distance of action from camera), camera angle, camera movement, focus, lens characteristics, and projection speed. Try to be aware of the way in which these elements are combined to create a completed product with the intended effect. Observe the way in which images are joined to one another through editing and cutting. Consider the impact of sound on emotional response, sensation, and interpretation. Language, sound effects, and music should all be seen as devices used by filmmakers to produce a desired reaction in an audience. Try to make judgments on how such filmmakers' techniques may or may not have influenced audience response. In sum, historical analysis can be enriched through an awareness of the elements of filmmaking.[4] You must learn to "read" a film. Sharpened visual literacy is an essential skill that not only opens the door to the past and its treasures, but also provides us with a valuable tool as we are confronted with media images in our own time. As you become more comfortable with analysis of the motion picture as primary source, you will develop the ability to screen information in the modern world of multiple visual images and conflicting ideas.

Historical Background: The Origins of the Motion Picture Industry

One of the most important technological developments of the late nineteenth century focused on the reproduction of faithful visual images, first by photography and finally through the introduction of moving images that seemed to capture life itself. From 1890 on, inventors on both sides of the Atlantic experimented with a variety of technologies that resulted in the introduction of the motion picture camera and the projection of moving images on the silver screen. This important technological change coincided with the social transition that accompanied the rapid industrialization of the United States following the Civil War. The mechanical reproduction of images in motion soon exerted a strong influence on the values, beliefs, and social behavior of early twentieth-century Americans. These images both appealed to and reflected the interests of early movie audiences.

The key personality in the United States was the brilliant inventor Thomas Alva Edison, whose laboratories in 1893 developed the basic motion picture technology that was to become a strong influence on American popular culture during the twentieth century. The first Edison kinetoscope machine was an instant success, but the inventor understood that because of the limited size of the images it created, other technologies would replace it. Once his firm had introduced a larger machine capable of projecting life-sized images on a screen, Edison worked to defeat several competitors who appeared in the mid-1890s. Always an aggressive businessman, he attempted to monopolize the field, with little success. By 1896, several systems competed with the Edison projection machine to provide commercial exhibition. In that year, Edison's system was used when the first commercially shown motion picture appeared at Koster and Bial's Music Hall next to Macy's on New York's Herald Square. A new and powerful technology had entered the field of commercialized mass entertainment.

Edison's attempts to control the market failed and by the early twentieth century, several firms had entered the field of motion picture exhibition, including the American exhibitors of the French Lumiere Brothers' machine and the American Mutoscope and Biograph Company. At first, the motion picture seemed a novelty, usually seen as an add-on to other forms of entertainment such as live vaudeville theater programs. For the first ten years, films projected were short subjects, perhaps eight to ten minutes in length. As a result, the earliest movies failed to develop clear story lines. It was not until 1903 that the first distinct and complete story line was to appear in *The Great Train Robbery*, a change that foreshadowed the motion picture's potential as an entertainment medium.

While the movie industry was in its infancy, the social and political climate changed in a way that helped create a sympathetic audience. From the 1880s on, the rising tide of immigration and a burgeoning industrial economy contributed to the rapid growth of America's cities. Urbanization and industrialization, in turn, expanded the size of the movie-going public. During the Progressive reform era of the early twentieth century, movie theaters provided a democratic site devoted to motion picture exhibition for a large working-class audience. At this time, the movies assumed greater social importance as an expression of a lively popular culture.

What made this development possible was the sharp increase in immigration into the urban communities of the United States in the late nineteenth and early twentieth centuries. Because the industrial economy required a larger labor force, millions of immigrants poured into the cities, where the younger generation, especially, sought new forms of popular amusement. The gathering places of the worker community included dance halls, saloons, music halls, sports events, and vaudeville houses, all of which aroused middle-class suspicions of the new mass entertainment. By 1905, small businessmen, often immigrants themselves, had begun to open motion picture exhibition spaces referred to as nickelodeon theaters, where for the five-cent admission fee, immigrant working-class audiences could be part of a truly democratic entertainment experience. These audiences, often multiethnic and poor, were actively drawn into the events portrayed on-screen. The movies were on the way to becoming the "peoples' entertainment."

Many new storefront theaters sprang up in the same working-class neighborhoods, where they competed fiercely with one another as well as other leisure entertainments. While movie theaters could be found in most small towns and mid-sized municipalities, the center of nickelodeon theater and immigrant presence was clearly the worker community of America's large cities. Because the movies and their audiences displayed immigrant working-class values, Progressive era reformers often found the nickelodeon theaters and other popular entertainment houses threatening. Due to their alleged moral deviance, open sexuality, earthy musical preferences, and robust ethnic diversity, immigrant audiences drew the attention of middle-class moralists. In order to force middle-class morality on the growing immigrant population, moral reform organizations and urban governments fixed their attention on the leisure behavior of the urban poor. To protect a middle-class definition of sexual behavior, brothels were eliminated, public health was emphasized, and nickelodeon theaters were subjected to the regulatory eye of local censorship boards. A clash of cultures had produced a challenge to the rapidly expanding motion picture exhibition business.

The increased attention devoted to nickelodeon film fare reflected important changes in film production and content. After 1905, ten-minute novelty films were gradually replaced by longer pictures featuring fuller plot development and the completion of a more complex story line in one or two reels. By 1909, motion pictures had begun to address such topics as sexual relationships, economic inequality, and violent behavior, all of which seemed inconsistent with middle-class morality. Equally disturbing to social reformers was the mingling in the storefront theaters of working-class men and women as well as the young and old. Some scholars believe that elite group disapproval also extended to the very idea that working-class people might have their own entertainment experiences, unregulated and unsupervised by the upper classes. This sensitivity to the democratic character of the early motion picture industry and the diversity of its audience was yet another factor in the moral reformers' concern over storefront theaters and film content. The end result was regular, sometimes heavy censorship of the motion pictures available to the audiences of Progressive America.

While moral reformers worried about the social threat posed by motion picture exhibition, business leaders tried to bring order to the very competitive movie industry that had developed by the early twentieth century. In a step typical of the business practices of the era, Edison and many of his competitors tried in 1909 to bring order to the young industry. In order to increase profit and limit competition, they combined to create the Motion Picture Patents Company, a business organization that soon threatened to monopolize film production and distribution. Created under Edison's leadership, the new company united his firm with Vitagraph, Biograph, Essanay, Pathé, Kalem, Selig, Lubin, and Melies. This organization (usually referred to as the "trust") hoped to shut out new competitors and return increased profits to member firms. The company combined production, distribution, marketing, and exhibition in a corporate giant capable of dominating this new form of mass entertainment.

A corporate combination that bucked the trend of Progressive era economic reform, the trust soon faced a strong challenge from independent businessmen who fought for a share of the profits generated by the expanding movie industry. By 1910, several independent companies resisted monopoly control by emphasizing the storefront nickelodeons now being neglected as the trust attempted to broaden its appeal to include middle-class theater audiences. The rise of the independents led to a series of bitter court battles in which the new competitors succeeded, which meant that several competing firms replaced the monopolistic Edison trust, which after 1914 no longer controlled the industry. The final blow came in 1915 when, led by the founder of Universal Studios, Carl Laemmle, the independent producers and distributors launched a successful restraint-of-trade lawsuit under the provisions of the Sherman Anti-Trust Act.

Even before the independents had beaten the trust in the courts, they shared power in the emergent industry. The younger, fresh competitors brought new energy to movie management and transformed the motion picture field through a series of production and distribution changes. In this period, film began to mature as an art form as feature length was extended to allow for full plot and theme development. For example, the revolutionary epic form was introduced with the release of *Birth of a Nation* in 1915. Equally significant were new marketing and advertising schemes such as chain distribution and the emergent star system that linked movie audiences with their favorite actors. Creative directors, such as the pioneering D. W. Griffith, experimented with new forms and techniques that permitted artists to showcase their talents in the most positive light. In the process, the independents lured the most talented actors and directors away from the more conservative trust firms.

As a result of the independents' initiative, new faces dominated the motion picture industry by the time of World War I, which itself provided a boost for the movies when

war-themed films drew new moviegoers to American theaters. As early as 1914, the inno-
vator Carl Laemmle shared the producers' spotlight with two aggressive newcomers,
William Fox and Adolph Zukor, both Hungarian Jews who had succeeded in the New
York entertainment industry. In fact, this second generation of movie executives was composed almost exclusively of immigrants who had accurately assessed the interests of the
largely immigrant working-class audiences that filled the theaters of urban America. Less
timid than the leaders of the trust, they explored sexual themes, humorous situations, war,
and other controversial topics on the screen. Similarly, they were open to the technical,
artistic, and business ideas that changed the motion picture industry in the second decade
of the twentieth century. They shared a determination to provide the entertainment
desired by audiences seeking diversion from the problems faced in their daily lives. For
this commitment to serve their clients, these young executives were to be amply rewarded
as the industry reached maturity during the "golden age" of the motion picture between
the 1920s and the 1940s. Fortified by wartime profits, industry leaders never looked back.

So it was that, by the 1920s, the motion picture industry had become one of the most
profitable business enterprises on the American economic scene. Recognizing the value of
large-scale operations, the industry's giants moved towards greater corporate concentration
after World War I. By 1930, this process had produced a group of firms that was to dominate
motion picture production and distribution until the 1950s. Paramount, Warner Brothers,
RKO, Fox, MGM, Columbia, Universal, and United Artists—these studios formed the
modern entertainment empire that created the democratic art we know as the movies.

After 1920 the capitol city of this empire could be found in the Hollywood hills of
Southern California. Yet in earlier years the motion picture production business had been
much less centralized. Early production facilities were to be found in such widely dis-
persed areas as New York, New Jersey, Chicago, Florida, Arizona, and, of course, California. Although movies were made in a variety of locations, the producers eventually
moved west, attracted by the perpetual sunshine that made year-round production possible. As a result, by 1930 the business was centralized in Hollywood, which became a
colony populated by the producers, directors, actors, writers, and other artists and technicians essential to what had become a major industry. The community also took on the
glitter that has long since been associated with the people who built the movies.

The glamour attached to the Hollywood image has long been linked to controversy
over the entertainment community and its influence on public morality. Over the years,
the industry's critics and defenders have debated the extent of that impact. Whether
movies influence or reflect social reality, since 1900 they have been the subject of cultural
controversy. As we have seen, Progressive-era social reformers expressed deep concern over
the potential sociocultural impact of the moving image. As a result, motion pictures were
sometimes banned, regularly censored, and often criticized in the period from 1905 to
1920. Middle-class concern over the allegedly damaging influence of movie morality
peaked in the 1920s in the wake of several Hollywood scandals that featured sex, violence,
and substance abuse. In an effort to defend themselves against public criticism, Hollywood
producers soon moved toward self-regulation by employing their own watchdog, former
United States Postmaster General Will Hays, who enjoyed wide authority over film
content and developed the industry's self-imposed standards designed to cleanse the
movies themselves while protecting the industry against social criticism. This set of standards, known as the Hays Code, controlled the movie product available to moviegoers from
the 1930s to the 1950s. When evaluating film content from this period, it is essential to

recognize the limitations imposed by the Hays Code as a factor in the presentation of a film's message. Only in the 1960s did Hollywood switch to the voluntary rating system familiar to modern film audiences. In recent years, the debate over film content resurfaced when Vice President Dan Quayle attacked the moral values displayed in the *Murphy Brown* television series. The continuing discussion of television and film content demonstrates that the issue of Hollywood's cultural influence remains unresolved in our own time.

From the beginning, therefore, the movies have sparked a wide-ranging social response. As we begin our examination of the film as primary source, be acutely aware of the motion picture as a cultural influence. Born at the intersection of Victorian and modern cultures, the movies of the early twentieth century provided Americans not only engaging mass entertainment, but also new cultural values that mirrored an industrial society in transition. It is your task to use the motion picture as a celluloid document that reveals the hopes, fears, concerns, problems, and preoccupations of men and women coping with rapid economic and social change. By subjecting selected films to close examination and analyzing film content in the light of supporting print evidence with an eye to historical context, you will gain a better understanding of several important themes in the history of the United States since 1900. In the process, you will also engage in the process of critical thinking about the past and its connection to the present. As you learn to "read" films produced by men and women of previous generations, you will develop critical skills that may be applied to the analysis of a variety of sources, whether print, visual, or material. All will guide you as you work to find meaning in the past.

Endnotes

1. I. C. Jarvie, quoted in J. Frederick Macdonald, "Film as Historical Document," Paper presented at American Studies Association, n.d. In possession of author.
2. For expanded treatment of these questions and their relevance for analysis of movies and the moviegoing experience as cultural phenomena, see Warren I. Susman, "History and Film: Artifact and Experience," *Film and History*, 15 (May 1985): 26–36.
3. For full discussion of the process by which a motion picture may be analyzed as a historical document, see John O'Connor, *Teaching History with Film and Television* (Washington, D.C.: American Historical Association, rev. ed. 1987), 7–9.
4. The visual language of film is fully discussed in O'Connor, 57–71.

Further Reading

Gabler, Neal. *An Empire of Their Own: How the Jews Invented Hollywood*. New York: Anchor, 1988.

Jowett, Garth. *Film: The Democratic Art*. Boston: Little, Brown, & Co., 1976.

O'Connor, John E., ed. *Image as Artifact: The Historical Analysis of Film and Television*. Malabar, Fla.: Robert E. Krieger Publishing Company, 1990.

Organization of American Historians. Film and History. *OAH Magazine of History*, 16 (summer 2002, special issue).

Powers, Stephen, et al. *Hollywood's America: Social and Political Themes in Motion Pictures*. Boulder, Col: Westview Press, 1996.

Sklar, Robert. *Movie-Made America: A Cultural History of American Movies*. New York: Vintage, rev. ed. 1994.

Chapter 1

Social Protest: *A Corner in Wheat* (1909) as Muckraking Film

By the dawn of the twentieth century, the American public had become aware of the social and economic consequences of industrialism and unrestrained capitalism. As the nation made the transition from an agricultural to industrial economy, it became clear that rapid industrial growth brought important changes in cultural and class relationships. The preceding generation had witnessed the dazzling advance of industrialization and urbanization, as well as the social upheaval that followed the collapse of the economy in the wake of the Panic of 1893. The Populist political rebellion of the 1890s, rooted in rural discontent but linked to the wider urban social crisis, focused popular attention on the increasing inequality in the distribution of wealth and power that resulted from rapid industrial growth. In this overheated social and economic atmosphere, social critics and intellectuals called attention to new problems that were to test the American commitment to democratic principles over the next generation. Memories of the labor disturbances of the 1890s, unemployment, and business failures encouraged reformers to explore new policies and institutions to defuse the social and economic conflicts and economic inequality that now threatened to shred the social fabric of industrial America.

The Historical Background

As a sweeping reconsideration of long-accepted principles such as laissez-faire economics and unbridled competition unfolded, Americans entered the age of Progressivism with a new openness to reform ideas. Progressive reformers worked tirelessly to humanize the workplace, democratize the political system, and reduce the human suffering that threatened social harmony. In order to accomplish the proposed reforms, it was necessary to build consensus behind policies and regulations that departed from nineteenth-century classical economics with its restrictive definition of governmental responsibilities. Crucial to this raised consciousness of social problems and proposed remedies was the work of journalists, novelists, and creative artists, who alerted mass audiences to the economic and social realities of the new era. Known as "muckrakers," these publicists explored the nation's most pressing social issues in literary works aimed especially at the new and broad middle-class audience of the Progressive era. Through such sensational works as Upton

Sinclair's *The Jungle* (1906), an exposé of the meatpacking industry, the muckrakers played a central role in developing public awareness of social abuses and popular support for new solutions to those problems. In the process, the print media of the Progressive era played a key role in the enactment of important reform legislation during the first two decades of the twentieth century.

As we have noted, the motion picture was one of the most dramatic media of communication to emerge in the early twentieth century as an influence on popular consciousness. Before the rise of the film industry, knowledge of the worst abuses of the general welfare had not always reached a wide public audience. Recent scholarship has shown that the film content of the silent era was much more political and socially conscious than that of later years. Among the topics addressed in Progressive era movies were the deadly Triangle Shirtwaist fire of 1911, the massacre of workers in the Colorado Fuel and Iron strike of 1914, and the sickening abuses in the meatpacking industry highlighted by Upton Sinclair in the film version of *The Jungle*. As noted by the National Board of Review in 1913, film was an influential outlet "for political, social, religious propaganda, for muckraking . . . [and] for revolutionary ideas."[1] As this statement suggests, the movies were employed as weapons in the class struggle in the early years of the motion picture industry's development. Film scholar Steven J. Ross correctly asserts that these early celluloid missiles struck with great force because they reached millions of viewers rather than the more limited audiences to whom the work of muckraking writers was addressed.[2] As you study the films of the Progressive era, think of their content within the context of that period's social reform movement as well as the contest for public sympathy and support.

Many Progressive era filmmakers chose to address controversial social issues in their work. One of the leading artists to employ such themes was the gifted director David Wark Griffith (D. W. Griffith) of Biograph Studios. Much of his early work dealt with worker culture and working-class problems in terms sympathetic to exploited farmers, workers, and their families. Griffith's films typically emphasized social and economic inequities, while characterizing the wealthy, privileged, and powerful as parasitic exploiters of defenseless workers. For example, he highlighted the problems of economic and sexual exploitation in such features as *The Lily of the Tenements* (1911) and *The Song of the Shirt* (1910). Always a gifted storyteller, Griffith filled his work with sharp social commentary. Consequently, you may compare him with equally effective muckrakers who communicated with a narrower audience through the print media.

Analysis of Griffith's classic morality tale, *A Corner in Wheat* (1909), must begin with its historical context and literary origins. The film's plot deals with one of the liveliest topics explored by the muckraking novelist Frank Norris in several of his works. Although Norris exposed the corruption and exploitative behavior of railroad and wheat monopolists in *The Octopus* (1901) and *The Pit* (1903), his short story "A Deal in Wheat" (1903), together with Channing Pollock's play, *The Pit* (1904), became the primary bases for the Griffith film.

Interest in the activities of monopolistic power brokers in the wheat industry and on the wheat exchanges actually dates from the concerns of the Populist Party, which in the 1890s had worked to expose the corrupt practices of wheat speculators, whom it attacked as enemies of both producers and consumers. After the return of higher grain prices in the late nineteenth century, the militancy of the farm rebellion declined. However, market manipulation by brokers, traders, and dealers continued to attract the attention of

Progressive reformers, who in 1910 introduced legislation to regulate grain speculators. While the intense heat of Populism had subsided, the interest of Progressive reformers in controlling financial manipulators made *A Corner in Wheat* a topical film after its release. It is within this context that you may best understand this film as a historical document of Progressive America.

Analyzing the Film

As you proceed with your examination of this film, it is important that you pay careful attention to the film structure, character development, and artistic techniques employed by the filmmaker in telling his story. Perhaps most significant are the editing and cross-cutting introduced by Griffith in *A Corner in Wheat*. Because the film blends three separate stories (the farmer, the wheat speculator, and the consumer), you should pay special attention to the ways in which the separate story lines are visually linked with one another through editing. Look for the central theme in the way in which the economic realities are perceived and experienced by the independent participants in a drama of greed and its consequences. Though the key figures do not confront each other directly, their lives and fortunes are closely interrelated. How does the film maker use sharp film cuts to establish a connection among farm, office, and marketplace? How does the tightly compressed plot work to show how the product of the fields is exploited by a ruthless commodities speculator to the disadvantage of the urban consumer unable to buy bread for her starving family? Consider the significance of the way in which the wheat king eventually meets his fate when, having cornered the world market, he accidentally slips into a bin of grain, buried in the object of his own greed.[3]

By examining the film's narrative structure and editing, it is possible to develop your critical skills while gaining a clearer understanding of the reform impulse so evident in early twentieth-century political life. Attention to cinematic technique may be combined with awareness of immediate historical context to strengthen your knowledge of American reform. *A Corner in Wheat* stands as a striking visual document of the social and economic consciousness of the Progressive era. Like the muckraking novels of this period, the picture demonstrates the impact of modern media on popular social and political awareness as Americans moved into the age of mass culture.

Thinking About Primary Sources

The best way to explore the muckraking themes evident in *A Corner in Wheat* is to begin with an examination of the primary sources contained in this chapter. A review of the excerpt from Frank Norris's "A Deal in Wheat" will familiarize you with one of the literary sources for Griffith's film. Be conscious of the relationship between the short story and the film based on it. In each case, try to assess the intentions of the work's creator and evaluate the respective outcomes. Next go beyond the work of Norris and Griffith to place their efforts in the larger historical context by considering the words of Senator Robert M. La Follette as a barometer of the Progressive era's political concerns. Determine how and where the film fits into the reform spirit of this historical period.

Finally, turn your attention to the marketing and reception of the film at the time of its release. Use the primary sources to detect the themes that were employed in advertising the picture. Since promotional materials often appeal to public taste, the advertising tear sheet will shed light on the producer's assessment of the potential market for the film. A comparison of the advertising copy and the film review could identify common themes that reflect the filmmakers' assumptions about viewers as well as elite group judgments about the target audience. The promotional campaign to "sell" *A Corner in Wheat* may be linked to the expanding advertising and public relations industries of the early twentieth century. Mass media and modern marketing, including alluring advertising appeals, were key features of the new age of mass culture. The film and the promotional activity surrounding its release were products of the modernization process well under way by the Progressive era. Critical analysis of this motion picture therefore sheds light on both the reform mentality and media culture shared by Americans in an age of transition.

Historical Perspective

Sincere as its moral statement may have been, *A Corner in Wheat* does not really offer clear solutions to the social and economic problems it discloses. Rather, the viewer of the Progressive era was able to cope with the emotional tensions created by this tale of exploitation through approval of the wheat king's unfortunate fate. As the viewer is left with the haunting image of the farmer sowing the seeds of future destruction, the film's deeper problem is left unresolved. Yet this film's biting social commentary had certainly shown the potential of the motion picture as a political weapon.

During the remainder of the Progressive era, the movie industry continued to project conflicting images of class harmony and social disruption. Not until the industry moved west to establish the Hollywood system would producers close ranks to deny class conflict, as their product was redesigned to fit the needs and worldview of an increasingly middle-class audience. By the 1920s, proponents of worker/labor films found that the resources necessary to the production process were often unavailable to those who boldly challenged the social assumptions that reinforced the business system.

As the moral outrage of Progressive consciousness weakened, most muckraking filmmakers of the prewar era turned to other pursuits. Creative artists like Griffith found that the national market was more open to epic films of sweeping scope and themes that increasingly stressed love, sex, violence, historical landmarks, and, during World War I , national glory and patriotic unity. As will be seen in Chapter 2, the brilliant D. W. Griffith was to continue his pioneering work in the movies by extending the sweep and dramatic structure of the feature film. His landmark production of *The Birth of a Nation* in 1915, while flawed by racism, would rewrite the rules of cinematic technique and address issues distinct from the social and economic questions raised by his earlier work. Yet the controversy surrounding *The Birth of a Nation* cannot obscure the Progressive commitment found in *A Corner in Wheat*, which stands as a visual reminder of that reform era's social consciousness. Griffith's muckraking achievement, when understood against the background of the literary product of its age, remains a revealing historical document of the humane vision that fired the first wave of twentieth-century reform.

Endnotes

1. Quoted in Steven Ross, *Working Class Hollywood: Silent Film and the Shaping of Class in America* (Princeton, N.J.: Princeton University Press, 1998): 35.
2. Ross: 36.
3. This analysis of the film's visual style and cinematic features is based in part on observations made in John O'Connor, *Guide to the "Image as Artifact" Video Compilation* (Washington, D.C.: American Historical Association, 1987). For further discussion of the picture's narrative and technique, see Tom Gunning, *D. W. Griffith and the Origins of American Narrative Film: The Early Years at Biograph* (Urbana: University of Illinois Press, 1994): 242–253.

The Primary Sources

A Corner in Wheat is based on two literary works by muckraking novelist Frank Norris, his novel *The Octopus* and the short story "A Deal in Wheat," a portion of which appears below. Like Norris, U.S. Senator Robert M. La Follette of Wisconsin focused on the predatory behavior of financial interests. In a speech before the Periodical Publishers' Association, La Follette, then considering a run as Progressive candidate for president in 1912, attacks financial manipulators, thus providing historical context for discussion of the issues dealt with in the film. The advertising tear sheet highlights the ideas used in promoting the film, while the review that follows reveals the picture's impact on critics and viewers at the time of its initial screening in 1909.

The Literary Inspiration
for *A Corner in Wheat*
The Bread Line
Frank Norris

The street was very dark and absolutely deserted. It was a district on the "South Side," given over largely to wholesale storage. . . . Every evening [the poor] began to gather about the side door. The stragglers came in rapidly, and the line—the "bread line," as it was called, began to form. By midnight it was usually some hundred yards in length, stretching almost the entire length of the block.

Toward ten in the evening, his coat collar turned up against the fine drizzle that pervaded the air, his hands in his pockets . . . Sam Lewiston came up and silently took his place at the end of the line. Unable to conduct his farm on a paying basis at the time when Truslow, the "Great Bear," had sent the price of grain down to sixty-two cents a bushel, Lewiston had turned over his entire property to his creditors, and, leaving Kansas for good, had abandoned farming and left his wife . . . with the understanding that she was to join him in Chicago as soon as he had found a steady job. Then he had come to Chicago and had turned workman. His brother Joe conducted a small hat factory on Archer Avenue, and for a time he found there a meager employment. But difficulties occurred, times were bad, the hat factory was involved in debts, the repealing of a certain import duty on manufactured felt overcrowded the home market with cheap Belgian and French products, and in the end his brother had assigned and gone to Milwaukee.

Thrown out of work, Lewiston drifted aimlessly about Chicago, from pillar to post, . . . and a park bench became his home and he "bread line" his chief makeshift of subsistence.

He stood now in the enfolding drizzle, sodden, stupefied with fatigue. Before and behind stretched the line. There was no talking. There was no sound. The street was empty. It was so still that the passing of a cable-car in the adjoining thoroughfare grated like prolonged rolling explosions . . . [they stood] absolutely still; a close-packed, silent line, waiting, waiting in the vast deserted night-ridden street; waiting without a word, without a movement, there under the night and under the slow-moving mists of rain.

Few in the crowd were professional beggars. Most of them were workmen, long since out of work, forced into idleness by long-continued "hard times," by ill luck, by sickness. To them the "bread line" was a godsend. At least they could not starve. Between jobs here in the end was something to hold them up—a small platform, as it were above the sweep of black water, where for a moment they might pause and take breath before the plunge.

The period of waiting on this night of rain seemed endless to these silent, hungry men; . . . The side door opened. Ah, at last. They were going to hand out the bread. But instead of the usual white-aproned undercook . . . there appeared in the doorway a new man—a young fellow who looked like a book-keeper's assistant. He bore in his hand a placard, which he tacked to the outside of the door. Then he disappeared within the bakery, locking the door behind him. A shudder of poignant despair . . . seemed to run from end to end of the line . . . owing to the fact that the price of grain has been increased to two dollars a bushel, there will be no . . .

Lewiston turned away, dumb, bewildered . . . he walked the streets, going on without purpose, without direction. But now at last his luck had turned. Overnight, the wheels of his fortunes had creaked and swung upon its axis, and before noon he had found a job in the street-cleaning brigade. In the course of time he rose to the first shift-boss, then deputy-inspector, then inspector . . .

But Lewiston never forgot. Dimly he began to see the significance of things. Caught once in the cogs of the . . . engine, he had seen—none better—its workings. Of all the men who had vainly stood in the "bread line" on that rainy night, he perhaps had been the only one who had struggled [to success] . . . . How many others had gone down in the great ebb? He had seen the two sides of a great wheat operation—a battle between bear and bull. . . . [While the speculator in wheat had profited], the working-man—he who consumed it—was ruined upon the other. But between the two, the great operators, who never saw the wheat they traded, bought and sold the world's food, gambled in the nourishment of entire nations, practiced their tricks, their chicanery and oblique shifty "deals," were reconciled in their differences . . .

SOURCE: Frank Norris, "A Deal in Wheat" (1903). New York: AMS Press, 1986.

U.S. SENATOR ROBERT M. LA FOLLETTE
ATTACKS FINANCIAL MANIPULATORS

The Centralized Control of Banking, Capital, and Credits

Robert M. La Follette

The country is only just beginning to understand how completely great banking institutions in the principal money centres have become bound up with the control of industrial institutions, the railroads and franchise combinations.

That there was a tendency on the part of great banking associations to merge and combine could not be overlooked. But while financial and economic writers had directed public attention to the fact and had even pointed out the opportunity and temptation for the use of this augmented power, in connection with the promotion of the speculative side of business organization, they were slow to believe that banking institutions could be so prostituted. Certain critical observers had, however, as long as five or six years ago, suggested the dangerous tendencies in this direction . . .

The plain truth is that legitimate commercial banking is being eaten up by speculative banking. The greatest banks of the financial centre of the country have ceased to be agents of commerce and have become primarily agencies of promotion and speculation. By merging the largest banks, trust companies, and insurance companies masses of capital have been brought under one management, to be employed not as the servant of commerce, but as its master; not to supply legitimate business and facilitate exchange, but to subordinate the commercial demands of the country upon the banks to call loans in Wall Street and to finance industrial organizations, always speculative, and often unlawful in character. Trained men, who a dozen years ago stood first among the bankers of the world as heads of the greatest banks of New York City, are, in the main, either displaced or do the bidding of men who are not bankers, but masters of organization.

The banks which were then managed by bankers as independent commercial institutions are now owned in groups by a few men, whose principal interests are in railroads, traction, telegraph, cable, shipping, iron and steel, copper, coal, oil, gas, insurance, etc.

This subversion of banking by alliance with promotion and stock speculation is easily traced.

There was every inducement for those who controlled transportation and a few great basic industries to achieve control of money in the financial centre of the country.

The centralization of the banking power in New York City would not only open the way for financing the reorganization and consolidation of industrial enterprises and of public utilities throughout the country, but would place those in authority where they could control the markets on stocks and bonds almost at will.

With this enormous concentration of business it is possible to create, artificially, periods of prosperity and periods of panic. Prices can be lowered or advanced at the will of the "System." When the farmer must move his crops a scarcity of money may be created and prices lowered. When the crop passes into the control of the speculator the artificial stringency may be relieved and prices advanced, and the illegitimate profit raked off the agricultural industry may be pocketed in Wall Street.

SOURCE: Robert M. La Follette, "Speech of Robert M. La Follette Delivered at the Annual Banquet of the Periodical Publishers' Association," Philadelphia, February 2, 1912, in Robert M. La Follette, *La Follette's Autobiography: A Personal Narrative of Political Experiences* (Madison, Wis.: The Robert M. La Follette Company, 1913: 776–777, 780–787.

THE SELLING OF *A CORNER IN WHEAT*

A Corner in Wheat: A Stirring Biograph Drama of the "Change"
Biograph Company

No subject has ever been produced more timely than this powerful story of the wheat gambler, coming as it does when agitation is rife against that terrible practice of cornering commodities that are the necessities of life. Laws are framed with a view of suppressing such nefarious transactions, and no more convincing argument could be shown than that set forth in this picture. Every phase of the question is illumined, beginning with an animated reproduction of Jean Francois Millet's masterpiece, "The Sowers." From the barn they start and with the grain sack hung from their shoulders, the two bent and knotted forms are seen trudging wearily over the plowed ground, their arms swinging in perfect chronometry with a slight gush of wheat grain pouring forth at each advance of the arm. In this scene we find the genesis of one of the mammoth industries of the earth. The foundation of life, for it is the foundation of the bread of life. How little do those poor honest souls realize the turmoil the fruit of their labors will incur. What a contrast is shown in the office of the Wheat King surrounded by his lieutenants, waiting for the word as he engineers the great corner, whereby he will obtain absolute control of the entire produce, not only of the present, but the future toiling of the poor sowers. Into the wheat pit on the "charge" we go, and there find a struggling mob of brokers with their all slowly but surely melting under the blast of the King's determination. At length the battle is won, and the Wheat King stands majestically amid the debris of wrecked fortunes. Here is the gold of wheat. He is lauded for his acumen, wined and dined and regarded as a man among men, little thinking of the misery and suffering his so called genius has induced. Ah! That is the chaff of the wheat. The baker is obliged to pay twice as much as formerly for his flour and so must charge twice as much for the loaf. Consequently, many a poor soul must go hungry. Furthermore the bread fund for the poor is cut down, and many a shivering wretch stands in the line only to be denied bread when his turn comes. There is no vengeance possible here but the hand of God, and God's vengeance when wreaked is terrible and unconditional, and one of the sins that cries to heaven for vengeance is denying food to the hungry. This cry is heard and as the King is showing his friends through the elevators into the bins of which are flowing the steady stream of his golden grain, he trips and falls into one of the bins and is buried. He has been called in before his God to answer. Our thoughts are carried back to the bent and knotted forms of the sowers trudging along, ignorant of the vengeance of the wheat.

Produced and Controlled Exclusively
by BIOGRAPH COMPANY

SOURCE: *A Corner in Wheat,* Advertising Sheet, Special Collections, Film Study Center, Museum of Modern Art, New York, in O'Connor, *Guide to the "Image as Artifact,"* Video Compilation, Document 13-C.

CRITICAL REACTION TO THE FILM
A Corner in Wheat
(*Biograph,* December 13)
New York Dramatic Mirror

This picture is not a picture drama, although it is presented with dramatic force. It is an argument, an editorial, an essay on a vital subject of deep interest to all. The theme is the rising cost of living, the inability of masses to meet the increase and the part played by the speculator in bringing about this unfortunate condition. No orator, no editorial writer, no essayist could so strongly and effectively present the thoughts that are conveyed in this picture. It is another demonstration of the force and power of motion pictures as a means of conveying ideas. It was a daring step for the Biograph producers to take, to thus step out of the domain of picture drama as they have done in this film and in the one last week, *The Redman's View,* but having taken the step and done so successfully, they are entitled to all the praise they will undoubtedly receive for having opened up a new vein for motion picture subjects. The film opens with an artistic farm scene after the style of Millet, showing the sowers of wheat, hopeless and worn down by hard work. From these depressing scenes we turn to the affair of the speculator where the great corner is being arranged. The master mind issues his orders and the brokers appear in the wheat pit, where we see them struggling like ravenous wolves to control the wealth they did nothing to create. The corner wins and the defeated gamblers are brushed aside like the chaff of the grain for which they had fought. Another change and we see the city poor paying the increased price for bread or going hungry for want of enough bread to buy. We get a glimpse of the dreadful breadline contrasted with the scenes of high life where the successful speculators are lavishing the money they have won. A sensational turn is given to the film when we see the speculator showing his friends through one of his elevators. He is handed a message telling him that he has cornered the world's supply and in the midst of his exultation he makes a misstep and falls to a terrible death in one of his own bins of wheat. We see him struggle and disappear from view in the dusty grain and we see again the breadline and the weary farmers. The film closes in the darkening night on the farm. The effectiveness of the subject is enhanced by the superb acting of the company. Every part is powerfully presented with telling truthfulness, except in one instance only, when we see the farmers sowing the wheat. No wheat would ever come up from the sort of sowing they do, but this slip is lost sight of in the artistic atmosphere of the scene and in the compelling pictures that follow.

SOURCE: "Review of Licensed Films," *New York Dramatic Mirror*, December 25, 1909, in O'Connor, Document 13-D.

Follow-Up Problems

1. The film review referred to the film as an "argument, an editorial, an essay." What did the reviewer mean? Does the film have a predominant theme? What does the review reveal about the filmmaker's intent?

2. In comparing literary sources with cinematic expression, what are the similarities and differences between the two?

3. What was the meaning of "muckraking" in the Progressive era? How do the values expressed in this film relate to the social and economic themes that were the hallmark of the reform mentality of the historical period of which it is a product?

4. What may be learned from this film and the supporting documentation about the institutional changes, pressures, and conflicts experienced by Americans in the age of mass culture?

Further Reading

Brownlow, Kevin. *Behind the Mask of Innocence*. Berkeley, Calif.: University of California Press, 1990.

Gunning, Tom. *D. W. Griffith and the Origins of American Narrative Film: The Early Years at Biograph*. Urbana, Ill.: University of Illinois Press, 1994.

Henderson, Robert M. *D. W. Griffith: His Life and Work*. New York: Garland Publishing, Inc., 1985.

May, Lary. *Screening Out the Past: The Birth of Mass Culture and the Motion Picture Industry*. Chicago: University of Chicago Press, 1983.

Ross, Steven J. *Working Class Hollywood: Silent Film and the Shaping of Class in America*. Princeton, N.J.: Princeton University Press, 1998.

Sklar, Robert. *Movie-Made America: A Cultural History of American Movies*. New York: Vintage, rev. ed. 1994.

Stokes, Melvyn, and Richard Maltby, ed. *American Movie Audiences: From the Turn of the Century to the Early Sound Era*. London: BFI Publishing, 1999.

Filmography

A Child of the Ghetto (Biograph, 1910).

Cry of the Children (Thanhouser, 1912).

Lily of the Tenements (Biograph, 1911).

The Celluloid Document

A Corner in Wheat (Biograph, 1909).

Chapter 2

Cultural History Through a Cloudy Lens:
The Birth of a Nation (1915) and the
Racial Climate of Progressive America

Perhaps no movie of the Progressive era so captured the imagination of a generation, yet stirred such bitter controversy as D. W. Griffith's epic portrayal of the Civil War and Reconstruction South, *The Birth of a Nation* (1915). Artistically inspired but factually flawed, the film laid bare the racial tensions of Wilsonian America and some ugly features of Progressivism at the height of its influence, including the then-dominant historical interpretation of the Reconstruction experience. Widely regarded as a motion picture classic, this landmark in movie history is also a revealing historical document that records the racism of many liberal reformers, historians included, who accepted the predominant racial assumptions of their era. At the same time, the battle that erupted over *The Birth of a Nation* documents a new spirit of African-American activism in challenging the long-held beliefs that had poisoned race relations since the Reconstruction settlement and the later establishment of segregation. Because it helped shape the values of a generation of moviegoers, it may be studied as not only a primary source and window into the mentality of Progressive America, but also as the source of tragically damaging stereotypes that harmed black Americans for many years to come. Its story reminds us that modern issues and problems cannot be well understood without knowledge of decisions and actions taken by men and women of earlier generations.

The Historical Background

To understand the origins of *The Birth of a Nation*, we must again return to the career and genius of the innovative D. W. Griffith. Griffith was born and raised in Kentucky, and his education and family experience had filled him with deep respect for traditional Southern values, including uncritical acceptance of the myth of the lost cause that had sustained many in the defeated South following the Civil War. Hence, he shared the perspective expressed by the romantic novelist Thomas Dixon in his sentimentalized treatment of the Reconstruction era, *The Clansman* (1905). Dixon's novel portrayed the salvation of the South as the result of heroic white resistance to Northern carpetbaggers and misguided blacks, most notably in the activities of the Ku Klux Klan. The novel's emphasis on Klan resistance to allegedly bestial African-Americans reflected Dixon's theme that the story of the South's resurrection was basically a racial narrative. After a series of black outrages, including political fraud, social climbing, and sexually aggressive behavior, Dixon's Klan saves both elite Southerners and their converted Northern sympathizers from further danger. Ultimately, reunion was achieved in the novel through sectional healing and extralegal violence, which together allegedly saved the South from a terrible fate.

Always alert to a marketable story, Griffith warmed to the tale, which so closely matched his own distorted beliefs about Southern history. Not surprisingly, therefore, the script treatment that adapted the novel to film followed its literary source very closely, as did the motion picture, crafted as it was by a director who accepted Dixon's premise and assumptions. The cinematic result was a film that featured uncivilized African-Americans, corrupt politicians, sexually predatory black males, uncultured freedpeople, and victimized white elites, whose women were in constant danger and whose political system lay in ruins. *The Birth of a Nation* fully accepted the "plantation illusion," a widely accepted though faulty impression of a victimized South that lived in the memories of defeated Confederates and their heirs. This version of Southern history featured the myth of a golden age of idyllic agriculture and happy slaves, which was destroyed by emancipation and Reconstruction after the Civil War.[1] The film embraced this belief in an explosive combination of Dixon's romantic sentimentalism and Griffith's artistry, reinforced by the filmmaker's own sympathies.

The picture was filled with historical inaccuracies, beginning with its depiction of the South Carolina legislature, including the crude, immature, and vengeful behavior of its black representatives. The film's account of Reconstruction stresses the lustful behavior of African-Americans allegedly relentless in their pursuit of innocent white womanhood, in the person of first the Cameron family's "little sister" and later Elsie Stoneman, daughter of radical congressman Austin Stoneman, who has come to exploit the defeated South. At all points, aggressive blacks challenge their former masters with disrespectful behavior that underscores the alleged social chaos created by emancipation. Moreover, political corruption prevails, as the scheming mulatto politician Silas Lynch exploits ignorant black voters in his drive for power and pursues the virginal Elsie. Rape, pillage, and murder all befall the helpless Southern white victims of the Radical excesses before symbolic union is achieved between former wartime enemies, Northern and Southern, whose salvation is guaranteed by a heroic rescue carried out by a triumphant Ku Klux Klan as the film reaches its conclusion. In short, the historical truth with regard to Reconstruction has been reversed.

The Birth of a Nation is therefore fatally marred by historical inaccuracy and laced with racial stereotyping. Despite these flaws, however, the film was typically well received by theater audiences, whose biases were reinforced by the visual images on screen. Produced at the considerable sum of $100,000, the film was also a breakthrough in style and artistry. A 12-reel feature, it was the longest picture ever made at the time of its production. Through creative editing and crosscutting, separate story lines were blended into a consistent narrative. In addition, an original musical score by Joseph Carl Breil combined classical themes with American Negro folk music to lend power to the visual images projected. The end result was an epic film bigger than life and gripping in its dramatic intensity.

Once preview showings were held, Griffith and Dixon sensed that they had created something truly new and revolutionary. The novelist expressed his personal excitement about the outcome in February 1915 at the New York preview, where he shouted across a crowded room to Griffith that its title (*The Clansman*) failed to express the film's scope and power, which would be more effectively communicated by the sweeping title, *The Birth of a Nation*.[2] It seemed clear that the retitled picture was destined to stimulate a lively response. Griffith, like Dixon, was elated at the preliminary reviews and early audience reaction.

Not all viewers shared Dixon's enthusiastic reaction to Griffith's achievement. Appalled at the film's distortion of African-American character, behavior, motives, and actual role in Reconstruction, the young National Association for the Advancement of Colored People (NAACP) complained bitterly and spearheaded a national protest against its distribution. Led by Moorfield Storey of the American Bar Association and Oswald Garrison Villard of the *New York Evening Post*, both liberals and NAACP activists, the organization expressed the views of many Americans, black and white, that *The Birth of a Nation* twisted the truth concerning the Reconstruction era and insulted all black people in the process. Taking aim at the film's blatant racism, the NAACP planned protest demonstrations in many cities, including Boston and Chicago. Determined to prevent nationwide showing of the film, its leadership called for a nationwide boycott intended to strangle its sponsors financially.

Despite the volatile reaction among racial liberals, Griffith and Dixon were not without their supporters. When Dixon and Woodrow Wilson, old schoolmates, discussed the movie, the president suggested a private showing. After a White House screening on February 18, 1915, the Southern-born Wilson reportedly described the film as "writing history with lightning." The scholar-president is said to have concluded that "[his] only regret [was] that it is all so terribly true." At another private screening, several members of Congress and the Supreme Court added their own positive responses. In endorsing the Dixon-Griffith account of the Reconstruction experience, the politicians echoed the dominant theme of Progressive era historical scholarship, which erroneously regarded the Reconstruction period as a "tragic era" of black domination in Southern political and social life. Their approval became a useful tool for the filmmakers as the battle over *The Birth of a Nation* grew more intense.

From the beginning, opinion was divided on the film's merits. Though audiences were usually sizable, mirroring an overwhelmingly positive critical and financial reception, controversy followed the film, especially in large urban centers. In Boston, for example, the NAACP led a vigorous protest, featuring five hundred demonstrators at the state capitol demanding that it be banned. The national organization went on to publish a pamphlet titled "Fighting a Vicious Film: Protest Against *The Birth of a Nation*," in which it denounced the picture as "three miles of filth." While the New York Board of Censors temporarily withheld approval, they reversed themselves upon learning of the Washington screenings, much to the disgust of board member Rabbi Steven Wise, who attacked *Birth* as an "indescribably foul and loathsome libel on a race of human beings." Joining Wise in criticism were numerous journalists, Jane Addams of Chicago's Hull House settlement, and the respected leader of black Americans, Booker T. Washington of Tuskegee Institute.[3]

Critical reviews in *The Crisis* by the NAACP's W. E. B. DuBois, the ongoing protests, and efforts to remove offensive scenes focused debate on an appropriate response to the distortions, inaccuracies, and stereotyping that liberals observed in a film which, despite the controversy, proved to be a huge financial success. Many of the film's opponents favored the idea of a national boycott intended to deny the picture's sponsors further revenues;

some hoped to eliminate the most offensive segments of the film through censorship, and others dreamed of a more sweeping reply through the cinema itself. Several groups, including Washington's Tuskegee organization, the NAACP, and their white allies, supported the idea of producing an independent motion picture that would in some way highlight the striving and progress of African-Americans on the road to full citizenship and participation in American economic and political life. After several false starts, these efforts resulted in the production of the little-known celluloid response, *Birth of a Race* (1918). By the time of its release, however, *Birth of a Race* had gone through numerous revisions that had largely eliminated its original celebration of black progress. Although this film was a critical and financial failure, its very production documents the powerful stimulus provided by *The Birth of a Nation*, which accurately records the racism that penetrated the public consciousness of Progressive America.

Analyzing the Film

When you approach *The Birth of a Nation* as a historical document, focus on the final segment of the film, which deals with the Reconstruction era. It will be useful for you to begin your analysis with a review of the Reconstruction period in American history, for without some idea of the historical realities, it is difficult to separate fact from fiction. Familiarize yourself with the factual background, including the economic, social, and political challenges faced by newly freed African-Americans. Note the role of both whites and blacks in the Reconstruction process, and examine the purposes of the first Ku Klux Klan. With this background, you should be able to assess the accuracy of Griffith's account of Southern history in the years after the Civil War. It will also be possible for you to grasp the difficulty of the black position in the Progressive era, by which time segregation had been institutionalized. During these years, intensified African-American race consciousness and a new commitment by some black militants, such as W. E. B. DuBois, to the demand for full equality existed side by side with the reality of increasing racism throughout American society, as expressed in the reactions of highly placed political leaders to the film previews.

It will be equally valuable for you to reflect further upon the historical context in which the film was produced and consumed. Note that in 1915 at least some Americans could remember slavery, the Civil War, Reconstruction, and even the Ku Klux Klan of the 1860s and 1870s. Recall also that in the year of *The Birth of a Nation*'s release (1915), a new, revived Ku Klux Klan made its appearance on the American scene, starting in Georgia and the South, but soon to expand throughout the United States. Be especially aware of the historical fact that the period from 1890 to 1915 was one of WASP supremacy in the United States, characterized by the appearance of the Jim Crow laws and their spread after the Plessy v. Ferguson decision of 1896, the climax of worldwide Anglo-Saxon imperialism, North-South reconciliation, and the symbolic return of the South to full participation in the Union with the election of the Southern-born Woodrow Wilson to the presidency. In short, Wilson's America was a socially structured, segregated, and race-conscious nation.

One of the important problems to be addressed in your analysis involves the Dixon-Griffith portrayal of Reconstruction. While their film understandably expresses the racial prejudice that penetrated the Progressive era, the filmmaker may be faulted for his own sins of omission and commission. Be alert to the clear distortions of fact, character, and behavior that are evident in *The Birth of a Nation*. Why does the filmmaker focus on Reconstruction as a solely Southern experience when, in fact, it was a national phenomenon? Turning to the South, which is the center of Griffith's attention, note the filmmaker's vision of the motives, character, and behavior of Radical Republicans, freedmen, and Southern elites. Finally, assess the movie's interpretation of the Ku Klux Klan and its role in Reconstruction. Concentration on these issues will enable you to evaluate the film as a portrayal of historical events and to place it within the context of Progressive era social values and racial attitudes, as well as the prevailing understanding of Reconstruction by historians at that time. In what way was this film a barometer of prevailing public attitudes towards minorities in early-twentieth-century America?

Moving to the more immediate historical context for the production and distribution of this motion picture, it may be useful to recall the place of Griffith and his artistry in the rapidly developing movie industry. Begin by asking what made this film different from the films that preceded it, with reference to cutting, length, sustained narrative, musical coordination, sequencing, epic scope, shot selection, and use of vignettes. Think about the ways in which technique and craftsmanship contributed to the reinforcement of socially explosive images and perceptions. Link the director's skill with the strengthening in the viewer's mind of the "plantation illusion" of a dignified aristocratic Southern society betrayed. Why did Griffith's characterization of the African-American people draw fire from the film's detractors? Exactly how did Griffith deliver his powerful social message?

Thinking About Primary Sources

Concentration on the portrayal of black characters throughout the film reminds us of the vigorous reaction of the nation's leading black organizations to this film. By exploring in detail their responses, it is possible to accurately place this picture in historical context. The primary sources provide rich detail on the counterattack against this film by the nation's leading African-American groups. Focus on the alternate strategies explored by African-Americans, their organizations, and allies within the white community in the effort to undercut or neutralize the impact of the film. Try to determine the origins of the counterattack against the picture. As you undertake this effort, the documents will be useful in gaining perspective on the depth of black revulsion against a movie that from a very early date began to reach a large national audience. Similarly, the primary sources provide evidence of collaboration between black elites and liberal whites. Yet the film's growing acceptance among white viewers lent urgency to the campaign against *The Birth of a Nation*, which included a failed boycott and the ill-fated production of a much less successful film, *Birth of a Race* (1918).[4]

Use the NAACP memorandum on the idea of a filmed response to explore the organization's objectives, as well as the source of the initiative behind this proposal. Note that, when finally released (1918), *Birth of a Race* was both commercially unsuccessful and devoid of the positive images envisioned by its original promoters. One important question to be examined involves the reasons for the failure of *Birth of a Race* and the significance of that result for our understanding of the racial climate of the late Progressive era. Think about the historical significance of the failed effort as a marker of prevailing racial assumptions in the early-twentieth-century United States.

Historical Perspective

The debate over *The Birth of a Nation* mirrored the social tensions and racial arrangements that prevailed in Progressive America, including the difficult accommodation made by African-Americans to discrimination and inequality. Despite all efforts made by the NAACP and its white liberal allies, the film was widely distributed and often praised. By 1928, a film made for $100,000 had grossed $10 million and become Griffith's most successful work. While the film was a financial success, it had been socially disruptive, as shown by the attempted boycott and an aggressive censorship effort, not to mention the commercial venture that resulted in *Birth of a Race,* which began as a chronicle of black racial progress but ended as a tribute to African-American participation in World War I. As a reply to the Griffith epic, the picture was a pale imitation of Griffith's film artistry and historical argumentation.

For his part, Griffith was deeply disturbed by the uproar over *The Birth of a Nation.* In an effort to satisfy the critics, he reluctantly agreed in 1915 to remove some of the most racist scenes in the original print. In his view, which was colored by his own assumptions and understanding of the past, the organized effort to censor and even suppress the film constituted an attack on the truth as he understood it. In 1916 Griffith's counterattack escalated with the publication of his pamphlet "The Rise and Fall of Free Speech," in which he asserted that the "integrity of free speech" had not been seriously attacked in the United States until the motion picture as an art form became "an excuse for an assault on our liberties." Finally, his next film, *Intolerance* (1916), aspired to protect mankind from man's inhumanity to man, including bigotry and intolerance. Essentially a commercial disaster, it failed to match *The Birth of a Nation,* either financially or artistically.

For students of history, the film remains a powerful artifact of the Progressive era, a document that records the period's blind spot on the issue of race. At the same approximate moment that white audiences applauded the Ku Klux Klan's rescue of the besieged victims in the movie's thrilling conclusion, the Klan was reorganizing for a new assault on personal freedoms as the Progressive era drew to a close. The racist assumptions embedded in *The Birth of a Nation* provide stark evidence of attitudes and beliefs that went to the heart of American thought on race relations in the early twentieth century. Similarly, the distorted view of Reconstruction expressed in the film matched the prevailing historical interpretation of the time. For the modern student, therefore, this landmark film opens a window into the past through which we can glimpse the limits of Progressive era biracial cooperation as well as the outlines of stereotypes that hindered racial accommodation for generations to come.

Endnotes

1. Everett Carter, "Cultural History Written with Lightning: The Significance of *The Birth of a Nation* (1915)," in Peter C. Rollins, ed., *Hollywood as Historian: American Film in a Cultural Context* (Lexington, Ky.: University Press of Kentucky, rev. ed. 1998), 12.
2. John Hope Franklin, "*The Birth of a Nation:* Propaganda as History," *Massachusetts Review* (1979), in Stephen Mintz and Randy Roberts, *Hollywood's America: United States History Through Film,* 2d ed. (St. James, N.Y.: Brandywine Press, 1999), 45.

3. For discussion of the controversy over the film, including the protests and attempted boycott, see Franklin, 46–47; Robert Sklar, *Movie-Made America: A Cultural History of American Movies*, (New York: Random House, rev. ed. 1994), 58–61.

4. Thomas Cripps, "The Moving Image as Social History: Stalking the Paper Trail," in John O'Connor, ed., *Image as Artifact* (Malabar, Fla.: Robert E. Krieger, 1990), 142–147.

THE PRIMARY SOURCES

The following documents focus attention on the controversy that erupted over the content of *The Birth of a Nation* at the time of its release. In the first letter, the NAACP acquaints several Hollywood motion picture companies with the issues raised by the film and calls upon the movie industry to respect the National Board of Review's decision to withhold approval. Not long thereafter, as revealed in the next document, the national NAACP wrote its local branches to organize protests against the film in cities where screenings were planned. In response to NAACP efforts, Theodore Mitchell, public relations representative for the producers of *The Birth of a Nation*, urges a *New York Post* executive to intervene with the NAACP's Oswald Garrison Villard in support of the film company's vision of free speech on the screen. Finally, in a confidential memorandum, Mary White Ovington of NAACP suggests a filmed response to *The Birth of a Nation*.

THE NAACP CHALLENGES HOLLYWOOD TO RESPECT THE WILL OF THE NATIONAL BOARD OF CENSORSHIP

Memorandum to Moving Picture Firms
NAACP

We know that you are very much interested in fighting the wave of legislation now sweeping over the country providing for legal censorship of motion pictures in every State, and that you are very anxious that this work should be left in the competent and trustworthy hands of the National Board of Censorship. In the publicity which the trade has sent out on this subject, you have laid great stress upon the claim that the motion picture manufacturers are loyal to the National Board of Censorship, and only too glad to abide by its rulings.

While we have had heretofore no reason for questioning the general truth of this position we want to call your attention to a very serious situation which has just arisen in the action of David W. Griffith in producing in this city and in Los Angeles "The Birth of a Nation" after the film had been disapproved by the National Board of Censorship. This picture is described in the current issue of the "Moving Picture World" as an "undisguised appeal to race prejudice." The reviewer goes on to say, "The tendency of the second part is to inflame the race hatred. The Negroes are shown as horrible brutes given over to beastly excesses, defiant and criminal in their attitude toward the whites and lusting after white women. Some of the details are plainly morbid and repulsive."

As you doubtless know, the National Board of Censorship through a subcommittee gave this picture a review and approval. When we informed the members of the General Committee of the Board, however, of the character of the picture the General

Committee itself reviewed the film and withdrew their approval, condemning certain offensive features of the first part and the entire second part of the film.

This raises a serious question in the minds of our Board: Is it true that the motion picture trade has no real respect for the National Board of Censorship, and no intention of abiding by its decisions when they become inconvenient and expensive? We are almost driven to this conclusion by the conduct of one reputed to be a leader in the motion picture field. Does the trade desire that the facts of this case shall come out in the several States where legal censorship bills are now pending?

NATIONAL ASSOCIATION FOR THE ADVANCEMENT OF COLORED PEOPLE

By

J. E. Spingarn   Oswald Garrison Villard
W. E. B. DuBois   John Hayes Holmes
Mary White Ovington   Florence Kelley
Mary Childs Nerney

SOURCE: NAACP, Memorandum to Moving Picture Firms, March 11, 1915, NAACP Papers, Box C-299.

NAACP MOBILIZES NATIONAL RESISTANCE TO THE SCREENING OF A RACIST FILM

To Our Branches and Locals
Mary Childs Nerney

April 7, 1915

To Our Branches and Locals:

Is the moving picture play, "The Birth of a Nation," based on Dixon's "Clansman," being played in your city? If not, is it advertised for production and on what date?

Has your city or state a local censoring committee or board. If so, send us immediately their names and addresses.

Has your city an ordinance regulating the production of moving pictures. What is it?

If the play is being produced or is advertised for production in your city you should immediately interest the local clergy, colored and white, civic organizations, welfare societies, secret societies, women's clubs, etc., to unite with you in protest. Letters signed by representatives of the branch and of these organizations should be sent to the Police Commissioner, to the License Commissioner and to the Mayor protesting against the play on the ground that it endangers public morals and may lead to a breach of the peace. Call attention to the fact that its prototype, "The Clansman" was stopped by executive order of Mayor Weaver in Philadelphia four years ago that the Mayor was sustained in his opinion by Judge Sulzberger of the Court of Common Pleas. It was also stopped in Boston. We can send you a copy of the Philadelphia decision.

In New York, at the request of this Association, Mayor Mitchell received a large delegation representing all elements among the colored people and many prominent white people and organizations interested in suppressing this play. After listening to the speakers the Mayor said he had seen the play, that he agreed with all that had been said against it, and that he advised the owner of the theatre and the owner and producer of the film that the most objectionable scenes must be cut out. These are the two rape scenes in the second part which represent a colored man attacking a white girl and a mulatto politician trying to force marriage upon the daughter of his white benefactor.

An amateur organization in New York known as the National Board of Censorship, approved, then disapproved and again approved this play. It is an unofficial body without authority or power and is now split in two factions as a result of their disagreement over this film. Their Chairman, Dr. Frederic C. Howe, who is also Commissioner of Immigration, and such important members as Dr. Charles S. Macfarland, General Secretary of the Federal Council of the Churches of Christ in America, are vehement in their open denunciation of the play, and Dr. Howe appeared before the Mayor with our Association to speak against it. He is also one of our witnesses in the legal case which we have brought against the owner and producer.

The following are some opinions of the play: Dr. Jacques Loeb, the eminent scientist, characterizes it as follows: "The play is in my opinion a glorification of homicidal mania with a special grievance against the Negro. It is an insult to this country to call that display of scenes of murder and its appeal to race hatred 'Birth of a Nation.'"

Miss Jane Addams, who witnessed the production at our request, in speaking of its historical value, says, "One of the most unfortunate things about this film is that it appeals to race prejudice upon the basis of conditions of half a century ago, which have nothing to so with the facts we have to consider today. It is both unjust and untrue. The producer seems to have fol-

lowed the principle of gathering the most vicious and grotesque individuals he could find among colored people, and showing them as representatives of the truth about the entire race. The same method could be followed to smirch the reputation of any race".

A writer in the New Republic of March 20 says, "Whatever happened during Reconstruction, this film is aggressively vicious and defamatory. It is spiritual assassination. It degrades the censors that passed it and the white race that endures it."

You should act at once. Make a special effort to secure the cooperation of all elements of colored people and prominent white people.

Sincerely yours,

Mary Childs Nerney

SOURCE: Mary Childs Nerney, "To Our Branches and Locals," April 7, 1915, NAACP Papers, Box C-299.

THE FILM'S PRODUCERS REACT TO THE THREAT OF CENSORSHIP

Response to Curwen Stoddard in *The Evening Post*
Theodore Mitchell

October 28, 1915

Mr. Curwen Stoddard,
The Evening Post,
30 Vesey Street, City.

Dear Mr. Stoddard:

After a trip over several of our routes which carried me into Virginia, Pennsylvania, New Jersey, Illinois and Ohio, I am positively convinced that the purposes of the society which Mr. Villard is interested in and which has been consistently opposing "THE BIRTH OF A NATION", are being diverted by scheming politicians and hangers-on to entirely different ends.

You will understand in the machinations of politics that these are things which cannot be specifically charged without involving interminable trouble and expense. It must be apparent however, that when offers of deals are proposed to this company that such

overtures are voluntary and that they have but one purpose—to blackmail us and in all this you find no sincere regard for the negro. These crooks however, do seize upon the opposition of the Colored Society—no matter how well intended their opposition may be in protesting against the production of our picture in different cities—to make capital out of it for their own profit. I have never heard one of them say anything but contemptuous things about the negro opposition and yet at the same time they seize upon it as a means to work their own little game.

All of this means expense to us and it must mean a futile expense to this colored society. In Virginia, I was approached with a proposition to deliver one of the leaders of the society over to us. In Ohio a powerful politician wanted a percentage of our production and in return, promised to deliver to us one of the very highest officials who represented the Negro society in the protest against our picture before the Censors. I can assure you that we never considered one of these propositions and that aside from the necessary legal expense of fighting for what we deem our rights, this company has not expended one cent to get "THE BIRTH OF A NATION" into any city or state in this country. As these crooked offers have been made you can form your own opinion of how disgusting it must be to us. My personal opinion is one of loathing for these contemptible crooks and one of deep regret that a society which apparently aims to help the advancement of the colored man in America should be made a cats paw for blackmail and extortion—for that is what they are after even if we have never submitted to either.

We recognize that there can be an honest difference of opinion on any question. You will recall that I have shown you statements from colored ministers, bishops and college men who think "THE BIRTH OF A NATION" is doing a great work for the enlightened colored man in showing him the way to a better station in life than to be the pawn and plaything of politicians and grafters—as was undoubtedly the case of many colored men in the days of the reconstruction period. Do you not think it is far better to reveal what education and work will do, as for instance the showing of the Hampton Institute pictures, than to patronize the negro and keep him mindful of his dependence upon the bounty of white men? In this I sincerely believe "THE BIRTH OF A NATION" is a good thing and the colored people are only robbing themselves of the fruits of this good impression by a hopeless endeavor to suppress the production. This belief was confirmed by the statement of a very prominent editor of one of the leading papers in Ohio made to

me personally that he was convinced after carefully canvassing the situation in Ohio that the barring of the picture from that state will cause a thousand times more feeling and prejudice against the negro than its presentation in every city and town in the state. I was in politics myself for a good many years in Ohio and I know the situation thoroughly.

But what is more directly to the point following up my conversation with you is that I feel sure Mr. Villard is not aware to what ends the well meant opposition of the Colored Society is being put. It reflects upon that society by making them a means to blackmail and I am convinced as a regular reader of the Post that Mr. Villard is one of the last men in the world who would want his good intentions distorted and put to such unworthy usage. It is for this reason that I think it is due him that these things be laid before him. You will understand my motives are the best. We are asking no favors and I feel confident that you are willing to substantiate this much of my statement after the years that you have been coming in contact with me in a business way.

Thanking you for your kindly consideration,

Yours sincerely,

Theodore Mitchell

TM:BC.

SOURCE: Theodore Mitchell (Epoch Producing Corporation) to Curwen Stoddard (*The Evening Post*), October 28, 1915, NAACP Papers, Box C-300.

NAACP CONSIDERS A FILM AS AN ANSWER TO *THE BIRTH OF A NATION*
Confidential Memorandum
Mary White Ovington

CONFIDENTIAL

The Birth of a Nation with its anti-Negro propaganda has captured the imagination of hundreds of thousands of people in the United States. It is proposed to present another scenario which shall treat the periods of slavery, the Civil War, and reconstruction with dignity and historic accuracy, and shall show the important and often heroic part that the Negro played during these difficult times. Such a scenario has been written by one of our most artistic and successful moving picture writers, Miss Elaine Sterne. It will be approved by America's foremost historian, Dr. Albert Bushnell Hart of Harvard University. It is full of thrilling and absorbing incidents, and brings out clearly the courage of the Negro who fled from slavery, the heroism of the Negro soldier, the faithfulness of the black men and women who guarded the plantations, and the self-denial of the Negro educator.

Miss Sterne was impelled to write this story after seeing the Birth of a Nation. She took it to the Universal Film Co. They approved it, but were unwilling to go to the great expense of producing a film to rival the Birth of a Nation without some outside capital. Miss Sterne then came to the National Association for the Advancement of Colored People to learn whether they would help finance the undertaking. The Board at once recognized that the Association could not enter upon any business undertaking. Whatever business was done must be by individual members. A committee was appointed consisting of Miss Mary White Ovington, Chairman; Mr. William English Walling, Mr. John Underhill and Miss Mary Childs Nerney to see what practical steps could be taken to assist in producing the scenario. Mr. Arthur Spingarn acted with the committee and the following offer was made by the Universal Film Co:

If the Committee would raise $10,000 the company would put in a sufficient sum to insure the production of a twelve-reel film on a scale as large as the Birth of a Nation. This, the Company estimated would mean an expenditure on their part of at least $60,000. They would return the $10,000 with the first profits, that is, the profit would be evenly divided until the $10,000 was paid off. A loan without interest would thus be made which would be returned unless the venture proved a failure.

The Committee is working on the basis of this proposition, and its members are endeavoring at once to secure pledges for the needed loan.

The scenario will be staged in Southern California where the Universal Film Co. has an enormous plant. The work, if it is to be done at all must start within two to three weeks.

The Committee will make sure that the film, when completed, shall be the same as that submitted by the writer of the scenario. They will guard against changes that might affect the impression of the Negro embodied now in the play.

The Association's Legal Committee will endeavor to protect, in every way possible, the interests of those advancing money to the company.

Mary White Ovington
Chairman, Scenario Committee

SOURCE: Mary White Ovington, "Confidential Memorandum," June 1915, NAACP Papers, Box C-300.

Follow-up Problems

1. Since Griffith was a strong proponent of social message films, how do you account for his involvement in a film like *The Birth of a Nation*, which contains elements of racism? What does this problem reveal to you about the values, attitudes, and objectives embraced by Americans of the Progressive generation?

2. What was Griffith's perspective on the Civil War and Reconstruction? How would you account for the flaws in this film as a depiction of the past?

3. Assess the film's portrayal of African-Americans as participants in the drama of Reconstruction. Which blacks were regarded as "good" and "bad"? Explain.

4. In what ways does the definition of "womanhood" play a role in Griffith's vision of the South and Reconstruction? Comment on the film's contrasting depictions of women (Northern/Southern, white/mulatto, white/African-American).

5. Identify the racial/racist stereotypes found in *The Birth of a Nation*. Today, some people believe that this film should not be shown in public. As historians and scholars, how should we deal with the problem created by the screening of images that might be offensive to a portion of the audience?

6. How do the primary sources clarify your understanding of the censorship issue as part of the struggle over *The Birth of a Nation*? How did white liberals who favored civil liberties justify their willingness to impose limits on free speech in film?

7. What is the significance of the film's commercial success? How did the widespread viewing of the movie

influence or reflect the values, opinions, and social perspectives of the national audience and the American people at the time of the film's release?

8. From an artistic point of view, how does this film compare with *A Corner in Wheat*? What elements of technique, editing, and visual imagery make the picture effective and persuasive?

Further Reading

Bernardi, Daniel, ed. *The Birth of Whiteness: Race and the Emergence of U.S. Cinema*. New Brunswick, N.J.: Rutgers University Press, 1996.

Bogle, Donald. *Toms, Coons, Mulattoes, Mammies, and Bucks*. New York: Continuum, 1997.

Carter, Everett. "Cultural History Written with Lightning: The Significance of *The Birth of a Nation* (1915)." In Peter C. Rollins, ed., *Hollywood as Historian: American Film in a Cultural Context*. Lexington, Ky.: University Press of Kentucky, rev. ed. 1998, 9–19.

Cripps, Thomas. *Slow Fade to Black: The Negro in American Film, 1900–1942*. New York: Oxford University Press, 1993.

_____. "Following the Paper Trail to *The Birth of a Race and Its Times*." *Film and History*, XVIII (September 1988): 50–62.

Franklin, John Hope. "*Birth of a Nation*: Propaganda as History." *The Massachusetts Review* 20 (1979): 417–434.

May, Lary. *Screening Out the Past: The Birth of Mass Culture and the Motion Picture Industry*. Chicago: The University of Chicago Press, 1983.

Filmography

Birth of a Race (Birth of a Race Photoplay Corporation, 1918).

The Celluloid Document

The Birth of a Nation (Epoch, 1915).

Chapter 3

Social Change and Sexual Politics: *Dancing Mothers* (1926) and Moral Ambiguity in the Jazz Age

With World War I behind them, Americans began the process of readjustment by focusing on domestic life and politics rather than foreign concerns. With the return of prosperity after a brief postwar recession, American citizens concentrated on economic gains and the acceleration of aggressive consumption that fueled the new economy. Although some groups, such as farmers and unskilled workers, did not benefit substantially from this economic growth, the wider availability of consumer goods together with the rise of installment buying did make it possible for many Americans to acquire the much-desired consumer items that became the symbols of the new era of prosperity. Within this environment, the entertainment industry flourished as disposable income was expended by urban dwellers in pursuit of pleasure. *Dancing Mothers* (1926) offers a case study in the complications associated with the search for personal satisfaction.

The Historical Background

The society inhabited by Americans in the 1920s differed dramatically from the simpler collection of self-contained communities known to many Americans in the years preceding World War I. For the first time, the census figures for 1920 revealed that the majority of citizens lived in places classified as "urban." To be sure, the demographic changes were the product of a long and gradual evolutionary process, but these statistics did record a momentous change. Not only was the nation more urbanized, but due to significant developments in the field of communications, nonurban communities were becoming more integrated into the fabric of a national community. As the new media developed in the 1920s, physical and social distance decreased. Telephone, radio, and motion pictures reduced the isolation of rural America by projecting aural and visual images far beyond their places of origin. The modern mass media provided instruction on social behavior, gender relations, sexual practices, generational differences, and consumption patterns that reduced community and personal independence while disseminating urban lifestyles throughout the nation. Americans had fully and finally entered the age of mass culture.

A key aspect of this new age of mass-produced pleasure was the rapid growth of the motion picture industry, which by the 1920s had migrated to the warm climes of Southern California. After 1920, movie attendance soared to new heights. By 1925, fifty million people a week viewed films, and the industry had become one of the most profitable businesses on the American economic scene. By this time, control of the industry had fallen to energetic immigrant Jews who had largely replaced the native-born Protestants who had competed successfully prior to World War I. During the 1920s, corporate consolidation resulted in the survival of the "Big Five"—Paramount, Warner Brothers, RKO, Twentieth Century Fox, and MGM, as well as the "Little Three"—Universal, Columbia, and United Artists. The executives who dominated the so-called "majors" were in a position to determine how the important social innovations of the postwar era would be projected on the movie screens of America.

In fact, the changes that seemed to be overturning traditional values in the twenties were not the product of a postwar revolution; rather, the new standards drew their origins from changing social patterns that had begun to appear in the Progressive era. New economic roles for women, the escalation of the divorce rate, increased premarital and extramarital sexual activity, expanded mobility, greater personal freedom for youth, and liberalized patterns of social behavior all had roots in the preceding generation. Though significant numbers of Americans accepted a more traditional value system, the spread of these social innovations and their popularization through the mass media left an indelible imprint on the millions of citizens, especially urbanites, who lived through what one scholar terms the "revolution in morals."[1] It is this image of American society in the "jazz age" that, despite the clear survival of old values, has often dominated the historical accounts of both contemporary social observers and historians.

While there were indeed many Americas in the twenties, the focus of the following account will be on those urbanites who experienced the social revolution most directly. No medium of communication played a more important role in advancing the new, urban-based patterns of moral behavior than the rapidly developing motion picture industry. A review of the Hollywood product in this era reveals a clear focus on themes that explored the new value system in all its dimensions. Experimental gender relations, more open sexual encounters, new strains on familial harmony, generational conflict, and shifting moral values all vied with tried-and-true traditional themes as Hollywood entered the early years of its "golden era." Careful analysis of one of these feature films, *Dancing Mothers* (1926), will reveal the depth of the social confusion experienced by Americans in the age of mass culture. Its conclusion underscores an unwillingness to completely abandon the moral standards so long embraced by most Americans. This picture offers many insights into the social tensions felt by men and women attempting to establish an updated value system as they made the transition to the modern era.

At the heart of this social revolution was the modern American woman and her portrayal on the screen. Many scholars have observed that from almost the beginning of the motion pictures, women have been featured prominently and have been central to the success of the industry. It is equally clear that their film treatment reflected real changes that women experienced in the decade of the 1920s. By the mid-twenties a "new woman" had emerged in urban America; sexually liberated, economically independent, emotionally free, and worldly-wise, the new woman controlled her own destiny as never before. Although the women who fit this profile were essentially an upper- and middle-class minority, it was this image that was often projected on the screens of America. Exceptional though it might have been, the "flapper" image of youthful and experimental freedom became one of Hollywood's female staples of the late silent era.

The new female screen image of the twenties was the product of an evolutionary process that had begun with the heroic child-woman of the prewar era and developed into the predatory and vaguely foreign "vamp" seen on the silent screen. By the 1920s, youth and sexual playfulness had supplanted the darker vamp image. Screen heroines were now portrayed as eager for sexual adventure, willing to flout the accepted rules of traditional gender relations, and prepared to expose an ample portion of the female body. Always ready for energetic dancing, illegal drinking, and forbidden romantic relationships, the female movie modern of the mid-1920s was typically open to what seemed risky sexual behavior.

Or was she? Further examination of the female screen images of the twenties reveals that in most cases, these adventurous heroines frequently married in the last reel. That is, the audience appetite for slightly lurid film content (not to mention suggestive movie titles) did not preclude a desire for a morally acceptable resolution of the sexual tensions and personal conflicts presented by the new value system. Nevertheless, despite the predominance of the conventional ending, there were films that raised more issues than they resolved. Moreover, the elaborate foreplay that marked the gender relations featured in these movies highlighted an exaggerated sexuality that was the hallmark of Hollywood's sexual fables and domestic dramas in this age of transition.

This focus on cute yet sexually charged attractiveness came to be called "it," in the language of the Hollywood publicist. "It" was a concept of female charm that suggested a magnetic quality at once highly sexualized and aggressively self-confident. Robust sex appeal was featured in a variety of romantic films and the promotional campaigns that sold them to a waiting public. The actress usually identified with this image, Clara Bow, was a key supporting player in *Dancing Mothers*. Herself the product of a hard childhood, Bow was attracted to the movies by the glamour of the Hollywood image, as well as its potential for financial success. In 1922, she began a film career that was to be built on an image of frank and healthful sexuality. Although she was not the featured player in *Dancing Mothers*, her first film for Paramount, Clara Bow cast a compelling image as the precocious and irresponsible young woman whose flirtation with a married man was the indirect cause of a parental separation. In this instance, "it" was the source of troublesome moral confusion and eventually the disruption of a dysfunctional family caught in the waves of the social revolution of the 1920s.

Analyzing the Film

This film, produced by Famous Players-Lasky in 1926, was in some ways a typical jazz age society drama that was part of a Hollywood cycle including *Our Dancing Daughters* (1928), *Our Modern Maidens* (1929), and finally, *Our Blushing Brides* (1930). *Dancing Mothers* stressed the disastrous consequences of questionable moral behavior on the part of a flapper daughter who openly flirted with an older man. The viewer is treated to a generous display of socially banned activities, including illegal drinking, a frankly presented extramarital relationship, and the strong suggestion of imminent divorce. By the final reel, a well-to-do family has been destroyed, lovers have parted, separation seems likely, and there is no apparent solution to the resulting social dislocation. In effect, the film ends with a bold question mark. *Dancing Mothers* therefore reflects the potential for social damage in the destruction of the traditional value system and uncertainty about the consequences. As you study this film, be aware of its significance as a historical document that records the social trauma experienced during the transition from the late industrial era to the age of mass culture and corporate capitalism.

When you think about that social disruption, pay particular attention to the ways in which *Dancing Mothers* explores shifting gender roles in the post–World War I United States. Examine the several female characters in the film and think about the social and legal choices available to emancipated women in the fluid 1920s, options that might have been closed off in previous generations. Explore the film's message with regard to the definition of healthy and fulfilled womanhood in this era.

The manner in which the status of women is dealt with in this picture also raises the question of the audience to which the film is addressed. Unlike many movies of this era, *Dancing Mothers* avoids the usual screen resolution, which would have constituted an evasion of reality. According to at least one reviewer, Paramount filmed an alternative conclusion in which the betrayed wife resolves her differences with her husband and daughter. The critic observed that the "happy" ending would in fact have damaged the fabric of the film by removing the dilemma presented by her self-discovery and development of a relationship outside her marriage. Such a resolution of conflict, the reviewer thought, might have been suitable for nonurban audiences (and may have been used in some locales). What does this reaction to the moral problem explored in *Dancing Mothers* (and the reference to the tastes of multiple audiences) reveal about urban-rural relationships in the 1920s and the differences between lifestyles found in distinct geographic and social communities within the United States at that time?

As you explore these issues, be aware of the ways in which the 1920s were a bridge between an older and a more modern America, including the conflicts found in the debate over values in that decade. Consider the role of the motion picture in forcing the reassessment of traditional values at this time, and speculate on the solutions explored by social theorists and motion picture executives to the moral issues raised by provocative film content. Ask whether movies influence the moral values of audiences, and assess the solutions to this threat advanced in the 1920s, culminating in the establishment of the motion picture production code in 1930. As you think about this debate, consider the meaning of the term "transitional" as applied to the decade of the twenties, and reflect upon the way in which *Dancing Mothers* contributes to your understanding of this concept.

Thinking About Primary Sources

In preparation for your viewing of *Dancing Mothers*, rely upon the primary sources to provide background for the social issues raised by the film. Use the documents bearing on the social changes of the 1920s to better understand the content of the celluloid evidence before you. Try to connect the commentary on divorce with the resolution of the conflicts highlighted by the film. Relate the film's setting to the social readjustments taking place in American society during the twenties.

Turning to the response to change, examine the excerpt from the movie industry's code of motion picture production principles. This document is sometimes referred to as the "Hays Code," since it was adopted under the vigilant administration of former United States Postmaster General Will Hays, who had been hired by the producers' association to insulate the producers and their product against charges of moral laxity. This code was an industry effort at self-policing in an effort to ward off government regulation. Under the leadership of Will Hays, the association first introduced a code to govern production in 1927. Administered by the association's Studio Relations Committee, this guideline combined the restrictions often imposed by domestic and foreign censors. Finally, in 1930 a new Production Code was announced under the leadership of the Hays Office, which gained new and sweeping authority over script review. Identify any connection between the issues raised in *Dancing Mothers* and the guidelines issued in the code and think about the principle of censorship thus raised. Link these concerns with the social realities explored in the domestic dramas that were such an important part of Hollywood output in the unsettled 1920s.

Historical Perspective

Throughout the 1920s, unsettling images of gender relations as well as the sexual content of motion pictures had been controversial. Partly as a result of a series of highly publicized Hollywood sex scandals in the immediate postwar period and partly due to the suggestive material contained in the films of the period, public attention was focused increasingly on the moral issues raised by the movies. While the questionable film content was innocent by modern standards, these films did have a profound impact on an audience whose entertainment experiences were more limited than those of later generations. Then, as now, public concern focused on the impact of the motion picture on the youth audience, which many observers assumed to be especially vulnerable to confusing moral messages. Whether forbidden sexual experiences or divorce was the topic, the movies addressed subjects not deemed suitable for youthful viewers. By the end of the 1920s, pressure from civic and religious groups on the producers and the Motion Picture Producers Association had escalated. These critics demanded that industry officials exert some kind of control over film content and the moral messages contained in the product of Hollywood.

There were at least two responses to the rise of concern over sexual images and the fears of undue moral laxity in American films. On one level, the producers and directors of the late silent era sometimes engaged in their own informal self-monitoring by communicating pious messages that justified the controversial imagery that filled American screens as well as movie advertising copy and theater displays. In these films, deviant behavior typically resulted in negative moral consequences for the wayward women who strayed from the straight and narrow path. More commonly, women who engaged in risky sexual escapades on screen chose morally acceptable alternatives in the final reel. The modern movie models may have tested the social limits, but marriage and family was still the last stop on their journeys of self-discovery. "Good" women ended up with husbands and lives of blissful domesticity.[2] In this respect, screen portrayals of the modern woman reflected the experience of many young women who broke into the workplace in the 1920s but failed to gain the full economic independence that would allow them true freedom and independence in the competitive world.

A second response that documented the insecurities of the Hollywood producers was a more formal and rigid self-censorship. By the end of the 1920s, a self-imposed regulatory system became institutionalized as industry officials closed ranks in self-defense. Fearful of new federal controls, studio leaders moved aggressively to protect themselves against charges of moral insensitivity. After a long battle with local censors dating from the Progressive era, the producers responded to the social critics by imposing their own set of standards on the movie industry, formally codified in the Hays Code of 1930.[3]

Though acceptance of code restrictions was voluntary, widespread compliance was destined to shape the content of the movies for years to come.

By the end of the 1920s, the moral experimentalism and social inquiry found in Hollywood's domestic dramas and romantic comedies had run their course. The unsettling social questions raised by the presence of the "new woman" and the social issues introduced in these films had proven too risky for an increasingly cautious industry intent on making its product acceptable to the new middle-class movie audience. It may be argued that as the motion picture industry reached for respectability, its product lost some of the social relevance that had surfaced in some of the films of the twenties. It is certainly true that, by the end of the decade, the excitement and optimism of the flapper figure had faded from the screen. Symptomatic of the change were the movie roles offered Clara Bow and Joan Crawford, the symbols of flapper madness. By 1930, Crawford was working on-screen to repair the social damage created by flappers out of control in *Our Blushing Brides*, while Bow had become a drag at the box office.

As the eventful 1920s came to a sour end with the devastating stock market crash of 1929, the increasing tendency to embrace domesticity found in the outcomes of the decade's films marked new realities faced by modern women. As Mary Ryan has noted, this period witnessed the "solidification of a new pattern of female roles characterized by a dynamic equilibrium between work, home, and consumer activities."[4] The motion pictures of the 1920s not only reflected the changes under way, but also exerted a powerful influence on women caught in this transitional process. Careful analysis of *Dancing Mothers* will enable you to explore some of the dramatic social changes that occurred when Americans entered the age of mass culture. As the film reaches its conclusion, none of the principal characters has found happiness in the new freedom of the new era; rather, social confusion has resulted from the clash between the old values and the new. The unsatisfying resolution of this domestic drama clearly reflected an element of ambivalence towards the new economic, technical, and social order identified by modern cultural historians. It is your task to discover and consider those points of conflict.

Endnotes

1. William E. Leuchtenburg, *The Perils of Prosperity, 1914–1932* (Chicago: University of Chicago Press, 1970), Chapter 9.
2. Mary P. Ryan, "The Projection of a New Womanhood: The Movie Moderns of the 1920s," in Jean E. Friedman and William G. Shade, eds., *Our American Sisters: Women in American Life and Thought*, 3d ed. (Lexington, Mass.: D. C. Heath & Co., 1982), 510.
3. Richard Maltby, "'To Prevent the Prevalent Type of Book': Censorship and Adaptation in Hollywood, 1924–1934," in Francis G. Couvares, ed., *Movie Censorship and American Culture* (Washington, D.C.: Smithsonian Institution Press, 1996), 104–105.
4. Ryan, 517.

THE PRIMARY SOURCES

The documents begin with an emphasis on women and marriage, starting with an excerpt from screenwriter Elinor Glyn's novel, *It* (1926), in which she summarizes the qualities identified with healthy sexuality in the 1920s. Novelist Fannie Hurst follows with a *New*

York Times interview describing companionate marriage, a more open relationship explored by some couples in this era. Suzanne La Follette, a member of a renowned political family, adds her endorsement of divorce as a necessary option. Turning to the movie industry's perspective on the social issues of the 1920s, social critic Frederick Lewis Allen's memoir (1931) notes Hollywood's move towards self-censorship under the leadership of Will Hays. The excerpt from the Hays Code addresses the troublesome moral issues of the period, with the industry's prescriptions for resolving them.

ELINOR GLYN DESCRIBES "IT"

It
Elinor Glyn

"To have "It," the fortunate possessor must have that strange magnetism which attracts both sexes. "It" is a purely virile quality, belonging to a strong character. He or she must be entirely unselfconscious and full of self-confidence, indifferent to the effect he or she is producing, and uninfluenced by others. There must be physical attraction, but beauty is unnecessary. Conceit or self-consciousness destroys "It" immediately.

SOURCE: Elinor Glyn, *It* (1926), http://www.mdle.com/ClassicFilms/rb2.htm.

A NEW MARRIAGE STYLE DISCUSSED BY FANNIE HURST

Interview
Fannie Hurst

"To begin with," she said, "My solution to the marriage problem is not the world's solution of the problem. I didn't set out to do that. I was not inspired with the ardor of the reformer who would bring peace to a badly organized world. There was none of that. I was interested in a highly specialized situation, peculiar to myself. . . . Mr. Danielson and I worked out a formula which seemed to meet our special and individual needs. It happens that we have hit on the right one. For ourselves, it has stood the test of eight years. It works.

"That doesn't mean that our solution must or will be the solution of the world. As long as human beings differ from each other each will have to work out his own salvation. But if we are going to treat the marriage business intelligently then we'll have to begin with acceptance of the idea that human beings are different. . . .

"Take marriage structure as it now stands. It's old fashioned, it's drafty, it's leaky, the roof sags, the timbers shake, there's no modern plumbing, no hardwood floors, no steam heat. We don't feel comfortable in it. We've outgrown the edifice, but we don't dare get out of it. . . .

"For some strange reason, social custom is the laggard of civilization. . . .

"Those of us who dare shiver at the cold of the old edifice, plan our structure differently. We study the plans of many architects and build our house to suit our own particular and peculiar needs. We put in hardwood floors, sanitary plumbing, steam heat, many windows. We retain much of the charm of the old-fashioned house. We keep the open fireplace, the handsome door, the good pictures, the things that bring ease and comfort and spiritual delight. It's all very wonderful. And very satisfying and sensible.

"Not the least satisfactory arrangement of the new structure, the new marriage structure, is the privacy it gives, the little self-respecting privacies which the old kind of marriage seems to revel in breaking down.

". . . Monogamy, however, is conceded to be a good thing for the social structure. Whether it is or not is not the point of this discussion. But granted that it is, what is the thing which is going to make us happy in a monogamous marriage? Illusion. Monogamy has to be pampered a bit; it has to be made to appear like a many-faceted jewel. A woman must be new to her mate, a man must be a not altogether known quantity to his. Neither can afford to let all the barriers *fall*.

"It is the partitions built up in the new edifice that help maintain the illusion, that help conserve and preserve it. Yet men are afraid to build it and women are afraid to live in it. Fear, fear of living. That is the cause of the slow step of progress in all avenues of life. . . .

"I have talked about this thing to women. I have talked it from the platform. I believe that marriage can be happy, but I am also convinced that the old pattern cannot be made to fit all. But women will not look at the problem from the point of view of the problem as a whole. They argue from the individual. . . .

"You speak about trial marriage. Trial marriage is logical solution for the problem for some people, but it's a waste of time to discuss it. People take it about as seriously as 'Yes, we have no bananas.' They refuse to consider it. You can't make any headway. It's important, but as long as people are ridiculed and shamed out of it, that won't be a solution to anything. . . .

"Do I think my solution is the solution for the young women who are aware of this wind before the dawn? Yes and no. There is no one solution for all, as I said before. But it's a solution as far as it can be adapted to individual needs. Keeping a double ménage is not a prime requisite of the arrangement. Keeping a sense of privacy and freedom is.

". . . Where there's actual freedom it is more likely to be used than abused. There is not so much to fear from a relationship of this sort, because both are kept on the *qui vive* for each other. There is everything to fear from the old-fashioned good-wife-and-mother relationship. It is contrary to the biological instincts of the human race. Its observation is based on the least admirable of human traits—fear of living!

". . . If a woman can sell insurance or run a paying beauty parlor or write a book, the chances are ten to one that she can hire vastly more efficient service to train her children than she could give them. Because I paint a picture, let us say, does not mean that I can bring up a child. . . .

"No, the place of the woman of intelligence is not inevitably in the kitchen worrying about pot and pan trifles, not at the front door every evening waiting tremulously for the step of her John and fearful lest the roast be not overdone. Her place is where she can give the most service and get the most out of life. . . ."

SOURCE: Fannie Hurst, Interview, *The New York Times*, December 9, 1923.

SUZANNE LA FOLLETTE DESCRIBES A NEW ATTITUDE ON DIVORCE
Women in the Modern World
Suzanne La Follette

The general acceptance of the idea of divorce at present is in great measure the result of woman's growing demand for reciprocity in her relations with men, and her refusal to be owned either economically or sexually. It may be regarded as an aspect of her general declaration of independence. That there are women who still make a profession of being owned, either in or out of wedlock, does not invalidate the general truth that as women have found themselves

in a position to make their demands effective, they have insisted upon elevating marriage to a higher moral plane. Divorce has been one of the means to this end. No doubt it is a means often abused; but no institution has been more often abused by unscrupulous people than that of marriage, and no one ever thought the abuse an argument against the institution. It is largely due to possibility of divorce that marriage now tends to be regarded as a voluntary partnership involving equal economic and spiritual obligations on both sides, and justly to be dissolved when those obligations have been violated by either party or have become onerous to either or to both. . . .

SOURCE: Suzanne La Follette, "Women in the Modern World," in Alvin Johnson et al., eds., *Civilization and Enjoyment, Man and His World Series* (New York: D. Van Nostrand, 1929), 58–60.

FREDERICK LEWIS ALLEN ASSESSES THE IMPACT OF THE MOVIES AND THE PRODUCERS' RESPONSE TO THE CRITICS

Movies and the Producers' Response
Frederick Lewis Allen

Crowding the news stands along with sex and confession magazines were motion-picture magazines which depicted "seven movie kisses" with such captions as "Do you recognize your little friend, Mae Busch? She's had lots of kisses, but she never seems to grow *blasé*. At least you'll agree that she's giving a good imitation of a person enjoying this one." The movies themselves, drawing millions to their doors every day and every night, played incessantly upon the same lucrative theme. The producers of one picture advertised "brilliant men, beautiful jazz babies, champagne baths, midnight revels, petting parties in the purple dawn, all ending in one terrific smashing climax that makes you gasp"; the vendors of another promised "neckers, petters, white kisses, red kisses, pleasure-mad daughters, sensation-craving mothers, . . . the truth—bold, naked, sensational." Seldom did the films offer as much as these advertisements promised, but there was enough in some of them to cause a sixteen-year-old girl (quoted by Alice Miller Mitchell) to testify, "Those pictures with hot love-making in them, they make girls and boys sitting together want to get up and walk out, go off somewhere, you know. Once I walked out with a boy before the picture was even over. We took a ride. But my friend, she all the time had to get up and go out with her boy friend."

A storm of criticism from church organizations led the motion-picture producers, early in the decade, to install Will H. Hays, President Harding's Postmaster-General, as their arbiter of morals and taste, and Mr. Hays promised that all would be well. "This industry must have," said he before the Los Angeles Chamber of Commerce, "toward that sacred thing, the mind of a child, toward that clean virgin thing, that unmarked slate, the same responsibility, the same care about the impression made upon it, that the best clergyman or the most inspired teacher of youth would have." The result of Mr. Hays's labors in behalf of the unmarked slate was to make the moral ending as obligatory as in the confession magazines, to smear over sexy pictures with pious platitudes, and to blacklist for motion-picture production many a fine novel and play which, because of its very honesty, might be construed as seriously or intelligently questioning the traditional sex ethics of the small town. Mr. Hays, being somewhat of a genius, managed to keep the churchmen at bay. Whenever the threats of censorship began to become ominous he would promulgate a new series of moral commandments for the producers to follow. Yet of the practical effects of his supervision it is perhaps enough to say that the quotations given above all date from the period of his dictatorship. Giving lip-service to the old code, the movies diligently and with consummate vulgarity publicized the new.

Each of these diverse influences—the post-war disillusion, the new status of women, the Freudian gospel, the automobile, prohibition, the sex and confession magazines, and the movies—had its part in bringing about the revolution. Each of them, as an influence, was played upon by all the others; none of them could alone have changed to any great degree the folkways of America; together their force was irresistible.

SOURCE: Frederic Lewis Allen, *Only Yesterday: An Informal History of the Nineteen-Twenties* (New York: Harper & Row, 1931), 84–85.

Motion Picture Production Code
Motion Picture Producers and Distributors of America

PLOT MATERIAL

1. *The triangle*, that is, the love of a third party by one already married, needs careful handling, if marriage, the sanctity of home, and sex morality are not to be imperilled.

2. *Adultery* as a subject should be avoided:
   a. It is *never* a fit subject for *comedy*. Thru comedy of this sort, ridicule is thrown on the essential relationships of home and family and marriage, and illicit relationships are made to seem permissible, and either delightful or daring.
   b. Sometimes adultery must be counted on as material occurring in serious drama.
   In this case:
   - It should not appear to be justified;
   - It should not be used to weaken respect for marriage;
   - It should not be presented as attractive or alluring.

3. *Seduction and rape* are difficult subjects and bad material from the viewpoint of the general audience in the theatre.
   a. They should never be introduced as subject matter *unless* absolutely essential to the plot.
   b. They should *never* be treated as comedy.
   c. Where essential to the plot, they must not be more than *suggested*.
   d. Even the struggles preceding rape should not be shown.
   e. The *methods* by which seduction, essential to the plot, is attained should not be explicit or represented in detail where there is a likelihood of arousing wrongful emotions on the part of the audience.

4. *Scenes of passion* are sometimes necessary for plot. However:
   a. They should appear only where necessary and *not* as an added stimulus to the emotions of the audience.
   b. *When not essential to the plot* they should not occur.

c. They must *not* be *explicit* in action nor vivid in method, e.g. by handling of the body, by lustful and prolonged kissing, by evidently lustful embraces, by positions which strongly arouse passions.

d. In general, where essential to the plot, scenes of passion should *not* be presented in such a way as to *arouse or excite the passions of the ordinary spectator*.

5. *Sexual immorality* is sometimes necessary for the plot. It is subject to the following:

GENERAL PRINCIPLES—regarding plots dealing with sex, passion, and incidents relating to them: All legislators have recognized clearly that there are in normal human beings emotions which react naturally and spontaneously to the presentation of certain definite manifestations of sex and passion.

a. The presentation of scenes, episodes, plots, etc., which are deliberately meant to excite these manifestations on the part of the audience is always wrong, is subversive to the interest of society, and a peril to the human race.

b. Sex and passion exist and consequently must *sometimes enter* into the stories which deal with human beings.
   - *Pure love*, the love of a man for a woman permitted by the law of God and man, is the rightful subject of plots. The passion arising from this love is not the subject of plots.
   - *Impure love*, the love of man and woman forbidden by human and divine law, must be presented in such a way that:
     a. It is clearly known by the audience to be wrong;
     b. Its presentation does not excite sexual reactions, mental or physical, in an ordinary audience;
     c. It is not treated as matter for comedy.

HENCE: *Even within the limits of pure love* certain facts have been universally regarded by lawmakers as outside the limits of safe presentation. These are the manifestations of passion and the sacred intimacies of private life:

1. Either before marriage in the courtship of decent people;
2. Or after marriage, as is perfectly clear.

In the case of pure love, the difficulty is not so much about what details are permitted for presentation. This is perfectly clear in most cases. The difficulty concerns itself with the tact, delicacy, and general regard for propriety manifested in their presentation.

But in the case of impure love, the love which society has always regarded as wrong and which has been banned by divine law, the following are important:

1. It must not be the subject of comedy or farce or treated as the material for laughter;
2. It must not be presented as attractive and beautiful;
3. It must mot be presented in such a way as to arouse passion or morbid curiosity on the part of the audience;
4. It must not be made to seem right and permissible;
5. In general, it must not be detailed in method or manner . . .

DETAILS OF PLOT, EPISODE, AND TREATMENT

Vulgarity

Vulgarity may be carefully distinguished from obscenity. Vulgarity is the treatment of low, disgusting, unpleasant subjects which decent society considers outlawed from normal conversation.

Vulgarity in the motion pictures is limited in precisely the same way as in decent groups of men and women by the dictates of good taste and civilized usage, and by the effect of shock, scandal, and harm on those coming in contact with this vulgarity.

1. *Oaths* should never be used as a comedy element. Where required by the plot, the less offensive oaths may be permitted.
2. *Vulgar expressions* come under the same treatment as vulgarity in general. Where women and chil-dren are to see the film, vulgar expressions (and oaths) should be cut to the absolute essentials required by the situation.
3. The name of *Jesus Christ* should never be used except in reverence.

Obscenity

Obscenity is concerned with immorality, but has the additional connotation of being common, vulgar and coarse.

1. *Obscenity in fact*, that is, in spoken word, gesture, episode, plot, is against divine and human law, and hence altogether outside the range of subject matter or treatment.
2. Obscenity should *not be suggested* by gesture, manner, etc.
3. An obscene reference, even if it is expected to be understandable to only the more sophisticated part of the audience, should not be introduced.
4. *Obscene language* is treated as all obscenity.

Costume

GENERAL PRINCIPLES:

1. The effect of nudity or semi-nudity upon the normal man or woman, and much more upon the young person, has been honestly recognized by all lawmakers and moralists.
2. Hence the fact that the nude or semi-nude body may be *beautiful* does not make its use in films moral. For in addition to its beauty, the effects of the nude or semi-nude body on the normal individual must be taken into consideration.
3. Nudity or semi-nudity used simply to put a "punch" into a picture comes under the head of immoral actions as treated above. It is immoral in its effect upon the average audience.
4. Nudity or semi-nudity is sometimes apparently necessary for the plot. *Nudity is never permitted.* Semi-nudity may be permitted under conditions.

PARTICULAR PRINCIPLES:

1. *The more intimate parts of the human body* are male and female organs and the breasts of a woman.
   a. They should *never be uncovered*.
   b. They should not *be covered with* transparent or translucent material.

c. They should not be clearly and unmistakably *outlined* by the garment.

2. *The less intimate parts of the body*, the legs, arms, shoulders and back, are less certain of causing reaction on the part of the audience.

Hence:

a. Exposure necessary *for the plot* or action is permitted.

b. Exposure *for the sake of exposure* or the "punch" is wrong.

c. *Scenes of undressing* should be avoided. When necessary for the plot, they should be kept within the limits of decency. When not necessary for the plot, they are to be avoided, as their effect on the ordinary spectator is harmful.

d. *The manner or treatment of exposure* should not be suggestive or indecent.

e. The following is important in connection with *dancing costumes:*

3. Dancing costumes cut to permit *grace* or freedom of movement, provided they remain within the limits of decency indicated, are permissible.

4. Dancing costumes cut to *permit indecent actions* or movements or to make possible during the dance indecent exposure, are wrong, especially when permitting:

a. Movements of the breasts;

b. Movements or sexual suggestions of the intimate parts of the body;

c. Suggestion of nudity.

Dancing

1. Dancing in general is recognized as an *art* and a *beautiful* form of expressing human emotion.

2. Obscene dances are those:

a. Which suggest or represent sexual actions, whether performed solo or with two or more;

b. Which are designed to excite an audience, to arouse passions, or to cause physical excitement.

HENCE: Dances of the type known as "Kooch," or "CanCan," since they violate decency in these two ways, are wrong. Dances with movements of the breasts, excessive body movement while the feet remain stationary, the so-called "belly dances"—these dances are immoral, obscene, and hence altogether wrong . . .

II. Sex

The sanctity of the institution of marriage and the home shall be upheld. Pictures shall not infer that low forms of sex relationship are the accepted or common thing.

1. ADULTERY, sometimes necessary plot material, must not be explicitly treated, or justified, or presented attractively. Out of regard for the sanctity of marriage and the home, the *triangle,* that is, the love of a third party for one already married, needs careful handling. The treatment should not throw sympathy against marriage as an institution.

2. SCENES OF PASSION must be treated with an honest acknowledgement of human nature and its normal reactions. Many scenes cannot be presented without arousing dangerous emotions on the part of the immature, the young or the criminal classes.

a. They should not be introduced when not essential to the plot.

b. Excessive and lustful kissing, lustful embraces, suggestive postures and gestures, are not to be shown.

c. In general, passion should be so treated that these scenes do not stimulate the lower and baser element.

3. SEDUCTION OR RAPE.

a. They should never be more than suggested, and only when essential for the plot, and even then never shown by explicit method.

b. They are never the proper subject for comedy.

4. SEX PERVERSION or any inference to it is forbidden.

5. WHITE SLAVERY shall not be treated.

6. MISCEGENATION (sex relationship between the white and black races) is forbidden.

7. SEX HYGIENE AND VENEREAL DISEASES are not subjects for motion pictures.

8. SCENES OF ACTUAL CHILDBIRTH, in fact or silhouette, are never to be presented.

9. CHILDREN'S SEX ORGANS are never to be exposed. . . .

SOURCE: "The Motion Picture Production Code," Second Section, 1930. Reprinted by permission of the Motion Picture Association of America.

Follow-Up Problems

1. What does this film reveal about women's life experiences in the 1920s? What does the betrayed wife's personal crisis indicate about family values and marital relationships in this era? What is the significance of her final decision?
2. What is "it," as represented in the character played by Clara Bow?
3. As you observe the images of consumption projected in this film, consider their significance in relation to the tastes and aspirations of the audience. What social and economic element in American society is dealt with in the picture? How are the experiences of the film's characters related to those of American moviegoers of the 1920s? What do these images of consumer behavior reveal about the economic changes of the era and the social function of the motion pictures?
4. In this film, what is the relationship of the young and the old? Do you find this conception of generational relationships credible?
5. What evidence do you see in *Dancing Mothers* of the clash between traditional and modern morality in the 1920s?

Further Reading

Brown, Dorothy. *Setting a Course: American Women in the 1920s*. Boston: Twayne, 1987.

Brownlow, Kevin. *Beyond the Mask of Innocence: Sex, Violence, Prejudice, Crime, Films of Social Conscience in the Silent Era*. Berkeley, Calif.: University of California Press, 1990.

Couvares, Francis G., ed. *Movie Censorship and American Culture*. Washington, D.C.: Smithsonian Institution Press, 1996.

Haskell, Molly. *From Reverence to Rape: The Treatment of Women in the Movies*. 2d ed. Chicago: University of Chicago Press, 1987.

Higashi, Sumiko. *Virgins, Vamps, and Flappers: The American Silent Movie Heroine*. Montreal: Eden Press, 1978.

May, Lary. *Screening Out the Past: The Birth of Mass Culture and the Motion Picture Industry*. Chicago: The University of Chicago Press, 1980.

Ryan, Mary. "The Projection of the New Womanhood: The Movie Moderns of the 1920s," in Friedman, Jean, and William G. Shade, eds., *Our American Sisters: Women in American Life and Thought*. 3d ed. Lexington, Mass.: D. C. Heath & Co., 1982.

Sklar, Robert. *Movie-Made America: A Cultural History of American Movies*. New York: Vintage, rev. ed. 1994.

Sloan, Kay. *The Loud Silents: The Origins of the Social Problem Film*. Urbana, Ill.: University of Illinois Press, 1988.

Filmography

Companionate Marriage (CM Corporation, Dist. First National Pictures, 1928).

Our Blushing Brides (MGM, 1930).

Our Dancing Daughters (MGM, 1928).

The Celluloid Document

Dancing Mothers (Famous Players, Dist. Paramount, 1926).

Chapter 4

The End of Romantic War:
All Quiet on the Western Front (1930) and
Disillusionment in the Interwar Era

For Americans in the 1920s and 1930s, the intervention of the United States in World War I had been an intensely moving experience. The enthusiasm of 1917 quickly turned to revulsion against a war of attrition that deeply impressed the young people who had been called upon to sacrifice in order to make the world "safe for democracy." Not only had veterans been shocked by the realities of trench warfare, but by 1919, many Americans had also concluded that the world system that grew out of the war was neither democratic nor very safe. Influenced by the political struggle that ended in American failure to ratify the Versailles Treaty, the public became deeply suspicious of idealistic pronouncements and hostile to foreign ties. Determined to preserve independence in foreign policy, both policy makers and the person on the street rejected hollow praise of patriotic war as well as the internationalist ideas that many saw as the key cause of a mistaken American effort to redeem the old world with the blood of the new. This disillusionment was captured in 1930 by *All Quiet on the Western Front*, a sensitive screen adaptation of Erich Maria Remarque's successful novel of the same name. Analysis of this film provides keen insight into American attitudes on foreign involvements in the interwar era.

The Historical Background

Given the smoldering resentment and deep-seated isolationism of the twenties, it is not surprising that Hollywood displayed interest in the human side of the Great War. By the mid-1920s, literary figures had already begun to explore the dark side of modern war and the apparent emptiness of Wilsonian idealism. Writers such as Ernest Hemingway and John Dos Passos recorded their own revulsion over the carnage and wasted humanity that were the by-products of the war for liberal democracy. As Michael Isenberg has noted, their works, though stunning in their realism, recorded an elite perspective on the wartime experience and its meaning for the future. In contrast, he argues, the wider public expressed mixed emotions about the war, which despite its brutalities had produced remarkable acts of heroism and self-sacrifice.[1] Because they had captured a mass audience, the motion pictures of the twenties may be viewed as barometers of non-elite opinion concerning the war's impact on those who fought and those who waited.

As early as 1924, director King Vidor and MGM producer Irving Thalberg had agreed that the human impact of the war would be an appropriate subject for a feature film that could tap the deepest feelings of an audience still sorting out its opinions about the wartime experience. Thalberg soon established a working relationship with author Lawrence Stallings, a veteran who wrote with passion of his own years of service overseas. For Stallings, the result was *Plumes*, a novel loosely based on his own experience with romantic war. This work, the literary source for Vidor's classic film *The Big Parade* (1925), expressed the conflicted attitudes of veterans who tried to find nobility in their personal sacrifices while confronting the futility of modern war. The film faithfully recreated this ambivalence towards the war and military service, which had produced only heartbreak for the wounded veteran whose story it told. Vidor's evenhanded treatment of the war and the veterans' response to combat connected with movie audiences from the outset. Always an important measure of a film's penetration of the public consciousness, the box office statistics make it clear that the film struck a chord with viewers in search of the war's meaning. After grossing over $15 million, *The Big Parade* was rereleased in 1931 with a new sound score that employed the latest technology to enhance its public appeal. The power of the film's blend of negative and positive images[2] was evident in its continued financial success.

By this time, however, another, more profoundly disturbing picture of the war had reached American screens. Carefully adapted from Remarque's brilliantly successful novel, *All Quiet on the Western Front* (1929), a sensitive film burst upon the American movie scene in 1930. Rightly recognized as the definitive filmic expression of antiwar sentiment, this picture helped shape public perception of World War I for a generation of Americans already disillusioned with Wilsonian idealism. One of the most successful films in Hollywood's long history, *All Quiet on the Western Front* has been seen by more than one hundred million people, a testimony to the lasting power of its clear message. For students of United States history in the interwar era, it documents the depth of isolationism in an American public unwilling to contemplate another foreign venture in internationalism.

Remarque's novel is partly autobiographical, derived largely from the author's wartime experience in the German army on the Western Front late in World War I. As such, it expressed the deep disillusionment of a generation of veterans who shared his loss of faith in governments, leaders, and empty patriotic ideals. Published in 1929, the book sold two million copies in its first year, a record that provides clear evidence of popular interest in antiwar themes. There can be little doubt that Remarque had successfully captured the sentiments of a postwar generation that rejected war as futile and expressed its anguish in a remarkably sensitive way. He spoke to and for an audience that bridged the nationality gap and shared a deep desire for a world without war.

Despite the novel's potential audience appeal, most American producers were unwilling to accept the challenge presented by its frank treatment of the war and its consequences. Several studios rejected the project as an unwarranted financial risk. Hollywood was in the business of entertainment, and this venture seemed likely to stimulate debate and upset audiences unnecessarily. Since the movies were by this time big business, it was not surprising that wary producers would seek to avoid themes that might anger foreign governments capable of disrupting the important overseas market for American films. In short, the nature of the business meant that there was little incentive for industry executives to risk financial failure by tackling controversial topics that endangered maximum distribution.

Yet one bold producer decided to take a chance on a novel that had been immensely successful. The result was the release in 1930 of Universal Pictures Corporation's production of *All Quiet on the Western Front*, a feature destined to become a film classic. The Hollywood adaptation of the Remarque novel reflected the judgment of the rising young producer Carl Laemmle Jr. of Universal Pictures, a German immigrant who was prepared to gamble on a clear antiwar argument. The film appeared at a critical moment in the history of the motion picture, the advent of sound; it was therefore revolutionary in its use of the new technology for maximum impact. Directed by the youthful Lewis Milestone and starring unknown actor Lew Ayres, *All Quiet on the Western Front* was the creation of a fresh group of Hollywood artists who were part of a postwar generation grown suspicious of authority and dubious about war as an instrument of national policy. The product of their efforts was a film that succeeded both critically and financially while becoming the major hit of 1930.

What distinguished this picture from other portrayals of World War I was not only an unvarnished antiwar stance bordering on pacifism, but also its unique portrayal of the combat experience from the perspective of young German recruits. By humanizing the former enemy, Milestone was able to universalize the horrors of modern mechanized warfare for a sympathetic audience. The disarmingly innocent Lew Ayres was a perfect fit for the character of Remarque's young antihero, Paul Baumer, who symbolized the helplessness of the little man caught up in the swirl of politics and the brutality of total war. There was a great distance between the ambivalence of *The Big Parade* in 1925 and the clarity of *All Quiet on the Western Front* only five years later.

Both the Remarque novel and the film professed nonpartisan objectivity. Quoting Remarque's introduction, the original version of the film began with a disclaimer. Its preface insisted that the story was "neither an accusation nor a confession" and certainly not an "adventure" since death was far from adventurous for those who faced it. Rather, the film promised to "tell of a generation of men who, even though they may have escaped its shells, were destroyed by the war." Despite the filmmakers' claims, it is difficult to view this powerful film without detecting an indictment of World War I and those who bore responsibility for the slaughter. This film truly engaged the past and drew contemporary meanings from history.

The clarity of the film's indictment of warfare in general and World War I in particular produced an immediate response. On the Left, both European and American liberals applauded its bold criticism of foreign policy and nationalism gone awry. Others were less complimentary. The searing images were too realistic and graphic for some observers, who charged the filmmakers with excess vulgarity. Of greater political significance were the reactions of conservatives who saw only too clearly the movie's potential for damaging nationalism. European politicians, later including the rising National Socialists in Germany, criticized the film as pacifistic propaganda that destroyed the national glory found in patriotic war. By emphasizing the human experience of combatants, they argued, this film robbed war of its political meaning and, by implication, its justification. These concerns led to censorship of the film in the German market and in 1931 forced Universal to delete several scenes in order to ensure exhibition in Germany. These efforts to accommodate the censors were ultimately fruitless, and, although *All Quiet on the Western Front* played to sellout crowds in England, by 1933 it had been banned in both Italy and Germany. Before the ban, future Nazi Propaganda Minister Joseph Goebbels encouraged street demonstrations and attacked the picture as "a Jewish film." In December 1930, forty thousand Nazis rallied in protest outside the Berlin theater where it was to be shown. Once Chancellor Adolf Hitler came to power in 1933, the film was subject to a total ban, which was not lifted in Germany until 1952. For other reasons, the film also encountered censorship in France, where it was not to reappear on the screen until 1962.

In the United States, on the other hand, the film fared much better, opening to positive reviews and widespread critical acclaim. The audience response was enthusiastic, which meant financial success. By 1931, it had garnered several awards, including the Academy Awards for Best Picture, Direction, Cinematography, and Screenwriting. Carl Laemmle Jr. was seriously suggested as a possible nominee for the Nobel Peace Prize. The enduring appeal of *All Quiet on the Western Front* was evident in its several rereleases after 1930, as well as in the steady revenue it produced over the years. It is still regularly incorporated into classic film series programs and is a staple on college and university campuses throughout the United States. The film contains a message for all seasons.

World War I, the first total war, brought an unprecedented level of bloodshed that left a permanent imprint on the generation of 1914. As the conflict expanded, unleashed technology overtook the men who had created the new tools of destruction. Given a sobering 13 million military dead and 34 million wounded, it is not an exaggeration to say that the war destroyed a generation and that its impact was disastrous for all nations and populations engaged. Through the magic of the moving image, Lewis Milestone, Carl Laemmle, Lew Ayres, and their comrades make it possible for modern viewers to step into the past to catch a glimpse of that conflict's character and consequences. Though these faded images are now 80 years old, they still possess the ability to captivate and horrify. Equally valuable is this film's capacity for taking modern students back to the late 1920s and reacquainting them with the sentiments of the movie audiences that reacted to these depictions of senseless human sacrifice. Careful examination of *All Quiet on the Western Front* makes the isolationism that dominated American public opinion in the late 1920s and early 1930s more understandable to modern observers. The horror of 1918 may be connected to the revulsion against war that permeated popular views on foreign policy as new overseas challenges arose in the wake of a failed war for democracy.

Analyzing the Film

From the very beginning of the film, viewers are drawn into the politics and nationalistic assumptions of a nation and people on the brink of destructive war. Watch for evidence of aggressive patriotism in the efforts of the elderly schoolteacher to inspire his young students to enlist in defense of the fatherland. In contrast, consider the meaning of Paul's words near the film's climax upon his return to the classroom. During the course of the film, moviegoers were exposed to the chaos, brutality, and waste of life in the trenches. Perhaps most telling was the depiction of slow death in the foxhole scene in which Paul confronts and finally kills a French soldier, whose utter humanity is revealed when Paul searches his wallet only to discover that he is a family man with dependents at home and suffers remorse at his own role in the outcome. In another sequence the brotherhood of all men is explored as combatants in the rear discuss the empty justifications for war manufactured by the politicians, thus underlining the meaninglessness of patriotic war. Impelled to kill by external forces, Paul himself meets his fate in the bittersweet final scene in which he is struck by a sniper as he reaches for a delicate butterfly above the trench he occupies, thus reinforcing the fragility of life and finality of death. The last schoolboy of 1914 has met his fate.

Because *All Quiet on the Western Front* was shot and completed early in the budding sound era, the new technology became an important feature of the production process. The film was, in fact, Lewis Milestone's first sound picture, which meant that he was engaged in an experimental production process. The result was a much more realistic representation of combat than had been possible in earlier features such as *The Big Parade*. As you analyze the film, ask yourself how the employment of sound contributed to the authenticity of the narrative that unfolds on the screen. What other elements of realism appear in the visual images you examine?

Careful examination of the film's primary focus will also lead to further thought about the targets of the criticisms leveled by both Remarque and Milestone. Look for the guilty parties singled out for ridicule or attack. Think about the nationality question and what the film's treatment of this issue reveals about the issue of responsibility for the human tragedy acted out on the field of battle. In this context, consider the sources of negative overseas reaction to the film during the 1930s, and account for those reactions. Notice the leadership issue. In what way does the film address the problem of governmental decision making?

Finally, place the film in the political context of the early 1930s by linking its argument and message to the foreign policy debates of the period. Try to connect the rise of fascism in Germany and Italy with American uneasiness about foreign entanglements. As you explore these political alterations and the controversy they initiated, assess the historical significance of *All Quiet on the Western Front* as evidence of deeply held beliefs and policy preferences expressed by American citizens in the interwar era. As you approach this task, try to grapple with the thorny question of the motion picture's relevance as either an influence on or reflection of the values and attitudes of the consumers who made up the movie audiences of the United States. In this way, you will again demonstrate the value of the motion picture as a primary source, in this case a document that records the sweeping noninterventionism that dominated the conduct and formulation of American foreign policy in the 1930s as the world began its march towards yet another war.

Thinking About Primary Sources

All Quiet on the Western Front is a celluloid document rich in content bearing on the public attitudes of Americans in the 1930s, many of whom remained shaken by the brutality of the trenches, the divisiveness of the war's political outcome, and the continuing disillusionment of an idealistic dream betrayed. The documents that follow, if read in conjunction with a critical viewing of the film, will contribute to a fuller understanding of the picture's meaning for the generation that first viewed this brilliant expression of the noninterventionist sentiment of interwar America. They also allow you to compare portions of the novel that gave life to the film with the screen adaptation of the author's initial work.

When you view the film, you will undoubtedly note that it is much more chronological in its structure than the novel, which employs flashbacks and memories of earlier times. The film narrative unfolds in a logical, sequential fashion. The movie proceeds from prewar education and enlistment to arrival at the front and the experiences encountered in the trenches. The final sequences focus on Paul's visit at home, his fatalism upon return to the front, and his ultimate death in combat. Try to account for the filmmaker's choice of the linear approach rather than the author's blend of memory and immediate experience.

Even more important for analytical purposes is your effort to link the ideas expressed in artistic form to the prevailing public attitudes on war at the time of the film's release. Use the documents to clarify the contemporary perception of World War I and its outcome. Connect the film's themes with the sentiments expressed in the Kellogg-Briand treaty and the film review. As you consider this question, try to identify the focal point of debate over warfare as an instrument of national policy. Think of this public discussion in the context of a distinction between sweeping universal truths and short-term ethical concerns. Use the visual imagery and the print sources to determine which category this film and its literary source belong in. One useful way to approach this task is to think about the film's emphasis on human experience as opposed to policy issues.

Finally, as you work to place this film in its historical context, think about the function of motion pictures as social indicators. Review the excerpts from Remarque's novel, and consider the author's and filmmaker's representations of reality. Determine whether it is possible for a work of art to be truly "realistic" in depicting the combat experience and the realities of war. Compare the novel and the film in terms of the literary artist's intent and biases, as well as the sometimes argumentative or "representational" aspect of the motion picture as a medium of communication. As you engage in this analysis, remain focused on the hopes, fears, and expectations of the American audience in 1930.

Historical Perspective

All Quiet on the Western Front left a deep impression on American audiences, whose members found it difficult to think of its characters as enemies beyond redemption. When Americans observed the plight of Paul Baumer and his unfortunate comrades, they saw the average man entrapped by politicians, patriots, militarists, and rulers. Their sympathy for the victims mirrored the public perception of the universal experience of servicemen caught up in the deadly serious business of physical survival. The popular response to the film in the early 1930s marked the high point of positive sentiment towards Germany in the interwar era. Likewise, American revulsion against what most regarded as the misguided intervention of 1917 contributed to widespread support for the policy of neutrality as Germany attempted to revise the Treaty of Versailles and reconfigure the geopolitics of the late 1930s.

The rise of Nazism in Germany was a reminder that not all parties, groups, or governments welcomed the message communicated in the novel and the film derived from it. Nazi attacks on Remarque's work and Milestone's adaptation successfully shut down German discussion of the human issues they had so forcefully raised. Similarly, the French censors banished the film from the visual record of the 1930s. In Europe, the politicians and military leaders rejected the wisdom of the previous generation, especially in Germany, a nation that had been humiliated by the shame of defeat in 1918.

When *All Quiet on the Western Front* swept the awards ceremonies at the time of its first release, *Variety* asserted that the League of Nations (which the United States had refused to join) should "buy up the master print, reproduce it in every language to be shown to every nation every year until the word *war* is taken out of the dictionaries." While the advice went unheeded in the unstable 1930s, the film retains its power as an antiwar statement and as an expression of the pathos of human sacrifice on the altar of nationalism. In 1964, Milestone recalled that his masterpiece had endured vicious cutting at the hands of censors and politicians, but that he was glad to report that "the picture proved to have a longer life than many a politician and is still going strong."[3] Without a doubt, this film's stark images of war on the Western Front have been significant in preserving the vivid memory of World War I for other generations. It is equally valuable as a primary source that documents the depth of American antiwar sentiment in the most isolationist juncture in the history of the interwar era.

Endnotes

1. Michael T. Isenberg, "The Great War Viewed from the Twenties: *The Big Parade* (1925)," in John E. O'Connor and Martin A. Jackson, eds., *American History/American Film: Interpreting the Hollywood Image* (New York: Frederick Ungar Publishing Co., 1979), 18–19.
2. The mixed messages in the film and the sources of its popular appeal are discussed in Isenberg, 22–32.
3. Detailed coverage of the controversy created by the film, including its censorship in Europe, may be found in Andrew Kelly, "*All Quiet on the Western Front*: 'Brutal Cutting, Stupid Censors, and Bigoted Politicos,' 1939–1984," *Historical Journal of Film, Radio, and Television* 9 (1989): 135–150, and John Whiteclay Chambers II, "*All Quiet on the Western Front* (1930): The Antiwar Film and the Image of the First World War," *Historical Journal of Film, Radio, and Television* 14 (1994): 377–412.

THE PRIMARY SOURCES

The first document, an excerpt from the Kellogg-Briand Peace Treaty of 1928, records the determination of the nations of the world to avoid another world war. Similar sentiments are reflected in the *New York Times* review of *All Quiet on the Western Front*, which appeared in 1930. Finally, a selection from Erich Maria Remarque's novel, *All Quiet on the Western Front* (1929) will enable you to compare the film with the literary work on which it is based.

DETERMINATION TO AVOID WORLD WAR

The Kellogg-Briand Peace Pact Records a Transnational Determination to Avoid Another World War
U.S. Statutes at Large

The President of the German Reich, the President of the United States of America, His Majesty the King of the Belgians, the President of the French Republic, His Majesty the King of Great Britain, Ireland and the British Dominions beyond the Seas, Emperor of India, His Majesty the King of Italy, His Majesty the Emperor of Japan, the President of the Republic of Poland, the President of the Czechoslovak Republic,

Deeply sensible of their solemn duty to promote the welfare of mankind;

Persuaded that the time has come when a frank renunciation of war as an instrument of national policy should be made to the end that the peaceful and friendly relations now existing between their peoples may be perpetuated;

Convinced that all changes in their relations with one another should be sought only by pacific means and be the result of a peaceful and orderly process, and that any signatory power which shall hereafter seek to promote its national interests by resort to war should be denied the benefits furnished in this treaty;

Hopeful that, encouraged by their example, all the other nations of the world will join in this humane endeavor and by adhering to the present treaty as soon as it comes into force bring their people within the scope of its beneficent provisions, thus uniting the civilized nations of the world in a common renunciation of war as an instrument of their national policy;

Have decided to conclude a treaty and for that purpose have appointed as their respective plenipotentiaries: . . .

Who, having communicated to one another their full powers found in good and due form have agreed upon the following articles:

ART. 1. The high contracting parties solemnly declare in the names of their respective peoples that they condemn recourse to war for the solution of international controversies, and renounce it as an instrument of national policy in their relations with one another.

ART. 2. The high contracting parties agree that the settlement or solution of all disputes or conflicts of whatever natures or of whatever origin they may be, which may arise among them, shall never be sought except by pacific means.

ART. 3. The present treaty shall be ratified by the high contracting parties named in the preamble in accordance with their respective constitutional requirements, and shall take effect as between them as soon as all their several instruments of ratification shall have been deposited at Washington.

SOURCE: *U.S. Statutes at Large*, Vol. XXXXVI, 2343.

Milestone's Achievement
New York Times

From the pages of Erich Maria Remarque's widely read book of young Germany in the World War, "All Quiet on the Western Front," Carl Laemmle's Universal Pictures Corporation has produced a trenchant and imaginative audible picture, in which the producers adhere with remarkable fidelity to the spirit and events of the original stirring novel. It was presented last night at the Central Theatre before an audience that most of the time was held to silence by its realistic scenes. It is a notable achievement, sincere and earnest, with glimpses that are vivid and graphic. Like the original, it does not mince matters concerning the horrors of battle. It is a vocalized screen offering that is pulsating and harrowing, one in which the fighting flashes are photographed in an amazingly effective fashion.

Lewis Milestone, who has several good films to his credit, was entrusted with the direction of this production. And Mr. Laemmle had the foresight to employ those well-known playwrights, George Abbott and Maxwell Anderson, to make the adaptation and write the dialogue. Some of the scenes are not a little too long, and one might also say that a few members of the cast are not Teutonic in appearance; but this means but little when one considers the picture as a whole, for wherever possible, Mr. Milestone has used his fecund imagination, still clinging loyally to the incidents of the book. In fact, one is just as gripped by witnessing the picture as one was by reading the printed pages, and in most instances it seems as though the very impressions written in ink by Herr Remarque had become animated by the screen.

In nearly all the sequences, fulsomeness is avoided. Truth comes to the fore, when the young soldiers are elated at the idea of joining up, when they are disillusioned, when they are hungry, when they are killing rats in a dugout, when they are shaken with fear and when they, or one of them, becomes fed up with the conception of war held by the elderly man back home.

Often the scenes are of such excellence that if they were not audible one might believe that they were actual motion pictures of activities behind the lines, in the trenches and in No Man's Land. It is an expansive production with views that never appear to be cramped. In looking at a dugout one readily imagines a long line of such earthy abodes. When shells demolish these underground quarters, the shrieks of fear, coupled with the rat-tat-tat of machine guns, the bang-ziz of the trench mortars and the whining of shells, it tells the story of the terrors of fighting better than anything so far has done in animated photography coupled with the microphone.

There are heartrending glimpses in a hospital, where one youngster has had his leg amputated and still believes that he has a pain in his toes. Just as he complains of this, he remembers another soldier who had complained of the same pain in the identical words. He then realizes what has happened to him, and he shrieks and cries out that he does not want to go through life a cripple. There is the death room from which nobody is said to come out, and Paul, admirably acted by Lewis Ayres, is taken to this chamber shouting, as he is wheeled away, that he will come back. And he does. The agony in this hospital reflects that of the details given by Herr Remarque.

. . .

Soldiers are perceived being taken like cattle to the firing line and then having to wait for food. There is the cook, who finds that he has enough rations for twice the number of men left in the company, and when he hears that many have been killed

and others wounded he still insists that these soldiers will only receive their ordinary rations. Here that amiable war veteran, Katczinsky, splendidly acted by Louis Wolheim, grabs the culinary expert by the throat and finally a sergeant intervenes and instructs the cook to give the company the full rations intended for the survivors and those who have either died or been wounded.

Now and again songs are heard, genuine melody that comes from the soldiers, and as time goes on Paul and his comrades begin to look upon the warfare with the same philosophic demeanor that Katczinsky reveals. But when the big guns begin to boom there are further terrors for the soldiers and in one of these Paul has his encounter with a Frenchman in a shell hole. Paul stabs the Frenchman to death and as he observes life ebbing from the man with whom he had struggled, he fetches water from the bottom of the shell hole and moistens the Frenchman's lips. It is to Paul a frightening and nerve-racking experience, especially when he eventually pulls from a pocket a photograph of the wife and child of the man he had slain.

. . .

Much has been made of the pair of boots and the soldier who wanted them and declared, when he got them from the man who passed on, that they would make fighting almost agreeable for anybody. Mr. Milestone has done wonders with this passage, showing the boots on the man and soon depicting that while they may have been comfortable and watertight, boots don't matter much when a shell with a man's name on it comes his way.

SOURCE: *The New York Times*, April 30, 1930.

ERICH MARIA REMARQUE SURVEYS WAR'S
<u>DEVASTATING IMPACT ON THOSE WHO SERVED</u>

War's Devastating Impact
Erich Maria Remarque

It is autumn. There are not many of the old hands left. I am the last of the seven fellows from our class.

Everyone talks of peace and armistice. All wait. If it again proves an illusion, then they will break up;

hope is high, it cannot be taken away again without upheaval. If there is not peace, then there will be revolution.

I have fourteen days rest, because I have swallowed a bit of gas; in the little garden I sit the whole day long in the sun. The armistice is coming soon, I believe it now too. Then we will go home.

Here my thoughts stop and will not go any farther. All that meets me, all that floods over me are but feelings—greed of life, love of home, yearning for the blood, intoxication of deliverance. But no aims.

Had we returned home in 1916, out of the suffering and the strength of our experience we might have unleashed a storm. Now if we go back we will be weary, broken, burnt out, rootless, and without hope. We will not be able to find our way any more.

And men will not understand us—for the generation that grew up before us, though it has passed these years with us already had a home and a calling; now it will return to its old occupations, and the war will be forgotten—and the generation that has grown up after us will be strange to us and push us aside. We will be superfluous even to ourselves, we will grow older, a few will adapt themselves, some others will merely submit, and most will be bewildered;—the years will pass by and in the end we shall fall into ruin.

But perhaps all this that I think is mere melancholy and dismay, which will fly away as the dust, when I stand once again beneath the poplars and listen to the rustling of their leaves. It cannot be that it has gone, the yearning that made our blood unquiet, the unknown, the perplexing, the oncoming things, the thousand faces of the future, the melodies from dreams and from books, the whispers and divinations of women; it cannot be that this has vanished in bombardment, in despair, in brothels.

Here the trees show gay and golden, the berries of the rowan stand red among the leaves, the country roads run white out to the sky line, and the canteens hum like beehives with rumours of peace.

I stand up.

I am very quiet. Let the months and years come, they can take nothing from me, they can take nothing more. I am so alone, and so without hope that I can confront them without fear. The life that has borne me through these years is still in my hands and my eyes. Whether I have subdued it, I know not. But so long as it is there it will seek its own way out, heedless of the will that is within me.

He fell in October 1918, on a day that was so quiet and still on the whole front, that the army report confined itself to the single sentence: All Quiet on the Western Front.

He had fallen forward and lay on the earth as though sleeping. Turning him over one saw that he could not have suffered long; his face had an expression of calm, as though almost glad that the end had come.

SOURCE: Erich Maria Remarque, *All Quiet on the Western Front*, 1929, trans. A. W. Wheen (New York: Fawcett Crest, rep. 1991), 293–296.

Follow-Up Problems

1. With reference to the problem of war, what is the primary target that this film aims at? What is the difference between "specificity" and "universalism" with regard to criticism of and opposition to war? Which approach do you think the filmmaker has taken in this picture?

2. What techniques, methods, and technologies has Milestone employed to replicate the combat experience? What does the film reveal about the nature of modern warfare?

3. How does this picture account for the origins of World War I (or other military conflicts)?

4. What was the significance of the film's focus on German armed forces during World War I? What was its impact on the American audience? How does this decision reinforce the objective of both novelist and filmmaker?

5. Both novelist and filmmaker professed to be "objective." To what extent did they achieve that goal? Explain.

6. As you know, *All Quiet on the Western Front* was subject to censorship in many countries, including France and Germany. What made this film so controversial that it was banned in Germany until the 1950s and France until the 1960s?

Further Reading

Barker, Christine R., and Rex W. Last. *Erich Maria Remarque*. New York: Barnes and Noble Imports, 1979.

Chambers, John Whiteclay II. "*All Quiet on the Western Front* (1930): The Antiwar Film and the Image of the First World War." *Historical Journal of Film, Radio and Television* 14 (1994): 377–412.

Doherty, Thomas. *Projections of War: Hollywood, American Culture, and World War II*. New York: Columbia University Press, 1993.

Isenberg, Michael T. *War on Film: The American Cinema and World War I*. Rutherford, N.J.: Fairleigh-Dickenson University Press, 1981.

Kelly, Andrew. "*All Quiet on the Western Front*: 'Brutal Cutting, Stupid Censors, and Bigoted Politicos,' 1930–1984." *Historical Journal of Film, Radio and Television* 9 (1989): 135–150.

Oehling, Richard A. "Germans in Hollywood Films: The Changing Image, 1914–1939." *Film and History* 3 (May 1973): 1–10.

Filmography

The Big Parade (MGM, 1925).

A Farewell to Arms (Paramount, 1932).

The Grand Illusion (R. A. C., 1937).

The Celluloid Document

All Quiet on the Western Front (Universal, 1930).

Chapter 5

Making It in Depression America: The Street or the Stage in *Gold Diggers of 1933* (1933)

Following the stock market crash of 1929 and the onset of depression, the American people and American capitalism underwent a crisis in confidence. With 25 percent unemployment rates, the loss of personal savings, and a massive withdrawal of investment capital, there was much to be feared. While movie producers worried, the introduction of sound pictures provided a short-term windfall that at least partly shielded them from the worst ravages of a failed economy. Nonetheless, as many individuals and families sank into the depths of despair, industry leaders wondered if the resultant reduction in disposable income meant an end to the prosperity that had sustained Hollywood's rapid rise as the center of a legitimate business enterprise. From almost the beginning of the economic crisis, movie executives expressed concern over stagnant revenues and then, ultimately, over the sea of red ink that engulfed them in 1931 and 1932. While the movies recovered much faster than most industries, most of the "big eight" moved aggressively to adopt preventive measures that would lure audiences back to the theaters in which their product was exhibited. Theater parties, dish nights, bingo nights, and other promotions lured moviegoers to motion picture palaces that allowed them to enjoy at least an evening's respite from the harsh realities of a depression economy.[1] While a variety of film genres met with audience approval, musical films, such as *Gold Diggers of 1933* (1933), were among the most popular of Hollywood's efforts to fill the social vacuum.

The Historical Background

Confronted by the crisis of depression, the motion picture industry moved quickly to regain its footing. By most accounts, the promoters were astonishingly successful. After the brief dip of the early thirties, the industry stabilized and prosperity returned to Hollywood, if not the rest of the nation. All evidence indicates that for most Americans, the movies mattered a great deal in the age of the Great Depression. By 1933, attendance had begun to increase as moviegoers returned to the theaters in large numbers. By one estimate, in 1937 more than 60 percent of Americans went to the movies at least once a week. Indeed, in the 1930s and 1940s, the motion pictures reached the height of their popularity as an entertainment medium. For a brief moment during the depression years, the movies enjoyed a close connection with the emotions of the American people not matched since. From a position at the center of the nation's consciousness, Hollywood played a role in sustaining the hopes and imagination of the public at a dark moment in the nation's economic history.

The reasons for the movie industry's success and the great popularity of its product are more complex than the simple escape function so often cited as the explanation. While the need for distraction was undoubtedly real and films often filled that gap, there were other reasons for Hollywood's stunning achievements in this era of economic peril. With the American dream in ruins for many and opportunity for personal achievement blocked as the result of impersonal economic forces, moviegoers looked to the screen for reassurance, hope, and a reaffirmation of the individual's capacity for success. In this chapter, it will be your task to examine the ways in which the hopes, fears, doubts, and criticisms of American citizens found filmic expression. By immersing yourself in the popular culture of the thirties, you will be able to know another side of the nation's past. For the movies spoke to those Americans, many of them not accustomed to recording their thoughts, who made up the population and provided the backbone of the nation's wounded economic system. Their interests and preferences drove the decisions of the Hollywood producers, who were engaged in an ongoing effort to meet consumer demand. It follows that content analysis of Depression era films will reveal much about the thoughts and aspirations of the American population during the greatest economic crisis the United States has ever experienced.

Scholars have often observed that the films of the 1930s frequently address the problem of limited economic opportunity. From the outset of the Great Depression, Hollywood recognized the importance of that issue to viewers whose own careers had been blocked by economic difficulties. One important response to the crisis came in the form of "social problem" films that probed the impact of social environment on the potential for success or failure in the American system. Another early reaction to this challenge came in the form of the popular gangster dramas of the early Depression era. In the period 1930–1932, as economic conditions worsened, it seemed to many observers that the long-accepted Horatio Alger success formula of hard work, intelligence, and moral behavior no longer worked for the rising man-on-the-make. For movie audiences, a new model for success was found in the calculating, brutal, and aggressive criminal of urban America who was intent on "making it" in his own way by openly violating the normal ethical rules. The gritty realism of these films, such as *Little Caesar* (1930) and *The Public Enemy* (1931), found a ready audience among those for whom opportunity had closed. By inverting the Alger myth, these outlaw "businessmen" found a way of achieving success in a society that limited individual accomplishment. The gangster was often a loner, whose temporary success was assured by the assertion of radical individualism. Despite their failures in the last reel, the gangsters upheld the tradition of individual freedom and free enterprise, if in a morally questionable way.[2]

In contrast to the gangster model of uncontrolled individualism, the musical films of the 1930s offered an alternative approach to economic success in a faltering economy. These movies, which since the advent of sound had successfully showcased the new technology, often stressed the value of collaboration in the pursuit of economic, creative, and marital happiness. Some scholars have seen these films as essentially escapist fare designed to provide diversion to an audience wearied by daily exposure to depression realities. The musicals, as Andrew Bergman notes, did allow viewers to lose themselves in waves of legs and costumes, not to mention improbable plots with pleasant outcomes. However, it is equally possible to study these productions for their social and political meaning, for they dealt with another avenue to the realization of the Alger myth and the payoff that came with success. One such musical comedy was Warner Brothers' *Gold Diggers of 1933* (1933), a film that embodied the success drive but proposed a collectivistic formula for achievement.

Live music was one of the many enhancements that came to the screen as a result of the sound revolution. The year 1933 produced a number of musical comedies, especially from Warner Brothers and MGM, that showcased generous portions of young womanhood, displayed for maximum impact. Among these productions were Warner Brothers' successful entries *42nd Street* and *Footlight Parade,* both of them tributes to the American dream of success through energy, hard work, and pluck, applied through collective action under firm leadership. Equally significant as a primary source was *Gold Diggers of 1933,* another tribute to the value of cooperation in pursuit of success. All of these successful films shared the "show within a show" theme, in which collaboration triumphs over economic hardship. While these movies certainly served an escapist function, they had a hard edge, too; as shown by scholars Mark Roth and Arthur Hove, they had a clear political dimension.[3]

It was not entirely coincidental that these reaffirmations of the American success myth appeared in the first year of Franklin Roosevelt's New Deal. As New Deal Democrats and contributors to the Roosevelt campaign, the Warner Brothers caught the spirit of optimism present during the early years of the Roosevelt presidency; consequently, the musicals of 1933 stressed the durability of a renewed American capitalism under decisive leadership, not to mention a clear liberal bias. However, this commitment to the existing economic system was expressed together with a sharp reminder of its shortcomings, including its breakdown in the wake of the great crash of 1929. *Gold Diggers of 1933* provides strong evidence that the Warner musicals were at once political and escapist, in equal measure.

Analyzing the Film

The dramatic concept of success in New York for aggressive young women with hopes of "making it" on the stage was tried and true. The Warners' production of *Gold Diggers of 1933* actually traces its origins to a Broadway play by Avery Hopwood, first produced in 1919. So appealing was its theme that the studio had released two versions, one silent (1923) and one sound (1929), prior to the Great Depression. By this time, the miracle of sound had already established the popularity of musical comedies with motion picture audiences. Shortly after the 1932 election, producer Darryl F. Zanuck launched the project by assigning a writer to adapt the script of the 1929 version for a recycled film titled *High Life.* After several rewrites, the shooting script was completed in February 1933, by this time including numerous musical numbers and dance sequences. The splashy production numbers were choreographed by the talented Busby Berkeley, who was to gain a reputation as the movie industry's leading dance director. His work was characterized by rhythmic, coordinated, and repetitious combinations of carefully matched chorus girls whose bodies were often displayed in perfect geometric designs. The completed film, under the direction of Mervyn LeRoy, appeared in June 1933. Featuring precision-coordinated dance numbers staged by Berkeley as well as a catchy musical score by Al Dubin and Harry Warren, *Gold Diggers of 1933* endorsed the collectivistic ethic while addressing the viability of the capitalist system. Not only is the "show within a show" successfully produced, but social healing is evident. How do the film's cross-class marriages reveal this theme? What is the connection between the upbeat tone of *Gold Diggers of 1933* and the popular optimism with which most Americans greeted the young administration of Franklin D. Roosevelt in the same year?

Despite the film's positive message, depression hardships were not ignored. The impact of the Great Depression is brought home in the film through the collapse of a Broadway show for lack of financial backing. Moreover, as the picture opens, Ginger Rogers and an army of beautiful chorus girls step lively to the tune of "We're In the Money," all the while insisting that they "never see headline about a bread line today." In an subtle reference to the grim meaning of the economic downturn, the women also assert that they have "a lot of what it takes to get along." Consider the double meaning of their words for Depression era audiences. But the clearest indicator that all was not well in America came with the climactic musical number featuring the "forgotten man." In this scene, marching soldiers are gradually replaced by crowds of unemployed men, whose wartime contribution to national security appeared to have been forgotten by an ungrateful nation. Reminiscent of the massive Bonus Army of 1932, which had gone to Washington to ask for early payment of a World War I bonus only to be ejected from the Capitol at bayonet point, the stark musical number stood as a vivid reminder of the historical context in which the film was produced and viewed. In what way does this scene shed light on the contention that *Gold Diggers of 1933* was indeed political as well as escapist?

As you consider the film's treatment of the coping strategies adopted by depression victims, think about their implications for gender relations. Early in the film, the female characters are cast as self-absorbed, if practical, hustlers seeking to entrap men into marriage or at least to separate them from their pocketbooks. This film contains imagery that continues a long tradition of sexual stereotyping found in the motion picture industry and the films it produced. These women exist on the border between companionship and prostitution in the eye of the viewer. In the final analysis, then, what was the key to their success? Try to decide whether these women controlled their own lives or were merely pawns in the marketplace.

As you review the issue of gender, ask whether portrayals of women in the films of the 1930s had changed from those that you observed when analyzing *Dancing Mothers*. The resolution of sexual, generational, and class tensions in *Gold Diggers of 1933* may be compared with the uncertainty with which the earlier film closed. In what way does the outcome in *Gold Diggers of 1933* relate to the pattern of marriage in the last reel, which characterized the fate of most movie models of the 1920s? Connect the upbeat conclusion of *Gold Diggers of 1933* to the public mood of the early Roosevelt years, and try to establish the relationship between film and cultural context.

As you think about context, be aware of the distinction between individualism and collectivism as approaches to the social and economic problems of the Depression era. Examine this film for evidence of one theme or the other, devoting special attention to the Berkeley choreography and the images projected in the dance numbers periodically inserted into the film's narrative. What is the relationship between the individual and the group in those portions of the film? Look for the survival of the Alger myth in the plot. Finally, think about the significance of strong leadership as it appears in the character of the show's director and the male lead. Try to connect these themes with the historical context for the film's production and release as well as the producers' objectives and estimate of the likely audience response.

Thinking About Primary Sources

As you examine *Gold Diggers of 1933*, pay particular attention to the many references to the social context of which it was a part. Consider the probable thoughts of men and women in the summer of 1933 concerning the economic problems they experienced every day, as well as the dramatic political events of the first hundred days of the Roosevelt administration. Connect the mood of the film with the popular response to the new president and the early stages of his program.

As you consider the atmosphere of hope and anticipation in 1933, be aware of the linkage between public sentiment and the themes of the picture. Try to relate that mood to the sentiments expressed in the documents included in this chapter. Compare the description of the Bonus Army's dramatic ejection from Washington, D.C., with the "exhilarating depression" of Franklin D. Roosevelt described in the memoir of writer Robert Bendiner. Notice the way in which director Mervyn LeRoy's memoir captures the spirit of that moment, and think about how it might have influenced the way in which he guided his cast and crew. Do the memories of social historian Frederick Lewis Allen shed any light on the director's intentions or the immediate impact of his film? Link these observations with the images projected in the movie.

When you attempt to connect the film with the historical context, pay careful attention to the debate over the social function of the motion picture in time of economic crisis. Be aware of the distinction between escapism and political awareness, and assess *Gold Diggers of 1933* as evidence to support one theme or the other. In this analysis, you should be especially conscious of the images of class relations found in both the documents and the film. Similarly, you must mine the film for hints of the filmmakers' views on solutions to the economic crisis of the Great Depression. How does the celluloid evidence reveal the inner concerns of moviegoers in 1933?

Historical Perspective

The Warner Brothers and the young producer Darryl F. Zanuck had their fingers on the pulses of moviegoers in the 1930s. Sensing that the 1920s operetta was less relevant to the modern audience than the fast-paced urbanity of the new musical genre, Zanuck and LeRoy embarked on this project with the assumption that audiences were ready for themes that mirrored the environment of the cities—what one observer called the "city gritty." The excitement of the city, the quick dialogue, the lively music and energetic dancing all helped create a special atmosphere of urban life that placed these films squarely in the context of Rooseveltian modern times. It is your task to identify those features and use them to enhance your understanding of the social impact of the Great Depression and the central place of the movies in the mass culture of the hungry thirties.

Whether this film was escapist, realistic, or both, one thing is certain: audiences responded positively to this Warner Brothers fantasy of class healing. In financial terms, *Gold Diggers of 1933* was one of the most successful movies of the year, an outcome that justified the optimism expressed by both Zanuck and LeRoy. Moreover, the critics found the film not only entertaining, but politically engaged. Some argued that for a musical, it was too socially relevant to succeed as entertainment. Correctly identifying the sharp political commentary in the climactic musical number, *The New York Times* criticized its "shabby theme of bogus sentimentality," which it saw favoring "legislative action." Ambivalent about the "forgotten man" sequence, Cy Caldwell of *The New Outlook* praised the film but thought the last reel's social realism in bad taste; war films were acceptable, but Caldwell "want[ed] none of them in musical comedies."

The critical responses show that the political dimension of *Gold Diggers of 1933* had not been missed by most observers. This film, like several of the year's musical entries by Warner Brothers, was very much a product of 1933 and the political and economic consciousness of that moment in history. With the memory of the Bonus March of 1932 fresh in the public mind, the picture had a sharp bite that counterbalanced the fable of cross-class romance and economic salvation that was so meaningful to moviegoers in 1933. For in the first year of the Roosevelt administration, the evidence was still out on the survival of American capitalism, and the words of "Remember My Forgotten Man" summarized the fear, despair, uncertainty, and cautious hopes of the times. But Roosevelt had been in office barely three months, and though optimism prevailed, cynicism and doubt were still in the background. This film, therefore, allows you to recapture the social consciousness and political awareness of a critical turning point in American history. Because the Warner Brothers musicals of 1933 were so directly related to the economic facts of life at the time of their release, *Gold Diggers of 1933* survives as a revealing historical document of fear and hope in American capitalism's darkest hour.

Endnotes

1. This summary is based on analysis provided by Andrew Bergman, *We're In the Money: Depression America and Its Films* (New York: Harper & Row, 1971), xix–xxiii.
2. Bergman, Chapter 1.
3. Mark Roth, "Some Warners Musicals and the Spirit of the New Deal," *The Velvet Light Trap: Review of Cinema* 17 (winter 1977): 1–7; Arthur Hove, ed., *Gold Diggers of 1933* (Madison, Wis.: University of Wisconsin Press, 1980), 26–31.

THE PRIMARY SOURCES

The documents begin with an account of the Bonus March of 1932 by Jim Sheridan, who provided oral historian Studs Terkel with a recollection of the veterans' expulsion from Washington, D.C. It is followed by an excerpt from liberal journalist Robert Bendiner's personal memoir of the Great Depression, which captures the spirit of optimism produced by the election of Franklin D. Roosevelt in November 1932. Similarly, director Mervyn LeRoy recalls his assessment of moviegoers' moods and desires in 1933. Finally, Frederick Lewis Allen adds his own retrospective assessment of Hollywood's early response to depression conditions, emphasizing the tendency to avoid social problems and embrace the audience's assumed middle-class aspirations.

A RECOLLECTION OF THE BONUS MARCH
Interview, Jim Sheridan
Studs Terkel

They had come to petition Hoover, to give them the bonus before it was due. And Hoover refused this. He told them they couldn't get it because it would make the country go broke. They would hold midnight vigils around the White House and march around the White House in shifts.

The question was now: How were they going to get them out of Washington? They were ordered out four or five times, and they refused. The police chief was called to send them out, but he* refused. I also heard that the marine commander, who was called to bring out the marines, also refused. Finally, the one they did get to shove these bedraggled ex-servicemen out of Washington was none other than the great MacArthur.

The picture I'll always remember . . . here is MacArthur coming down Pennsylvania Avenue. And, believe me, ladies and gentlemen, he came on a white horse. He was riding a white horse. Behind him were tanks, troops of the regular army.

. . .

As night fell, they crossed the Potomac. They were given orders to get out of Anacostia Flats, and they refused. The soldiers set those shanties on fire. They were practically smoked out. I saw it from a distance. I could see the pandemonium. The fires were something like the fires you see nowadays that are started in the ghettoes. But they weren't started by the people that live there.

The soldiers threw tear gas at them and vomiting gas. It was one assignment they reluctantly took on. They were younger than the marchers. It was like sons attacking their fathers. The next day the newspapers deplored the fact and so forth, but they realized the necessity of getting these men off. Because they were causing a health hazard to the city. MacArthur was looked upon as a hero.

And so the bonus marchers straggled back to the various places they came from. And without their bonuses.

*General Pelham D. Glassford

SOURCE: Interview, Jim Sheridan, in Studs Terkel, *Hard Times: An Oral History of the Great Depression* (New York: Avon, 1971), 27, 30–31.

THE EXHILARATING DEPRESSION OF FDR
The Exhilarating Depression
Robert Bendiner

Almost as soon as the nomination was safely in Roosevelt's hands, however, he moved to change the atmosphere dramatically. Violating the hoary protocol that a nominee had to wait for a delegation to solemnly apprise him of his selection before he could open his mouth, Roosevelt flew out to the convention in Chicago to symbolize a fresh approach to the country's dire problems: "Let it be from now on the task of our party to break foolish traditions." In his acceptance speech the "forgotten man" was thor-

oughly remembered, dwelt upon, and courted, and for the first time we heard the promise of a "new deal." The beaming self-confidence that was gradually to warm a shaken people in the campaign, the cigarette holder that was tilted at an angle that was to convey the verve of the man in countless newspaper photographs and newsreels, the vibrant voice that was to make of radio a first-class political weapon, the gallantry with which he minimized his physical affliction, and, above all, the pledges to deal specifically and from above with all the country's agonies—all these burst on a nation starving for leadership and imagination. It would be months before St. George could be duly vested with power to take on the dragon, and meanwhile things could and would get worse. But, all the same, bands across the country were playing "Happy Days Are Here Again," and even if they weren't quite here yet, there was a widespread disposition to believe they were on the way.

. . .

On Broadway the ladies of the cast of *Strike Me Pink,* which had just opened the week the banks had closed, first bemoaned in song the dire effect that the world Depression had been having on their income of diamonds and mink. And then, arms raised high, they burst into a paean of hope and confidence: "We depend on Rose-a-velt! We depend on him!" Covering the show, Robert Benchley was of the opinion that not even the economic fates could withstand such impudence. "It was so staggering, even shocking, in its brashness in the face of a national emergency unequaled since the firing on Fort Sumter that the Forces of Darkness collapsed then and there out of sheer chagrin."

The mingling of relief, admiration, and excitement in that first week was infectious. It set the national tone for the next year or so, even if the plight of a great many individuals was not to be soon or greatly changed. Suddenly, after years of bucolic languor under Coolidge and chilled remoteness under Hoover, Washington had become the swirling, raucous, highly personal center of American life. . . .

. . . Motion picture houses, which did extremely well as havens of escape from the realities of depression, figured to still do better with the aid of homey come-ons. Whereas a family might feel conscience-stricken about going twice a week merely to dance again with Ginger Rogers and Fred Astaire, to follow in Hitchcock's Thirty-Nine Steps, or to take a fantasy bus ride with Clark Gable and Claudette Colbert, they could justify taking a chance on a lucky ticket number that might bring them some new dishes or a few dollars in cash. The result was that even in New York a visit to the movies took on something of the character of a turkey raffle. Tuesday was usually Bank Night, which one could take part in only if he had registered his name and address on a previous visit to the theatre. Shortly before nine o'clock the manager would appear on stage, pick a child from the audience, and have him, blindfolded, draw a coupon from a revolving drum. The number was then checked against the registration list and the name of the winner announced. If he was not on hand, the prize was forfeited and went to sweeten the following week's pot . . . .

. . . For theatres that did not sign up with Bank Night there were pale imitations. Some had Dish Night, though I never understood the attractiveness of this particular bait (why not cigarettes or aspirin?), and others might offer a session of bingo. Since admission to neighborhood theatres ran around 25 or 30 cents, one could make a reasonable investment and at the same time retreat from a still shaky world—all at the mere sacrifice of having to sit through a double feature, a painful institution just then coming into vogue.

SOURCE: Robert Bendiner, *Just Around the Corner: A Highly Selective History of the Thirties* (New York: E. P. Dutton, 1967), 28–29, 37, 42–43.

DIRECTOR MERVYN LEROY ASSESSES THE MARKET
Mervyn LeRoy: Take One
Mervyn LeRoy

"In 1933, my instinct was working overtime. I could feel the public was surfeited, temporarily at least, with the films of realism that had flooded the market since I opened the gates with *Little Caesar.* Now, with the Depression coming to an end, I felt they wanted something gayer, splashier, more lavish. I know I had the urge to make that kind of movie. I had my chance with *Gold Diggers of 1933.*"

SOURCE: Mervyn LeRoy, *Mervyn LeRoy: Take One* (New York: Hawthorn, 1974), quoted in Arthur Hove, ed., *Gold Diggers of 1933* (Madison, Wis.: University of Wisconsin Press, 1980), 31.

Avoidance
Frederick Lewis Allen

As for the movies, so completely did they dodge the dissensions and controversies of the day—with a few exceptions, such as the March of Time series, the brief newsreels, and an occasional picture like "I Am a Fugitive from a Chain Gang" or "They Won't Forget"—that if a dozen or two feature pictures, selected at random, were to be shown to an audience in 1960, that audience would probably derive from them not the faintest idea of the ordeal through which the United States went in the nineteen-thirties.

Upon these movies were lavished huge sums of money. For them the stage was robbed of half its ablest actors and playwrights; the literary world, of many of its ablest writers—to say nothing of the engineering and photographic skill which brought to adequacy that cacophonous novelty of 1929, the talking picture, and which toward the end of the decade was bringing more and more pictures in reasonably convincing color. A large number of excellent pictures were produced, with capital acting—whether comedies like "It Happened One Night," or adventure stories like "Mutiny on the Bounty," or historical dramas like "The Life of Emile Zola," or picturizations of fictional classics like "A Tale of Two Cities"; and there was a far greater number of pictures which, whatever their unreality, served as rousing entertainment for an idle evening. . . .

The capital invested in the movies preferred to steer clear of awkward issues, not to run the risk of offending theatre-goers abroad or at home. The moralists must be placated; as a result of the campaign of the Legion of Decency in 1934, Joseph Breen had been installed in the office of the Motion Picture Producers and Distributors of America, ready to censor before production any picture which showed too prolonged a kiss, which showed small boys bathing naked, which permitted a character to say "damn" or "hell." . . .

Not merely did the movies avoid temptations to thought about the condition of the country; in effect their producers played, half unwittingly, a gigantic joke upon the social salvationists, and particularly upon those men and women who would have liked to make the American masses class conscious. For the America which the movies portrayed—like the America of popular magazine fiction and especially of the magazine advertisements—was devoid of real poverty or discontent, of any real conflict of interests between owners and workers, of any real ferment of ideas. More than that, it was a country in which almost everybody was rich or about to be rich, and in which the possession of a huge house and a British-accented butler and a private swimming pool not merely raised no embarrassing questions about the distribution of wealth, but was accepted as the normal lot of mankind. . . .

While the writers and artists in whom burned a fierce desire to reveal to their fellow-countrymen the inequalities and miseries of their lot were resolutely addressing a public numbered in the thousands, another public numbering *eighty-five millions each week* was at the movies watching Gary Cooper, Clark Gable, Myrna Loy, Katharine Hepburn, Ronald Colman, Carole Lombard, and the other gods and goddesses of Hollywood disporting themselves in a dreamland of wide-sweeping stairways, marble floors, and magnificent drawing-room vistas. And these eighty-five millions were liking it.

Was not the lesson of all this that America was not—or not yet, if you prefer—proletarian-minded? True, its citizens were capable of organizing hotly to redress wrongs and secure themselves benefits, were quite ready to have these wrongs redressed and these benefits provided by the government if no other agency would do it; and some Americans might even fight, if need be, to get what they wanted. Yet still in the back of their minds there was room for an Horatio Alger paradise where young men of valour rose to the top and young women of glamour married the millionaire's son, and lived happily ever after.

Source: Frederick Lewis Allen, *Since Yesterday: The 1930s in America, September 3, 1929–September 3, 1939* (New York: Perennial, 1939), 222–224.

Follow-Up Problems

1. In what ways does *Gold Diggers of 1933* introduce the issue of class differences in American life? What attitudes towards wealth and poverty are expressed? What solutions for the problem of inequality are advanced?

2. How does this picture address the status and roles of women? What images of women and/or gender relations are projected by the film?

3. In what way are authority figures presented in this film, including workplace leaders, political authorities, the legal profession, and governmental figures?

4. Compare the images of collectivism and individualism projected by this film. How are these concepts linked to the historical context in which the film appeared?

5. Discuss the elements of escapism and realism as they appear in *Gold Diggers of 1933*.

6. Can you identify any connection between the themes present in the film and the historical context of New Deal America? What do you think is the purpose of the "show within a show" device, as it is used in this film? How does the outcome of this sub-theme relate to the political context in 1933?

Further Reading

Bergman, Andrew. *We're In the Money: Depression America and Its Films*. New York: Harper & Row, 1971.

Doherty, Thomas. *Pre-Code Hollywood: Sex, Immorality, and Insurrection in American Cinema, 1930–1934*. New York: Columbia University Press, 1999.

Fehr, Richard. *Lullabies of Hollywood: Movie Music and the Movie Musical*. Jefferson, N.C.: McFarland, 1993.

Giovacchini, Saverio. *Hollywood Modernism: Film and Politics in the Age of The New Deal*. Philadelphia: Temple University Press, 2001.

Hove, Arthur, ed. *Gold Diggers of 1933*. Madison, Wis.: University of Wisconsin Press, 1980.

Roddick, Nick. *A New Deal in Entertainment: Warner Brothers in the 1930s*. London: British Film Institute, 1983.

Roffman, Peter, and Jim Purdy. *The Hollywood Social Problem Film: Madness, Despair, and Politics from the Depression to the Fifties*. Bloomington, Ind.: Indiana University Press, 1981.

Rosen, Marjorie. *Popcorn Venus: Women, Movies, and the American Dream*. New York: Avon, 1974.

Roth, Mark. "Some Warners Musicals and the Spirit of the New Deal." *The Velvet Light Trap: Review of Cinema* 17 (June 1977): 1–7.

Rubin, Martin. *Showstoppers: Busby Berkeley and the Tradition of Spectacle*. New York: Columbia University Press, 1993.

Schindler, Colin. *Hollywood in Crisis: Cinema in American Society, 1929–1939*. London: Routledge, 1994.

Sklar, Robert. *City Boys: Cagney, Bogart, Garfield*. Princeton, N.J.: Princeton University Press, 1992.

Filmography

Footlight Parade (Warner Brothers, 1933).

42nd Street (Warner Brothers, 1933).

Little Caesar (Warner Brothers, 1930).

The Public Enemy (Warner Brothers, 1931).

The Celluloid Document

Gold Diggers of 1933 (Warner Brothers, 1933).

6 Chapter

The Resilient People:
The Grapes of Wrath (1940) Exposes
Poverty in the Land of Plenty

The Great Depression resulted in widespread economic distress and human suffering in both urban and rural America. Among the most striking images of social and economic hardship were the stark but vivid representations of the tenant farmers and sharecroppers unfortunate enough to inhabit the "Dust Bowl" of the Southwest. Their story formed the basis for John Steinbeck's very successful novel of social protest, *The Grapes of Wrath* (1939). One year later Darryl Zanuck and John Ford of Twentieth Century Fox transformed Steinbeck's words into striking visual images in a film that familiarized a wide American audience with the human and ecological disaster that befell the Great Plains and its inhabitants in the "dirty thirties."

The Historical Background

Due to a blend of capitalist pressure, human greed, and exploitative agriculture, a large portion of Oklahoma, Arkansas, North Texas, Kansas, Colorado, and New Mexico was transformed into a semiarid wasteland. The residual effect of this ecological tragedy was the mass dislocation of hundreds of thousands of plains dwellers who moved west in search of employment in the fields of golden California and other parts of the West. Penniless and demoralized, these Dust Bowl refugees, labeled "Okies" by native-born Californians, drew national attention as a major social and economic problem in the late 1930s. For these poverty-stricken transients there was little alternative but to offer their labor to the growers of the West, who were quick to seize an opportunity to profit at their expense.

The problem created by the "Okie" migration was actually a product of several developments that coincided in the 1930s. The primary cause of their plight was to be found in a combination of wasteful agricultural practices, poor land-use decisions, and the cyclical scarcity of precipitation in an area subject to periodic drought. Overuse of the soil, including the cultivation of submarginal lands, made the swirling dust storms of the mid-1930s brutal in their impact. In their wake, once-productive acreages now assumed a desertlike appearance. A further complication stemmed from the combination of increased mechanization on the farm, which displaced a large number of marginal farmers, and the shortage of capital available to small producers. The problem thus created was magnified by the unintended effects of New Deal agricultural policies that encouraged acreage restriction and caused landowners to withdraw tenant and sharecropper lands from production.[1] Landless and homeless, the rural dispossessed joined a mass migration that enlarged the California population and produced social tensions as newcomers and natives clashed in the fertile valleys of the West.

By the mid-1930s, the Roosevelt Administration had already turned its attention to the economic and social problems of the Dust Bowl, including the human casualties. In 1935, for example, the progressive Resettlement Administration (RA) decided to produce a film intended to call attention to the errors that had created this ecological problem. Arguably the New Deal's most radical agency, the RA, along with its director, the agricultural economist Rexford Tugwell, asked film critic Pare Lorentz to plan, shoot, cut, and finish a documentary "film of merit" focusing on the Dust Bowl crisis. In the motion picture that resulted, *The Plow That Broke the Plains* (1936), Lorentz and his crew succeeded in capturing the root causes of the Depression era environmental problem in the Southwest, as well as the tragic social dislocation and family disruption that followed. Controversial from the start, the film was criticized as New Deal propaganda, though Lorentz insisted that his concern had always been to advance the film as art form while presenting an important social message. After a hotly contested political battle, the film was withdrawn from circulation in 1938, not to resurface until the 1960s.[2]

Another literary artist who took note of the Dust Bowl migration was the native Californian, novelist John Steinbeck. An important figure on the literary Left, Steinbeck was part of a radical culture that dedicated itself to the exposure of American economic problems and the promotion of social change. A contributor to progressive journals such as *New Masses,* Steinbeck joined Ernest Hemingway and John Dos Passos in the vanguard of intellectuals committed to political activism. As a result, he was sometimes confronted with allegations of Communist affiliations.

Already a moderately successful writer by the mid-1930s, Steinbeck crafted stories often set in the California he knew so well. After a breakthrough success with *Tortilla Flats* in 1935, he set about the task of recording the experiences of the Dust Bowl refugees who were streaming into the western states, blown out by the great dust storms of the mid-thirties. As was frequently his practice, Steinbeck went to the source, traveling to Oklahoma and joining a group of migrants moving to California. After reaching California, he remained with them and observed their contacts with growers, police, local citizens, and government authorities. Deeply impressed by his brush with social reality, Steinbeck was radicalized to the point of action. While publishing a few articles on the problem, he threw himself into the task of penning a novel that would focus public attention on the issue in a way that could not be ignored. The result was a powerful work that raised serious questions about the fairness and viability of American capitalism.

The Grapes of Wrath (1939) was highly successful in its first year. Published in March 1939, it topped the best-seller list by May. At first subject to criticism for its sexual content, the book soon became controversial due to its political themes. Native Californians, community boosters, and the growers bristled at Steinbeck's hard-hitting portrayal of their exploitation of the migrant population. Management groups objected to the clear prolabor stance taken in the book. Threatened by the charges made, the growers launched a vigorous counterattack aimed at censorship. Often masking their motivations with charges of obscenity, the critics insisted that the book was spreading untruths about California and ignoring the many efforts made to aid the transient population. Banned in Kern County, California, the book became even more well known as public curiosity increased. In short, the anti-Steinbeck campaign in California was largely ineffective; it did, however, focus public attention on the social abuses and antilabor practices that made life miserable for migrant workers in the West.

Given the composition of the forces arrayed against Steinbeck, it was perhaps inevitable that the assault on his work take a harshly political turn. Because he had laid bare the seamy side of capitalism, Steinbeck's political motives soon came under fire. Under the leadership of the Associated Farmers of California, the assault took on an increasingly anti-Communist tone. One publication sponsored by this organization charged that *The Grapes of Wrath* must be challenged as an open attempt to promote class warfare and "hatred of class against class." Yet, despite the increasingly shrill ideological attacks on the book, it continued to grow in stature, both critical and financial. For more than a year after its publication, it remained on the best-seller list. The public receptivity to the book's indictment of capital was consistent with the lingering suspicions of the business system that were embedded in the mass culture of the late 1930s.

Given the ties between business, finance capital, and the motion picture industry, Darryl Zanuck's decision to purchase the movie rights to the book one week after its publication may seem remarkable. Indeed, the idea that such a novel would ever be faithfully adapted to the screen was questionable. Yet *The Grapes of Wrath* was clearly a hot property. Always a shrewd businessman, Zanuck understood the cultural implications of the novel's widespread popularity. More than this, he recognized that the book's strong indictment of capitalism could be transformed into an uplifting affirmation of a system undergoing national reassessment at the time.

When Zanuck approached the widely respected director John Ford with a proposal that he consider making a film based on Steinbeck's work, Ford eagerly swallowed the bait. In response to the initial inquiry, Ford assured Zanuck that if he could get a little time to finish his current projects, he "would leap at the chance of doing 'Wrath.'"[3] Ford's biographer notes that the director detected in the saga of the Joad family's cross-country journey echoes of his own Irish forebears evicted from the land in the wake of the great famine. The product of Ford's commitment was a film that, while it softened some of Steinbeck's more radical themes, does mirror outrage against the treatment of the Dust Bowl refugees.

Analyzing the Film

The Grapes of Wrath was not the first Hollywood look at the dark side of Depression America. There had been several efforts to highlight the shortcomings of the system, such as *Wild Boys of the Road* (1933), *Our Daily Bread* (1934), and *Dead End* (1937), films that addressed unemployment, transients, agricultural problems, urban slums, and juvenile delinquency. These films, however, lack the power and emotional impact of Ford's work.

In view of box office statistics, financial returns, and critical reaction, no other Depression era attempts at social criticism appear to have approached the stature and influence of *The Grapes of Wrath*. Nor do previous screen entries adopt the openly sympathetic stance on the aspirations of labor and unions that is so evident in this film.

Determined to capture the social realism that marked Steinbeck's novel, Ford insisted on authenticity wherever possible. Seeking to replicate the Joad family's cross-country journey, he sent a camera crew out to shoot roadside footage on Highway 66 under the falsified film title *Highway 66*. Intent on honesty and accuracy, Zanuck relied on private detectives to check Steinbeck's objectivity in reporting. These operatives went through the migrant camps and farmed out on jobs with the workers. Later, Ford and all the leading cast members visited the camps to become acquainted firsthand with the people whose lives they were portraying. All the principal players read the book and, according to lead actor Henry Fonda, felt "nothing but sympathy for the situation of the people." The cast shared Zanuck's commitment to "tell the truth."[4]

At first, Steinbeck worried that Zanuck and Ford would rob his work of its radical socioeconomic content. Although Zanuck had assured the author that he was willing to take any reasonable gamble with the material, there was reason for concern because of Fox Studios' links with eastern finance capitalists, including Chase Manhattan Bank. As Ford biographer Joseph McBride has noted, however, the financiers were willing to have Zanuck develop the project, and the result was a beautifully crafted film that revealed the flaws of capitalism without rejecting the fundamental structure of the system. While the film toned down some of the novel's more radical political content, it was sufficiently honest to expose the system's shortcomings as well as man's inhumanity to man. Even Steinbeck was reportedly satisfied with Ford's treatment of his work. While modern critics have faulted the film for its optimism and de-emphasis on the brutal realities so frankly dealt with in the novel, this picture came as close as any Hollywood film ever produced to addressing the inequities in American life.

It is your task to identify these weaknesses, as revealed in the film. Consider, for example, the significance of the flashback scene in which Muley recounts the experience of being tractored off the land. What does it reveal about the frustrations experienced by the discards of the capitalist system? Similarly, think about the stark realism of Ford's portrayal of the migrant camps, including the senseless murder of a woman by a guard spraying bullets around a crowded community area. In what way does the film expose the brutality of antiunion tactics and the manipulation of hungry workers into acts of class betrayal? Finally, be aware of the film's perspective on management's transparent attempt to undercut worker organizations with charges of Communist inspiration. How did screenwriter Nunnally Johnson and John Ford attempt to soften the story's radical edge without losing the novel's sense of outrage?

The Grapes of Wrath provides a vivid portrait of the many problems confronting the migratory workers of the Dust Bowl, sketched through the story of the hard-pressed Joad family, which had been evicted and tractored off its ancestral land and forced into the trek to golden California. Along the way they face death, desertion, violence, and exploitation at the hands of capitalists in collusion with insensitive local authorities. Watch for a change in Tom Joad's social and political philosophy as he flees the authorities in order to carry on the struggle for social and economic justice towards both his people and all those oppressed by a failing system.

Perhaps the critical theme developed in the film involves the fate of the family. While the Joad family is mired in the process of disintegration, Tom is learning from Preacher Casy the ideology of the larger family of all men and women. What is the political meaning of Tom's declaration to Ma Joad, made just before his hasty departure, that he is joining a fight for the integrity of a family that transcends the collapsing Joad clan? Initially, Ford had planned to end the film with Tom's escape, but Zanuck persuaded him to incorporate the final scene in which the surviving family members are off for another work opportunity. Reflect upon the thematic importance of Ma Joad's assertion that the group has been down, but they are by no means out, because they are "the people." Have the abuses, dishonesty, and exploitation endured by the Joads and witnessed by the audience damaged the family? What did this scene imply, with regard to faith in the system?

While modern film critics and literary scholars have sometimes dealt harshly with the film's conversion of a social protest novel into a picture that essentially validates capitalism, *The Grapes of Wrath* retains its power to inspire. In its semidocumentary realism, brilliant photography, subtle sympathy for labor, stunning use of light and shadow, and rhythmic dialogue, this film helps students and scholars to recapture the suffering of the Dust Bowl migration and the people caught up in that mass movement. Did it lose the radical edge of the novel? No less an authority than John Steinbeck, himself, delivered the surprising verdict in December 1939 when he previewed Ford's masterpiece: "Zanuck has more than kept his word. He has a hard straight picture in which the actors are submerged so completely that it looks and feels like a documentary film and certainly it has a hard, truthful ring. No punches are pulled—in fact, with descriptive matter removed; it is a harsher thing than the book, by far. It seems unbelievable but it is true."[5] It is this uncompromising truth that makes *The Grapes of Wrath* an enduring document of its times: that moment in American history when, for some Americans, the system failed and the future seemed uncertain. This film, together with the gripping novel that gave it life, played an important role in alerting Americans to sharp inequities in a broken agricultural system.

Your effort to evaluate the film and its impact will be enhanced by careful attention to the techniques employed by the filmmakers and the talented artists who collaborated to make *The Grapes of Wrath* one of the finest social-problem films ever to come out of a typically timid Hollywood film community. How does Ford achieve a semidocumentary feel for the subject? Be aware of cinematographer Gregg Toland's brilliant work, as well as the effective use of light and shadow that contribute to the often somber mood conveyed by the narrative. Similarly, you should explore the ways in which sounds, silences, and music are employed to reinforce the film's themes. What was the overall impact of these technical and artistic decisions on the ultimate cinematic outcome?

Most important, however, as you subject this movie to critical analysis, focus your attention on the historical context in which it appeared. Connect the solutions explored in both the novel and film with approaches to economic and social betterment that were tried in the 1930s. Link Tom Joad's troubles to those faced by farmers, transients, and workers in the Depression era, and assess the Roosevelt administration's efforts to meet the needs of rural migrants. As you do so, look for evidence of the filmmakers' view of government as a means of meeting the needs the film addresses. Do you see any connection between the issues dealt with in this film and those stressed in the documentary films produced by the Resettlement Administration in the 1930s?

Another aspect of thirties America explored in this film was the labor movement as an approach to social improvement. Relatively few Hollywood films have so endorsed the cause of workers as did *The Grapes of Wrath*. Examine the movie for evidence of the film-makers' perspective on unionism as a solution to the clear exploitation of workers and their families. Try to determine whether the film really embraces labor unions as institutions or as the means to restore a lost agrarian community. What, if any, are the elements of collectivism evident in this picture? What type of an ideal community does the film argue for? What would its social and ethnocultural composition be? As you consider these questions, think about the presence or absence in the movie of realistic political solutions to the social and economic problems it addresses.

Problematic in terms of clear political direction, *The Grapes of Wrath* falls back on the strong family and rural community as prescriptions for communal salvation. Consequently, the film is rich in images of women as heroic figures. Notice the role that women play as the cement of family unity and think about that characterization as evidence of the filmmakers' social vision. Can you link this aspect of the film to social changes that were occurring in many American families during the Great Depression? This dimension of the film's argument connects directly with the picture's larger concern with the survival of the system. The family and benevolent government as complementary institutions go hand in hand as the subtext in this film. It is your responsibility to locate evidence of these assumptions.

Your examination of the film's representation of government will raise a larger question about the future of capitalism in the face of systemic failure. As previously noted, Steinbeck's work had a sharply critical edge in its questioning of capitalist institutions. Think about both novel and film as expressions of a viewpoint with regard to the survival of democratic capitalism as a system of production and distribution. Pay particular attention to the way in which they arrive at their respective conclusions. Consider the implications of Ma Joad's reassurances with regard to the durability of the family and the American people as a larger family. In the last analysis, you must decide whether this movie embraces or dismisses capitalism as a structure for the organization of an economy and society. Once you have made your decision on this issue, return to the question of the motion picture and the movie industry as reflections of the society of which they are a part. Try to understand the function of film as an element of the larger social and economic order.

Thinking About Primary Sources

Your analysis of *The Grapes of Wrath* must be based on an effort to familiarize yourself with the literary source from which this extraordinary celluloid document is drawn. If you have never read the novel, be sure to examine closely the excerpts reprinted in the documents section that follows. This reading will enable you to make an independent judgment as to whether or not Steinbeck's more radical social and economic observations were softened in the process of producing the film. You may also study the striking visual image created by the talented government photographic artist Dorothea Lange, whose work was sponsored by the Farm Security Administration. Think about the contemporary impact of this photograph on a public first gaining an awareness of the Dust Bowl crisis and its casualties. As you analyze the images created by these government artists, consider them in comparison with the visual imagery projected in the Hollywood version of Steinbeck's work. You might also assess music as an expression of social protest, focusing your attention on the words of folksinger Woody Guthrie, whose lyrics spoke for a generation of Dust Bowl refugees. Compare the visual images and music with the written word as vehicles for the expression of social protest. At this point, you should assess the motion picture *The Grapes of Wrath* (1940) as a statement of protest on film. Evaluate the various media as tools for sharpening public awareness of social evils. Which do you consider most effective?

The documents shed light on the reaction to Steinbeck's novel as well as the film that grew from it. Identify the sources of opposition to the novel and try to determine what factors lay behind the negative reaction to a book considered by some critics to be one of the most important of its era. Think about the impact of this heavy public criticism, including its influence on audience attitudes concerning the film. How would you account for the movie's box office success? You should also examine the film for clues to the controversy it caused. Do you think that the picture offered a truthful representation of a social problem or biased propaganda? Be sure to provide evidence to support your conclusion.

This film and the print sources offer a wonderful opportunity to link the spoken and written word with on-screen images as influences on social attitudes in the age of mass culture. Moreover, *The Grapes of Wrath* records, through sharp visual representation, the environmental disaster of the Great Plains in the 1930s. As you apply your critical skills, rigorous thought about these documents and the film they address will open a window through which you may observe the public questioning, self-doubt, and fervent hopes for a better future that were found in an economically damaged nation.

Historical Perspective

The overwhelmingly positive response to *The Grapes of Wrath* came as a surprise to the tentative Steinbeck. The film was a clear economic success, grossing over $1.1 million, a substantial sum by the standards of the time. Critically acclaimed, it received seven Academy Award nominations and won two Oscars, Jane Darwell's Best Supporting Actress award for her powerful portrayal of the matriarchal Ma Joad and John Ford's Best Director award. Sentimental though it may be, this picture was in large measure true to its literary source and dealt honestly and realistically with the social and economic toll taken by the Great Depression on one brutally exploited segment of the American population. Though Ford denied political intent, the film struck viewers as a ringing political statement; and its emotional and intellectual impact has not lessened with the years.

Despite this enduring quality, some critics have argued that *The Grapes of Wrath* is an imperfect vehicle for the expression of social protest. The uplifting final scene, in which Ma Joad extols the family and the people, may well undercut the radical content of the novel. By implication, at least, the outcome seems to say that the system will endure. To be sure, many of Steinbeck's indictments of the capitalist system have been retained and the viewer is properly shocked by the social abuses thus revealed. Yet ambiguity on the labor movement as a solution to social evil and evasiveness on an explicit political remedy for the inadequacies of American capitalism suggest an endorsement of the shaken economic system. Like most film fare of the Depression era, then, *The Grapes of Wrath* offered reassurance to an anxious public that hoped for an end to the social crisis of the troubled thirties.

The conclusion was regarded by some observers as a "New Deal ending," a view that underscores the link between film and historical context. Even in Oklahoma, where Steinbeck's novel had sparked political controversy with its portrayal of human suffering, this conclusion and the film's overall treatment of the "Okies" as tough and resilient people were important in winning over a skeptical public. For many Americans of the 1930s, Ford's film reflected hard reality and underscored the nobility of the human spirit. Unwilling to acknowledge the truthfulness of Steinbeck's observations, however, many Californians continued to criticize the film and novel as distortions of reality. The sharpness of this reaction reminds us of the motion picture's usefulness as a primary source. Both film and novel are vivid historical documents that provide modern students with a colorful sketch of a portion of American society in the Great Depression, as well as a statement of political consciousness that still makes a strong impact. As you analyze this film, try to place it and the mood it expresses within the context of the late Depression years. By so doing, you will be able to link the changing economy with the purposes of the filmmaker in an explanation of the movie's underlying thesis.

Endnotes

1. The origins of the Dust Bowl ecological disaster are discussed in Donald Worster, *Dust Bowl: The Southern Plains in the 1930s* (New York: Oxford University Press, 1979).
2. John E. O'Connor, *Image as Artifact: The Historical Analysis of Film and Television* (Malabar, Fla: Robert E. Krieger Publishing Co., 1990), 289–292.
3. John Ford to Darryl Zanuck, July 17, 1939, John Ford Papers, Lilly Library, Indiana University, Bloomington, Indiana, Box 1, 1939 File.
4. Interview, John Ford; Interview, Henry Fonda, both in Ford Papers, Box 11.
5. Quoted in Joseph McBride, *Searching for John Ford: A Life* (New York: St. Martin's Press, 2001), 314.

THE PRIMARY SOURCES

The documents provide historical background against which you may understand the social problems addressed in *The Grapes of Wrath*. The striking photograph by Dorothea Lange is drawn from the Resettlement Administration/Farm Security Administration collection in the library of Congress, which includes many powerful images of the people and topography of the Dust Bowl. Think about the lines of experience etched in the migrant mother's face as you review the excerpt from John Steinbeck's novel, *The Grapes of Wrath*, which highlights the author's perspective on the impact of rural poverty on its victims. Contrast Steinbeck's moving portrayal of migrant grievances with the cold response to the Dust Bowl migration in the California Citizens Association's 1939 report. In the final selection, folksinger Woody Guthrie, himself a Dust Bowl refugee, endorses the film in 1940 as an authentic expression of his people's story.

A MIGRANT MOTHER

Destitute Pea Pickers in California
Dorothea Lange

SOURCE: "Destitute Pea Pickers in California," Nipomo, Calif., February, 1936. Photograph by Dorothea Lange, Library of Congress, LC-USZ62-95653.

JOHN STEINBECK DESCRIBES THE MIGRANT EXPERIENCE

Excerpt from *The Grapes of Wrath*
John Steinbeck

And in Kansas and Arkansas, in Oklahoma and Texas and New Mexico, the tractors moved in and pushed the tenants out.

Three hundred thousand in California and more coming. And in California the roads full of frantic people running like ants to pull, to push, to lift, to work. For every manload to lift, five pairs of arms extended to lift it; for every stomachful of food available, five mouths open,

And the great owners, who must lose their land in an upheaval, the great owners with access to history, with eyes to read history and to know the great fact: when property accumulates in too few hands it is taken away. And the companion fact: when a majority of the people are hungry and cold they will take by force what they need. And the little screaming fact that sounds through all history: repression works only to strengthen and knit the repressed. The great owners

ignored the three cries of history. The land fell into fewer hands, the number of dispossessed increased, and every effort of the great owners was directed at repression. The money was spent for arms, for gas to protect the great holdings, and spies were sent to catch the murmuring of revolt so that it might be stamped out. The changing economy was ignored, plans for the change ignored; and only means to destroy revolt were considered, while the causes of revolt went on.

The tractors which throw men out of work, the belt lines which carry loads, the machines which produce, all were increased; and more and more families scampered on the highways, looking for crumbs from the great holdings, lusting after the land beside the roads. The great owners formed associations for protection and they met to discuss ways to intimidate, to kill, to gas. And always they were in fear of a principal—three hundred thousand—if they ever move under a leader—the end. Three hundred thousand, hungry and miserable; if they ever know themselves, the land will be theirs and the gas, all the rifles in the world won't stop them. And the great owners, who had become through their holdings both more and less than men, ran to their destruction, and used every means that in the long run would destroy them. Every little means, every violence, every raid on a Hoover-ville, every deputy swaggering through a ragged camp put off the day a little and cemented the inevitability of the day.

The men squatted on their hams, sharp-faced men, lean from hunger and hard from resisting it, sullen eyes and hard jaws. And the rich land was around them. . . .

The moving, questing people were migrants now. Those families which had lived on a little piece of land, who had lived and died on forty acres, . . . had now the whole West to rove in. And they scampered about, looking for work; and the highways were streams of people, and the ditch banks were lines of people. Behind them were more coming. The great highways streamed with moving people. There in the Middle- and Southwest had lived a simple agrarian folk who had not changed with industry, who had not farmed with machines or known the power and danger of machines in private hands. They had not grown up in the paradoxes of industry. Their senses were still sharp to the ridiculousness of the industrial life.

And then suddenly the machines pushed them out and they swarmed on highways. The movement changed them; the highways, the camps along the road, the fear of hunger and the hunger itself, changed them. The children without dinner changed them, the endless moving changed them. They were migrants. And the hostility changed them, welded them, united them—hostility that made the little towns group and arm as though to repel an invader, squads with pick handles, clerks and storekeepers with shotguns, guarding the world against their own people.

In the West there was a panic when the migrants multiplied on the highways. Men of property were terrified for their property. Men who had never been hungry saw the eyes of the hungry. Men who had never wanted anything very much saw the flare of want in the eyes of the migrants. And the men of the towns and of the soft suburban country gathered to defend themselves; and they reassured themselves that they were good and the invaders bad, as a man must do before he fights. They said, These goddamned Okies are dirty and ignorant. They're degenerate, sexual maniacs. These goddamned Okies are thieves. They'll steal anything. They've got no sense of property rights.

And the latter was true, for how can a man without property know the ache of ownership? And the defending people said, They bring disease, they're filthy. We can't have them in the schools. They're strangers. How'd you like to have your sister go out with one of 'em?

The local people whipped themselves into a mold of cruelty. Then they formed units, squads, and armed them—armed them with clubs, with gas, with guns. We own the country. We can't let these Okies get out of hand. And the men who were armed did not own the land, but they thought they did. And the clerks who drilled at night owned nothing, and the little storekeepers possessed only a drawerful of debts. But even a debt is something, even a job is something. The clerk thought, I get fifteen dollars a week. S'pose a goddamn Okie would work for twelve? And the little storekeeper thought, How could I compete with a debtless man?

And the migrants streamed in on the highways and their hunger was in their eyes, and their need was in their eyes. They had no argument, no system, nothing but their numbers and their needs. When there was work for a man, ten men fought for it— fought with a low wage. If that fella'll work for thirty cents, I'll work for twenty-five.

If he'll take twenty-five, I'll do it for twenty.

No, me, I'm hungry. I'll work for fifteen. I'll work for food. The kids. You ought to see them. Little boils, like, comin' out an' they can't run aroun'. Give 'em some windfall fruit, an' they bloated up. Me, I'll work for a little piece of meat.

And this was good, for wages went down and prices stayed up. The great owners were glad and they sent out more handbills to bring more people in. And wages went down and prices stayed up. And pretty soon now we'll have serfs again.

. . .

And the companies, the banks worked at their own doom and they did not know it. The fields were fruitful, and starving men moved on the roads. The granaries were full and the children of the poor grew up rachitic, and the pustules of pellagra swelled on their sides. The great companies did not know that the line between hunger and anger is a thin line. And money that might have gone to wages went for gas, for guns, for agents and spies, for blacklists, for drilling. On the highways the people moved like ants and searched for work, for food. And the anger began to ferment.

SOURCE: John Steinbeck, *The Grapes of Wrath* (New York: Viking, 1939; reprint, Penguin, 1986), 306–307, 362–365.

CALIFORNIANS REACT TO STEINBECK'S PORTRAYAL OF GOLDEN CALIFORNIA

California Citizens Association Report
Bakersfield, California, July 1, 1939
California Citizens Association

Despite optimistic announcements of a decline in the number of migrants coming to California principally from Oklahoma, Arkansas, Texas, and Missouri, the burden on the taxpayers of our state has become more acute. It is now that the local and state relief rolls are being filled with artificially created "residents," subsidized by the Farm Security Administration for the year's required eligibility. It is now that we are feeling the financial pressure of building new schools for the migrants' children.

It is *now* that we are paying.

Records of the Kern County Hospital show that 44 per cent of the patients taken care of there during the past year were nonresidents, and the origin of 77 per cent of that number was in the four states mentioned. In this period more than 110,000 cases were treated free.

These migrants are not farmers who have been dispossessed. Even the Farm Security Administration, which once claimed evidence to the contrary, now admits that they were either sharecroppers or laborers in their home states. It is plain that there was no place for them here when there were already five unemployed for every available agricultural job in California.

. . .

The United States Employment Service is authority for the fact that no effort was made by any California farm group to bring labor here, by advertising or by other means. The farmers neither needed nor wanted additional workers, nor did they want the tax cost of supporting unneeded migrants.

California has always maintained the highest farm wages of any area in the world, but it cannot continue to be oppressed by taxes to feed these surplus workers and still uphold this standard.

The author, John Steinbeck, in his novel, *Grapes of Wrath*, did great injustice both to Californians and to the migrants themselves. These hapless people are not moral and mental degenerates as he pictures them, but victims of desperate conditions—conditions which can bring to California the same tragedy that drove them from their home states.

The recounting by Steinbeck of incidents in which violence was used upon the transients is based upon nothing more than the envisionings of an overworked imagination. It is absolutely untrue.

A deep-set prejudice seems to be the only explanation for the involving of the American Legion in a fictionally-created harassment of these people.

The California Citizens Association, made up of various organizations, presented to the Congress petitions signed by hundreds of thousands of people, directing the attention of the government to the fact that no further migration could be endured by the people of California. The record of the California Citizens Association has been one of sympathy for these people, but one that must now be tempered by a deep desire to maintain our standard of living and by the natural law of self-preservation.

SOURCE: California Citizens Association Report, Bakersfield, July 1, 1939, from Marshall V. Hartranft, *Grapes of Gladness* (Los Angeles: De Vorss, 1939), 124–125, in Warren French, ed., *A Companion to "The Grapes of Wrath"* (New York: Penguin, 1963), 138–139.

People's World
Woody Guthrie

Seen the pitcher last night, Grapes of Wrath, best cussed pitcher I ever seen.

The Grapes of Wrath, you know is about us pullin' out of Oklahoma and Arkansas, and down south, and a driftin' around over state of California, busted, disgusted, down and out, and a lookin' for work.

Shows how come us to be that a way. Shows the dam bankers men that broke us and the dust that choked us, and comes right out in plain old English and says what to do about it.

It says you got to get together and have some meetins, and stick together, and raise old billy to hell till you get youre job, and get your farm back, and your house and your chickens and your groceries and your clothes, and your money back.

Go to see the Grapes of Wrath, pardner, go to see it and don't miss.

You was the star in that picture. Go and see your own self and hear your own words and your own song.

SOURCE: Woody Guthrie, *People's World*, 1940, in Guthrie, *Woody Sez* (New York: Grosset and Dunlap, 1975), 133. http://www.geocities.com/Nashville/3448/tomjoad.html

Follow-Up Problems

1. Define the terms radicalism, liberalism, and conservatism. As you reflect upon your viewing of *The Grapes of Wrath*, which of these terms would most accurately represent the themes and messages communicated in this film? In what ways does the film address the future of the capitalist system? What does the film's perspective on capitalism's survival reveal about the function of the motion picture industry in times of national economic crisis?

2. How does the film attempt to infuse this movie with a sense of realism? What techniques are used to lend authenticity to the problems addressed in this film?

3. What evidence do you find in this film to clarify the filmmakers' perspective on Franklin D. Roosevelt and the New Deal? How does the film relate to the political and economic innovations of the 1930s?

4. Compare and contrast the social commentary in Steinbeck's novel with the social and political content of Ford's film.

5. What perspective does the film adopt concerning the role of labor unionism and organizational activity in addressing capitalist exploitation of workers? How would you account for this attitude?

6. It has been argued that this film was more a stimulus to nostalgic memory of agrarian community than a realistic program for the post-agrarian future society emerging in the United States by 1940. What is your view of this question?

Further Reading

Bluestone, George. *Novels into Film*. Berkeley, Calif.: University of California Press, 1957.

Bodnar, John E. *Blue Collar Hollywood: Liberalism, Democracy, and Working People in American Film*. Baltimore: Johns Hopkins University Press, 2003.

Crowder, Laura. *Rousing the Nation: Radical Culture in Depression America*. Amherst, Mass.: University of Massachusetts Press, 1998.

Maland, Charles. *American Visions: The Films of Chaplin, Ford, Capra, and Welles*. New York: Arno Press, 1977.

McBride, Joseph. *Searching for John Ford: A Life*. New York: St. Martin's Press, 2001.

Roffman, Peter, and Jim Purdy. *The Hollywood Social Problem Film: Madness, Despair, and Politics from the Depression to the Fifties*. Bloomington, Ind.: Indiana University Press, 1981.

Sobchack, Vivian C. "*The Grapes of Wrath*: Thematic Emphasis through Visual Style." In Peter Rollins, ed., *Hollywood as Historian: American Film in a Cultural Context*. Lexington, Ky.: University Press of Kentucky, rev. ed. 1998.

Schindler, Colin. *Hollywood in Crisis: Cinema and American Society, 1929–1939*. London: Routledge, 1996.

Filmography

Black Fury (Warner Brothers, 1935).

Cabin in the Cotton (Warner Brothers, 1932).

Dead End (United Artists, 1937).

Our Daily Bread (Viking, 1934).

Wild Boys of the Road (Warner Brothers, 1933).

The Celluloid Document

The Grapes of Wrath (Twentieth Century Fox, 1940).

Chapter 7

Thinking of Intervention:
Foreign Correspondent (1940)
and the Winds of War

In testimony before a Senate subcommittee investigating interventionist propaganda in American motion pictures, isolationist Senator Gerald P. Nye of North Dakota argued in September 1941 that the motion picture industry was actively promoting the entry of the United States into the war then raging in Europe and other parts of the world. Angered by alleged bias towards England and the allies, Nye claimed that in industry circles observers spoke "not of the foreign policy of the United States," but rather of "the foreign policy of Hollywood."

The bitterness expressed by the senator and like-minded colleagues reflected the realities of a heated debate then underway between advocates of intervention and steadfast opponents of American involvement in the European conflict. Since the mid-1930s the American public had been hesitant about the prospect of a misguided intervention into the political and military disputes of Old World nations that seemed bent on repeating the mistakes of the preceding generation. As your examination of *All Quiet on the Western Front* demonstrated, this widespread public uneasiness over the possibility of another world war was evident in the warm response to that film in the United States. The film had accurately captured the predominant mood of the American public in the early 1930s, a revulsion against war rooted in the widely held belief that the decision to intervene in 1917 had been a disastrous mistake.

By the end of the decade, however, the international situation had changed, and the advance of fascism had come to alarm many American citizens, as well as President Roosevelt and some key advisors in his administration. As Germany, Italy, and Japan proceeded on the path of conquest, a significant and growing segment of the American policy elite became alarmed at the danger thus posed to national security. By mid-1940, the noninterventionist America First Committee and the internationalist Committee to Defend America by Aiding the Allies were locked in heated debate over the American response to the war that had raged in Europe since the Nazi invasion of Poland in September 1939. The informed public, then, was engaged in a national discussion of policy alternatives on the eve of the 1940 presidential election. By this time, internationalists, including Republican presidential candidate Wendell Willkie and journalist William Allen White of the Committee to Defend America by Aiding the Allies, had endorsed

Roosevelt's prudent steps towards intervention. It is this shift in public opinion that provides the background for your analysis of *Foreign Correspondent* (1940), a hard-hitting Hollywood attack on isolationism and the foreign policy of neutrality that had dominated the thirties.

The Historical Background

National discussion of the neutrality issue was matched by a lively foreign-policy debate in the movie capital that featured a perceptible shift in film content towards engagement in the European conflict. Until 1939, interventionist messages had rarely been found in the product of Hollywood. Convinced that there was little audience interest in propaganda films and fearful of lost markets in fascist countries, the industry avoided controversial issues. When independent producer Walter Wanger succeeded in making *Blockade* (1938), a subtle pro-Loyalist treatment of the Spanish Civil War, he was confronted with a boycott of this cautious antifascist film. Outcomes such as this did little to advance the cause of Hollywood interventionists, who hoped to explore serious political issues on the screen. Not until mid-1939 would a motion picture clearly and unequivocally enter the escalating national foreign-policy debate.

　　Not surprisingly, it was the pro-Roosevelt Warner Brothers, a studio that had compiled a distinguished record of socially conscious problem films, that first took a risk with an open attack on German fascism. Following the betrayal of Czechoslovakia at Munich in 1938 and the brutal suppression of the Czech nation that followed in early 1939, Hollywood activists increased their lobbying activities through the Hollywood Anti-Nazi League and later the "Committee of 56," which demanded that the administration end economic relations with Germany. Led by actors Melvin Douglas, Edward G. Robinson, and Gale Sondergaard, the Committee of 56 worked closely with the Roosevelt administration to publicize its interventionist foreign-policy line. The ranks of Hollywood interventionists were reinforced by an infusion of non-Americans, some of them refugees, who had a very personal interest in the war's outcome.

　　Alerted by administration figures to the activities of an active Nazi spy ring in the United States, Jack Warner assigned writer Milton Krims to prepare a screenplay for a film that was to mark a turning point in Hollywood's treatment of European fascism. The result was a semidocumentary feature film that told the story of Nazi espionage in the United States. Based on the reports of FBI agent Leon Turrou, *Confessions of a Nazi Spy* (1939) leveled a broadside against the activities of German agents as well as their domestic collaborators in the militant pro-Nazi German-American Bund. The film's message is clearly stated in the words of its central character, a clever FBI agent (played by the politically committed Edward G. Robinson), who flatly concludes that "it looks as if Germany is at war with the United States."

　　Like *Confessions of a Nazi Spy*, Walter Wanger's provocative *Foreign Correspondent* attempts to stay abreast of rapidly escalating world events. The film was loosely based on journalist Vincent Sheean's successful memoir, *Personal History* (1935), which recorded the rise of fascism from the perspective of a working newspaper correspondent. Arguably the first feature to assume an unconditional prowar stance, this picture provides an excellent illustration of filmmakers' efforts to be topically relevant, not to mention the significant and close relationship between Hollywood and transplanted British artists intent on serving their home country's cause in England's hour of need. Directed by Alfred Hitch-cock and influenced by a production crew that included English writers Charles Bennett, Joan Harrison, Robert Benchley, and James Hilton, the film explored the threat of international fascism and warned that inaction on the part of the democratic nations would have disastrous consequences. It tells the story of an innocent and somewhat naive American journalist, Johnny Jones, who seems to symbolize noninterventionist America. By the last reel, Jones has undergone a conversion that leads him to warn his listening audience to "keep the lights burning," by covering them with steel, guns, battleships, and planes.

Released in August 1940, *Foreign Correspondent* could hardly have been more relevant to contemporary events. Already reeling under the emotional impact of Hitler's victories in France and the low countries, the American public first viewed Hitchcock's work at the same approximate moment as it witnessed the heroic resistance of England and the British people during the dramatic Battle of Britain in the fall of 1940. Originally set in preoccupation Paris, the final shooting script relocated the scene of Jones's radio appeal to the American people to London under siege, a shift that reflected the lightning speed with which international events were unfolding as the German war machine rolled on. The broadcast from London had contemporary meaning for radio audiences in the United States already familiar with Edward R. Murrow's messages beamed to them from England in the summer of 1940. The blending of historical fact and Hollywood fiction lent an eerie immediacy to film content. Indeed, the producer's original goal of making an effective propaganda feature based on the Sheean account was now achieved against a backdrop that seemed to confirm the wisdom of the journalist's account of the fascist menace. Like other features released in 1940, including *The Great Dictator* and *The Mortal Storm,* Wanger's film called on Americans to make a choice in the battle of ideas that had engulfed the world.

Analyzing the Film

Although Hitchcock was uneasy about the idea of open propaganda, it is clear that he made the most of his opportunity to acquaint the American audience with the dangers of fascism and the imminence of war. Despite personal reservations about "message" pictures, he crafted a film that served the British cause in the United States. The stunning Nazi victories of 1940 added a new urgency to the task of awakening the American public from its isolationist slumber. While some scholars have argued that the film's final appeal for preparedness is not really pro-British propaganda, it is difficult to view the concluding sequence without grasping the interventionist message. One thing is certain: the isolationist senators who attacked Hollywood in 1941 for pushing the United States towards war saw this film as a prime example of Hollywood's alleged campaign to promote American intervention in the European conflict.

The film narrative, which departs significantly from its literary source, revolves around the awakening of the central character to the fascist menace. Ignorant of European politics, the foreign correspondent must learn in painful steps of the dangerous forces at work in the effort to undermine the peace of the world. Sent to observe the activities of the European peace effort, he uncovers a plot to destroy the movement by kidnapping its leader and wrecking a planned peace conference. In the process, internal subversion is exposed as English conservatives conspire to betray their country and the cause of peace. While the plot is foiled, the peace initiatives are overtaken by the march of events, including the fall of Paris and the bombing of London. The closing scene, which Hitchcock later dismissed as simplistic and overdramatic, marked the passage of time and the collapse of international cooperation. If Hitchcock is to be believed, the final scene was not the product of his imagination, but rather the result of rewriting, including the work of Wanger himself. Melodramatic though it was, the final speech drew the endorsement of the Roosevelt administration, which was delivered in a personal congratulation from the president and his personal advisor, Harry Hopkins. They, too, understood the value of the motion picture as an influence on public opinion on international events and American foreign policy. Their interest in the film stands as evidence of *Foreign Correspondent*'s relevance as a primary source that documents a raging public debate as the United States edged slowly towards intervention into World War II.

Your analysis of *Foreign Correspondent* should be informed by careful examination of the filmmaker's techniques of persuasion and creative methods. Explore Hitchcock's effort to lend authenticity to the story he tells, including on-location shooting, historical references, the uses of light and shadow, and other tricks of the artist's trade. Consider those aspects of the movie that re-create the atmosphere of Europe on the brink of another war. Think about the concentration on feverish and fruitless attempts by the film's politicians to forge a diplomatic solution to problems that defied resolution and to cope with national leaders who resisted peacemaking efforts. How do these efforts relate to historical context? Finally, be aware of Wanger's decision to shift the setting for the picture's final scene.

As you study the film's character development, watch for the filmmaker's use of his male lead as a mirror for world affairs and the place of the United States in the diplomatic activity of the late 1930s. How are the attitudes expressed by Johnny Jones with regard to international events related to the stance of the United States government and the policy preferences of the American people as Europe descended into military confrontation? Likewise, observe the evolution of Jones's thinking and consider its relevance to the state of American opinion in mid-1940. As you think about this transition, evaluate Nye's argument that there was a "foreign policy of Hollywood." Determine which groups in the movie industry worked to advance a political argument and explore their reasons for doing so. Link the film content in *Foreign Correspondent* to Wanger's personal view of the motion picture and its social function.

With this film, Alfred Hitchcock rewarded England's leaders with an engaging and powerful, yet subtle, anti-Nazi statement. Not only did *Foreign Correspondent* document the influence of British transplants in Hollywood, but it also demonstrated the movie industry's growing recognition of the fascist menace to American security. Close analysis reveals that Wanger, like many other Hollywood liberals, had clearly become engaged in the national dialogue over the American response to the deterioration of peace in Europe. By placing the film in its immediate historical context, it is possible for the student to revisit the last years of American neutrality and to experience again the intensity of the debate over foreign policy in the year before Pearl Harbor changed the United States and its role in world affairs forever.

Thinking About Primary Sources

The documents will enable you to place *Foreign Correspondent* squarely in the context of the battle between interventionists and isolationists in the late 1930s. Note the concerns expressed by Wanger over the issue of censorship and the pressures exerted on those filmmakers engaged in the production of topical films. Be aware of the difference between Sheean's original story and the narrative line chosen by the screenwriters and the production team, as well as the reasons for those departures. What factors made a faithful replication of the literary source impractical in the summer of 1940?

As you consider the primary sources, pay particular attention to the relationship between leaders in the American movie industry and British citizens and officials. Probe the documents for evidence of British interest in the Hollywood product, both before and during American intervention in World War II. There is evidence to indicate that Hitchcock remained in the United States at least in part at the behest of the London government, which was convinced that the director could best serve the Allied cause by working to counteract American isolationism. Dissect the sources for indications that Hitchcock and his countrymen played a role in the dissemination of propaganda in the United States.

The documents are also rich in insight concerning the domestic debate in the United States over the proper American stance on the changing geopolitics of Europe in the late 1930s and early 1940s. Search the sources for evidence of this political and popular disagreement over American foreign policy as the era of isolationism came to an end. Consider the political affiliations and preferences of Hollywood internationalists and try to determine what actions these antifascist liberals took to influence or support the increasingly interventionist policies of the Roosevelt administration. As you do so, think about the reaction to this film and the other political films of the late prewar era on the part of the Senate isolationists. Be alert to the factors that may have led liberals like Walter Wanger, Jack Warner, and others to adopt a belligerent stance, as well as the explanation for the attitudes of Roosevelt's Senate critics. Always be aware of hidden motives as well as openly expressed views.

As you examine the motivations of government and political leaders in the United States, you should also think about the reaction to the film and others like it overseas as well as at home. The primary sources contain important clues concerning the needs and psychology of nations at war. Consider the impact of total war on both government public-information policies and the public affected by full mobilization on both sides of the Atlantic. In at least one instance, the documents enable the historian to look back at the neutrality period from the perspectives of movie industry and government figures during wartime. Does this retrospective vantage point make it easier to clarify the intentions of filmmakers and the influence of their productions on the viewing public? The central question to be considered involves the growing impact of the communications media in the age of mass culture.

Historical Perspective

The reaction to *Foreign Correspondent* was almost uniformly positive. Most critics had praise for the film as a work of art, a judgment that reflects Hitchcock's arrival as a master of suspense and intrigue. It is also important to note that most reviewers linked it to the international politics and military conflict unfolding at the time of its release. In the words of John Mosher of *The New Yorker*, this spy thriller was so relevant that "you have the sense of turning from a paragraph in the current news and finding it dramatized for you upon the screen."[1] As the script revisions and dramatic conclusion demonstrate, the film was as current as the Battle of Britain and the bombing of London that American radio correspondents were reporting on as the summer of 1940 came to an end. Hitchcock and Wanger had crafted an antifascist statement without ever actually mentioning Germany, which may have been a factor in the Production Control Administration's willingness to grant the film its needed seal of approval.

Because of its topicality and distinctly prowar stance, *Foreign Correspondent* did not escape the attention of the Senate isolationists who were on a mission to expose Hollywood's tilt towards interventionism. North Dakota's Republican Senator Gerald P. Nye became engaged in a running battle with the industry, launching an assault that became even more shrill in 1941 as it took on a darkly anti-Semitic character. As early as January 1941, Nye's Senate colleague, Democrat Burton K. Wheeler of Montana, threatened the Hays office with legislative controls if the movie industry failed to contain the interventionism of some of its leading studios. So it was that in August of 1941, a Senate resolution created a subcommittee to investigate "propaganda disseminated by motion pictures and radio or any other activity of the motion picture industry to influence public sentiment in the direction of participation by the United States in the present European War."[2]

Not surprisingly, one of the films identified by the Senate isolationists was *Foreign Correspondent*. When the Motion Picture Producers Association was asked to assemble information on film content, Walter Wanger Productions responded with a detailed summary of the film's plot and narrative, as well as the difficulties experienced in making a film as the historical situation evolved before the eyes of the production team. Going beyond the requirements of the inquiry, the company defiantly enclosed a copy of the film's final speech, which it described as a "stirring radio scene appeal to America to defend itself with a ring of steel."[3] Wanger was not backing away from his commitment to interventionism.

In preparation for the Senate hearings, the Producers Association shrewdly selected former Republican presidential candidate Wendell Willkie as their legal counsel. Himself an outspoken interventionist, Willkie succeeded in casting the argument in terms of free expression and a threat to civil liberties, as well as abuse of Senatorial power. Outflanked and under vigorous assault from the press, the committee beat a hasty retreat and the hearings came to an end with a victory for the motion picture industry. While the industry emerged unharmed, the very fact of the hearings was disturbing to thoughtful social observers, who saw government intervention in a medium of communication on the horizon. As will be evident in subsequent chapters, this would not be the last time that Hollywood was to draw the attention of powerful political critics bent on exposing the industry's alleged efforts to influence the American public on important public issues.

For the moment, however, the motion picture industry was moving in step with Franklin D. Roosevelt and an administration gradually and deliberately moving towards war. In 1941, Wanger used his position as head of the Academy of Motion Picture Arts and Sciences to solidify government ties with the studios. While Hollywood cooperated with Washington in the production of training films and other military documentaries, the year's feature films took on a more interventionist tone. After a number of pictures stressing Anglo-American ties had appeared, the September premiere of the quietly understated *Sergeant York* marked a fitting climax to the foreign policy of Hollywood by reminding the public of moral responsibility in crisis times. By recounting the World War I story of war hero Alvin York, this Warners production emphasized the primacy of patriotic duty in times of national danger. The transition to outspoken interventionism was complete.

By the eve of Pearl Harbor, therefore, an important segment of the film community had taken up arms in the effort to warn the American public of the dangers of fascism. Alarmed by the advance of Nazi Germany and the racist policies it followed, many Hollywood producers, directors, and their creative teams had spoken out in an effort to influence the public debate over the appropriate American response to aggression in Europe. At the forefront of these efforts was the ardent New Deal Democrat Walter Wanger, whose timely production of *Foreign Correspondent* advanced the public discussion by publicly advocating preparedness as well as support for the hard-pressed British in an alliance of the surviving democracies. Careful examination of this powerful film within its immediate historical context places the student historian at the heart of a foreign-policy debate that was to end in American intervention and change the course of World War II.

Endnotes

1. *The New Yorker*, August 31, 1941, quoted in John Rossi, "Hitchcock's *Foreign Correspondent*," *Film and History* XII (May 1982): 33.
2. Quoted in James J. Lorence, "The Foreign Policy of Hollywood: Interventionist Sentiment in the American Film," in Robert Brent Toplin, ed., *Hollywood as Mirror: Changing Views of 'Outsiders' and 'Enemies' in American Movies* (Westport, Conn.: Greenwood Press, 1993), 109.
3. "Questionnaire," n.d., Walter Wanger Papers, Madison, State Historical Society of Wisconsin, Box 186.

THE PRIMARY SOURCES

This set of primary sources provides an inside look at the way in which the personal agendas of producers and directors drove film content. The documents open with an excerpt from a question and answer session following a speech made by producer Walter Wanger at the University of Southern California in April 1940 during the production of *Foreign Correspondent*. Examine this source for evidence of the censorship issue's impact on filmmaking. The following document, an internal memorandum from the vice president of Walter Wanger Productions, emphasizes the importance of combining topical entertainment with propaganda messages in a successful marketing program for the film. Business concerns aside, Walter Wanger's personal letter to President Franklin D. Roosevelt constitutes a clear endorsement of the president's internationalist foreign policies as of August 1941. At the same approximate moment, Senator Gerald Nye's extended remarks in the United States Senate reveal his conviction that Hollywood was encouraging a drift towards American intervention in the European conflict. Emphasizing the function of the motion picture industry in wartime, Wanger's 1942 letter to Gardner Cowles of the Office of War Information explores the importance of film as a psychological weapon and sheds light on his objectives in the prewar completion of *Foreign Correspondent*.

Questions for Mr. Wanger
Walter F. Wanger

Q: Do you know what the response of the public was to your article?

A: I don't know whether there was much public response or not.

Q: Would you give us a few of the problems involved in your attack on "Personal History"?

A: I bought "Personal History" in a moment of enthusiasm about four years ago when, as you know, it was one of the first books to appear with more-or-less the "confessions" of a foreign correspondent. A number of them appeared later and I felt that a first picture really showing what an American correspondent went through should have a good market. I have been confirmed in that because there have been a great many of them since. They all have the same pattern and they end up with more or less the same conclu-sion: that if we want to participate we should know what it is about. The war began to move so rapidly and it became impossible to produce anything like what Sheean wrote. Another picture I made caused such havoc that the exhibitors refused to take "Personal History" and I have re-written it. The result is there is more Gallagher and Sheean than of the author in it but, as a matter of fact, there is so little of Sheean left that I am going to change the title. There are none of the incidents or the characters that were in the original. It could never have been made with the original idea and nobody in his right mind today would do the incidents as Sheean portrayed them.

SOURCE: "Questions for Mr. Wanger," in Walter Wanger, "The Social Significance of the American Film," Speech, University of Southern California, April 1, 1940, Wanger Papers, Box 36.

Memorandum
Clarence Erickson

MEMO FOR MR. WANGER
Re – FOREIGN CORRESPONDENT

1/25/41

Contact - ? Mr. C.E. Pettijohn
Mr. Mallett
Mr. Corcoran

re Minister of Information.

Ascertain who is Minister of Propaganda or Information or proper person to contact theatres who have signed for the Defense Program.

Theatre-goers get tired of out-right propaganda. Foreign Correspondent contains the utmost in entertainment plus *what might happen here*.

Re-dating and re-playing Foreign Correspondent in key cities would offer perfect springboard for newspaper and magazine editorials on "*what could happen here.*"

From Clarence Erickson, Director, VP, Treasurer, of Walter Wanger Productions

SOURCE: Clarence Erickson, Vice President and Treasurer, Walter Wanger Productions, "Memo for Mr. Wanger," January 25, 1941, Wanger Papers, Box 8.

Open Letter
Walter F. Wanger

To Franklin D. Roosevelt
The President of the United States

Dear Mr. President:

I am a private citizen with no political ambitions. My motive in addressing you is to express what I believe millions of Americans are thinking and feeling; to let you know that we respect your courage and strength in this great crisis and to assure you the rank and file of Americans, regardless of party, are solidly behind you and your administration.

. . .

Mr. President, we think you have done a great job the past eight months; the greatest job in the hardest time during your long service as a public servant. You have shown great tolerance of the arguments of those who have disagreed with you. But we don't want you to be mistaken about the way we feel about what is happening in the world. We want you to know we are getting disgusted with long winded arguments, theories and talk that stop us from doing things to ensure our own safety. We think it is time for action, and we don't want you to go slowly in any idea that we aren't ready for it. We are ready for it. We are not asking you to guarantee the future of the American people, because we know the only future that can be guaranteed to us is the one we ourselves are willing to assume.

When we hear some of these politicians talk and tell us to play safe and try to get along with these world aggressors, we wonder if this is the same America in which we were born and brought up. We do not like the sound of advice like that, Mr. President. We are not blind to what China has done for herself because she had the courage to go ahead. There was a time when the British Commonwealth played safe, but every American is thrilled by what she has accomplished against the enemy—starting from scratch after she found out her mistake. Why, know-

ing what we do and seeing what we have seen, should we make any mistake about it now? We are told that there is nothing we can do but make peace with Hitler. This sort of advice was followed by the Czechs; it paved the way for the downfall of France and the low countries. Are we, ostrich-like, to follow such apostles of fear? Or worse still, surrender our heritage of freedom obtained by such great sacrifice by our forefathers?

There are a few men in our Senate, Mr. President, who have been hypnotized by Hitler's "Mein Kampf" and believe that they can imitate him successfully in this country. They should join Hitler and leave those of us who cherish our liberties the right to fight for them, unhampered by their fears and un-American influences. It is hard for the ordinary citizen to debate or argue with these irresponsible Senators whose utterances are malicious, tricky and cunning. But we the people are waking up to these methods. We distrust them and the people who use and support them, and we are not going to accept them or their misleading doctrines in this country. . . .

We want to do the right thing and we know that the right way is the courageous way.

You have the facts. Your duty is to protect the United States of America and the nations of this hemisphere. We have all pledged ourselves to that. To insure that protection, we have pledged all-out aid to those nations who believe in the things we believe in.

If you and your staff believe the United States Navy can help win the essential battle of the Atlantic, Mr. President, it is your duty to use it, and use it now when it will be the greatest help.

If you and your staff believe the United States Army can protect us by taking more outposts, and more advanced aerial bases, we ask you as Commander in Chief to give the orders and take them.

Your problem is serious, Mr. President, but so was the problem faced by Abraham Lincoln. He did not ask Congress whether he should relieve Fort Sumter. As Chief Executive of the nation, he had the facts and he went ahead and acted in the full responsibility of his office. He gave the order to relieve Fort Sumter, while Congress was still arguing. The politicians did not stop him from action to save the union.

The American people know what must be done. How it is to be done they leave to you, who know the facts. If there is any confusion among them, it comes from inactivity, and action can cure it. Americans prefer peace to war, Mr. President. But they are not foolish enough to think that they can buy peace.

They know it has to be won and maintained by keeping strong and watchful. They are willing to fight for it if that is the only way it can be obtained. If some of us are too soft to fight for it, it's time the rest of us found it out now. . . .

And we, the people, say—you are our Commander in Chief.

God bless you, Mr. President.

SOURCE: Wanger, "An Open Letter to Franklin D. Roosevelt, President of the United States (A Broadcast by Walter F. Wanger Under the Auspices of the Committee to Defend America)," August 2, 1941, Wanger Papers, Box 36.

Remarks
Gerald P. Nye

To carry on propaganda you must have money. But you also must have the instruments of propaganda. And one of the most powerful, if not the most powerful, instrument of propaganda is the movies. In Germany, Italy, and in Russia—the dictator countries—the government either owns or completely controls and directs the movies. And they are used as instruments of government propaganda. In this country the movies are owned by private individuals. But, it so happens that these movie companies have been operating as war propaganda machines almost as if they were being directed from a single central bureau.

We all go to the movies. We know how, for too long now, the silver screen has been flooded with picture after picture designed to rouse us to a state of war hysteria. Pictures glorifying war. Pictures telling about the grandeur and the heavenly justice of the British Empire. Pictures depicting the courage, the passion for democracy, the love of humanity, the tender solicitude for other people, by the generals and trade agents and the proconsuls of Great Britain, while all the peoples who are opposed to her, including even courageous little Finland now, are drawn as course, bestial, brutal scoundrels. . . .

Why do they do this? Well, because they are interested in foreign causes. You cannot doubt that. Go to Hollywood. It is a raging volcano of war fever. The place swarms with refugees. It also swarms with British actors. In Hollywood they call it the "British Army of Occupation." The leaders are almost all heavy contributors to the numerous committees of all sorts organized, under the guise of relief to Britain, Greece, or Russia, to propagandize us into war.

. . .

What I would like to know is this: Are the movie moguls doing this because they like to do it, or has the Government of the United States forced them to become the same kind of propaganda agencies that the German, Italian, and Russian film industries have become? I have excellent reason to believe that this governmental influence has prevailed. . . .

Americans, we want to be strong and ready always to effectively defend ourselves against the worst that any part of the world might choose to bring against us, of course. We want to leave no stone unturned that will aid in guaranteeing such a defense.

But, likewise, we ought to want freedom from foreign influence in times like these. Let's have courageous American thinking, not the kind which finds us waiting for the cue that Churchill gives; not the kind that has to be painted and pictured by propagandists or by forces whose profits are dependent upon foreign causes.

Let's be Americans because of and for causes that are American. Let us bury forever the thought that real Americanism is determined only by those who both hate Hitler most and love Britain best. Let us be giving larger thought to what is best for America. . . .

SOURCE: Gerald P. Nye, "Our Madness Increases As Our Emergency Shrinks," Extension of Remarks of Hon. Gerald P. Nye of North Dakota in the Senate of the United States, Monday, August 4, 1941, in Gerald P. Nye Papers, West Branch, IA, Herbert Hoover Presidential Library, Box 58.

WANGER RECALLS HIS OBJECTIVE IN THE PRODUCTION OF *FOREIGN CORRESPONDENT*
Letter to Gardner Cowles, Jr.
Walter F. Wanger

July 30, 1942

Mr. Gardner Cowles, Jr.
Office of War Information
Washington, D.C.

Dear Mike:

Only last Saturday George Gallup, Ogilvie and I were lunching and discussing the problem of the motion picture. George said, "What I would give to sit down and talk this all out with Mike Cowles"—so it seemed quite timely that your letter and the report should arrive.

I hasten to answer you because I have been struggling with the problem of motion pictures and mass enlightenment ever since the last war and I am delighted to give you my views.

First of all, I wish to say I found the report you sent me excellent and agreed with it in many instances. My disagreements will become apparent in my own statements.

Accepting the fact that psychological warfare is necessary in this crisis, then the American film is our most important weapon as no country has developed its film industry to compete with ours. The problem of enlightenment of the masses is a major problem and admittedly the film is the greatest visual educational factor accepted by the masses. The other great American means of communication, the radio and the press, are more limited. Very few people read American papers abroad and those you want to reach by short-wave radio cannot afford the sets. So you are back to the film again,

The film is of enormous value during the *war*, but its importance will multiply in the *post-war* period when our doctrine will have to be spread rapidly to counteract enemy propaganda. Beyond that, in the rebuilding of the world, the film uses are too many to be listed. . . .

Kindest personal regards,

Hastily and sincerely,

P.S. As you know, I have been very much interested in making pictures that will help the situation. It was for that reason I made FOREIGN CORRESPONDENT, which met with a great deal of resistance at the box-office because the exhibitors called it propaganda. . . . I am not alone in wanting to do this type of picture nor alone in being able to do them, but if we had more cooperation and better coordination a much more successful program could be achieved. There are so many pictures in production by the different studios that require this coordination and assistance and if you look favorably upon this report I hope you will be able to put a plan in effect immediately.

Source: Wanger to Gardner Cowles Jr., July 30, 1942, Wanger Papers, Box 14.

Follow-Up Problems

1. What is the primary message in this film? What cinematic techniques are used to lend credibility to the argument advanced in the picture? In what way did it attempt to influence or address the policy debates underway in the United States in 1940?
2. German Propaganda Minister Joseph Goebbels is said to have responded positively to this film. As you think about its portrayal of the Western democracies, can you see any reason why he would have reacted in this way?
3. What is the symbolic significance of the lead character (foreign correspondent Johnny Jones) in this film?
4. How would you account for Walter Wanger's intense interest in the production of antifascist films?
5. How was the making of the film itself influenced by the onrush of events in Europe?

Further Reading

Brewer, Susan A. *To Win the Peace: British Propaganda in the United States During World War II*. Ithaca, N.Y.: Cornell University Press, 1997.

Dick, Bernard F. *The Star-Spangled Screen: The American World War II Film*. Lexington, Ky.: University of Kentucky Press, 1985.

Giovacchini, Saverio. *Hollywood Modernism: Film and Politics in the Age of the New Deal*. Philadelphia: Temple University Press, 2001.

Koppes, Clayton R., and Gregory D. Black. *Hollywood Goes to War: How Politics, Profits, and Propaganda Shaped World War II Movies*. New York: Free Press, 1987.

Lorence, James J. "'The Foreign Policy of Hollywood': Interventionism in the American Film, 1938–1941," in

Robert Brent Toplin, ed., *Hollywood as Mirror: Changing Views of 'Outsiders' and 'Enemies' in American Movies*. Westport, Conn.: Greenwood Press, 1993, 95–116.

Roffman, Peter, and Jim Purdy. *The Hollywood Social Problem Film: Madness, Despair and Politics from the Depression to the Fifties*. Bloomington, Ind.: Indiana University Press, 1981.

Rossi, John. "Hitchcock's *Foreign Correspondent* (1940)," *Film and History* XII (May 1982): 25–35.

Schindler, Colin. *Hollywood Goes to War: Films and American Society, 1939–1952*. Boston: Routledge & Kegan Paul, 1979.

Filmography

Confessions of a Nazi Spy (Warner Brothers, 1939).

The Great Dictator (United Artists, 1940).

The Mortal Storm (MGM, 1940).

Sergeant York (Warner Brothers, 1941).

The Celluloid Document

Foreign Correspondent (United Artists, 1940).

Chapter 8

Government Persuasion: *Prelude to War* (1943), *The Negro Soldier* (1944), and the Issues of the War

As noted in Chapter 7, Hollywood and Washington had worked together since 1939 in several ways, including both informal discussion of feature film production and cooperation in the production of training films for the armed services. After Pearl Harbor, this collaboration became even closer with the establishment of the Hollywood War Activities Committee, which assisted in the marketing of government productions through the theater chains. Moreover, the movie industry increased its service to Washington by expanding its assistance in the production of training and information films designed for both military uses and public distribution. The smooth government-business relationship soon became more tense as the armed forces launched their own production programs designed to meet national defense needs. Yet even these government production programs relied heavily on Hollywood expertise, thus demonstrating the dramatic impact of total war on American social and economic institutions. This chapter explores the opportunities and perils inherent in the wartime marriage of public and private energies through analysis of the United States Army's brilliant orientation film *Prelude to War* (1943) and an equally significant effort at social engineering, *The Negro Soldier* (1944). Together, these films reveal the power of the motion picture as an instrument of propaganda in time of war.

The Historical Background

Even before the United States was a belligerent, the Roosevelt administration public information program had produced what historian Richard W. Steele terms "a propaganda din so pervasive and so diverse in its sources that by the end of 1941 it had become an unexceptional element of daily life." Working through the Office of Government Reports, the Division of Information, and the Office of Facts and Figures, administration propagandists provided information, withheld information, and shaped information, all of which tended to "numb the resistance to war."[1] These efforts were to some degree hampered by widespread public suspicions stemming from World War I and the zeal of the Committee on Public Information (CPI), the Wilson administration's propaganda office. Recalling the earlier experiment in public information programming, President Roosevelt was at first reluctant to support a propaganda agency with broad powers such as those once exercised by the CPI.

The need for an informed public in time of war, as well as increasing interagency competition, ultimately persuaded Roosevelt that a centralized information bureau would serve the national interest. Consequently, in June 1942 a new Office of War Information (OWI) assumed the functions of the prewar agencies. Under the leadership of news commentator Elmer Davis of CBS Radio, the OWI coordinated a broad propaganda campaign that reflected the administration's view of the war. Portraying the United States in a positive light to domestic and foreign audiences alike, OWI communicated American confidence with the message, in the words of Davis, "that we are coming, that we are going to win, and that in the long run everybody will be better off because we won." The agency's Bureau of Motion Pictures (BMP), headed by former journalist Lowell Mellett, became a key point of contact between Hollywood and Washington, distributing government films, guiding the movie industry's steps to support the war effort, and sometimes producing its own pictures. While BMP consistently strove to move the industry towards a more inspiring portrayal of democracy's war aims, Hollywood resisted censorship efforts and sometimes balked at voluntary script review. The result was a tension-ridden relationship.

An additional government effort to communicate the war aims of democracy through film arose from another source and reflected different objectives. In no instance were motion pictures more powerful propaganda instruments than in the Army's seven orientation films that constituted the critically acclaimed *Why We Fight* series, produced under the supervision of Major Frank Capra between 1942 and 1945. This ambitious project originated in military concern over a generation of draftees filled with revulsion against war and schooled in the rhetoric of 1930s isolationism. Facing a morale problem, the Army responded in 1940 and 1941 with a lecture-based orientation program designed to acquaint recruits with the reasons for the outbreak of World War II. Dissatisfied with the results, Chief of Staff George C. Marshall concluded that reliance on the motion picture and the movie industry's trained personnel was the key to effective teaching of history. Marshall's idea reflected the thinking of the War Department's Morale Branch, which in August 1941 had recommended the adoption of several propaganda devices, including reliance on film and collaboration with the motion picture industry towards that end. As long as the nation was at peace, however, an army indoctrination program remained a sensitive issue; but after Pearl Harbor these concerns no longer stood in the way. Consequently, in February 1942 the Morale Branch recruited Hollywood director Frank Capra to produce a film series that was to write a new chapter in the history of American motion picture propaganda. Convinced that "to win this war we must win the battle for men's minds,"[2] Marshall played a personal role in persuading Capra to accept a commission and assume leadership of the Army's indoctrination film program.

Capra was an inspired choice to carry out the assignment. A talented artist with a record of achievement at Columbia Pictures behind him, he had established a reputation for his directorial celebration of the democratic spirit through the resilience of the little man arrayed against entrenched economic and political power. Some of his films, such as *Mr. Deeds Goes to Town* (1936) and *Mr. Smith Goes to Washington* (1939), had established his ability to convey populist messages to a mass audience. His work contained inspiring accounts of success against odds as well as an awareness of the dark side of human nature and the reality of oppression. Although he had never made a documentary film, he was by temperament and experience well suited to the task of developing instructional films that would clarify the issues of the war.

Once he had signed on, Capra threw himself into the work with the same enthusiasm that had marked his career at Columbia. As he warmed to the task, he exploited existing film resources, mined the available Nazi documentaries, and used his experience in the Hollywood community to assemble a crew of talented artists and technicians whose skills would contribute substantially to the ultimate success of the project. He also gave considerable thought to the challenge of capturing audience attention with exciting celluloid history lessons. To Capra, there were "no rules in filmmaking, only sins," and of these, "the cardinal sin was dullness."[3] His commitment to the concept of high energy and constant stimulus was evident in most of the films produced under his supervision during the war.

Analyzing the Films

The first film in the *Why We Fight* series, *Prelude to War* (1943), attempted to accomplish what the failed orientation lectures had been unable to do—namely, to describe the collapse of peace as a result of previously ignored events that had occurred in far-removed geographic locations between 1931 and 1941. The entire film revolves around an answer to the question, why are Americans being called to war?

In answer to this question, the film moves beyond the obvious argument that Axis criminality and injustice must be defeated to make the positive case that the war was in fact a struggle for liberty and equality on a worldwide scale. Like all the series entries, *Prelude to War* promises to secure freedom in a world safe for diversity. Dominated by the pointed narration of the widely respected actor Walter Huston, it combines words and visual images to create a persuasive argument for every American's stake in the war.

From the very beginning, the film follows a narrative structure based upon the theme of contrast: the clear distinction between polar opposites labeled "the free world" and "the slave world." These concepts are reinforced by sharp photographic and celluloid images, as well as brilliant animated sequences crafted by the Walt Disney Studios. Insisting that America's enemies are identical in ideology, origins, and aggressive character, the filmmakers proceed to blur distinctions as they describe the German, Japanese, and Italian people as herd creatures who had willingly surrendered their individuality as subordinate cogs in the wheel of the dominant state. In each instance, government leaders had destroyed democratic political, religious, educational, and cultural institutions. With the image of the slave world set firmly in mind, the film turns to the contrasting imagery of the free world with its democratic characteristics. By the end of the last reel, the distinctions have been drawn so clearly that no viewer could have missed the central point about the two worlds and the urgency of Allied victory.

Prelude to War was actually released for training purposes in October 1942. Marshall regarded it as a "wonderful thing," while Secretary of War Henry L. Stimson wrote that it was "a most powerful picture." Even more significant, President Roosevelt was so "thrilled" and "moved" by the film that he proposed its release to a wider civilian audience. After considerable political opposition, including some from within his own administration, *Prelude* reached theater audiences in May 1943, a development that marked the administration's crossover into the territory of film propaganda for the civilian population.

While Mellett opposed this step as an unnecessary challenge to Hollywood, the industry, and the War Activities Committee, public distribution was consistent with the goals of the Army, which included an effort to use film to communicate its message to the wider American audience. From the outset of the war, Army officials had worried about what it saw as the general public's lack of enthusiasm for the struggle, which it thought resulted from a poor understanding of the issues at stake in the battle against fascism. Because these attitudes made it difficult to train recruits, the Army and its civilian supporters argued that it was unwise and shortsighted to limit morale-building propaganda to the military audience. In the last analysis, the combination of the Army's interests and the perceived political advantages of screening the film overcame the stubborn resistance mounted by Mellett, and the film was released for public distribution, aided by a promotional campaign by the Hollywood War Activities Committee. While the film was an underachiever at the box office, it was widely distributed and won the Academy Award for Best Documentary of 1942. Moreover, for millions of recruits, it became a powerful introduction to the issues that justified the heroic sacrifices that they were asked to make in the battle between the "slave world" and their own.

While *Prelude to War* addressed the issues of the war dramatically and convincingly, it skirted one of the critical social questions of the 1940s, the matter of race relations and the place of African-Americans in the war effort. The combined interest of the Army, the black community, optimistic social scientists, and Hollywood liberals in the "correct" portrayal of African-Americans on the screen and in the war resulted in a significant effort to reshape the image of America's largest wartime minority in the minds of a people engaged in democratic warfare. This effort became even more important in light of the problems faced by African-Americans who faced discrimination in defense hiring and segregation in the armed forces. As early as March 1942, Capra appealed to the War Department's Research Branch for guidance on the screen depiction of African-Americans. In response, he received detailed advice on the avoidance of stereotypes and the importance of positive cinematic portrayals of black citizens and soldiers. This guideline, prepared by Sociologist Donald Young, reflected the conviction that it would be possible to restructure public attitudes through the application of social science techniques—what David Culbert has labeled "social engineering."[4]

The most notable outcome of Capra's attempt to influence social attitudes with regard to the race issue may be found in his targeted orientation film, *The Negro Soldier*, released in 1944. Given wartime racial tensions in the cities, the reality of segregation in the military, pressures from black organizations such as the March on Washington Movement (which forced Roosevelt to ban discrimination in the defense industry), and the militant "Double Victory" campaign against home-front racism mounted by the black press, it was essential that the Army deal with the rising hopes of black inductees as well as the larger African-American community. The race question was aggravated by discrimination and intimidation at wartime military bases, as well as the reality of periodic urban rioting, as in the bloody Detroit race riot of 1943. As blacks called for a victory over racism at home as well as abroad, the urgency of the War Department's attempt to deal with a potential morale problem increased.

In May 1942, work on the script began with a first draft by Marc Connelly, a liberal best known for his work as a writer for the critically acclaimed *Green Pastures* (1930). As the script evolved, several screenwriters, including Ben Hecht, Jo Swerling, and Carlton Moss, had a hand in the project. Of these, the most important was the African-American writer, Carlton Moss, who eventually played the key role of the preacher-narrator in the finished product. Moss brought a burning commitment to the project, a reflection of his personal experiences in a racist society and firm determination to make a statement that might elevate the moral level on which the war was fought. After considering the experienced William Wyler as director, Capra chose for the job a relative unknown who had done some film work on racial themes, Stuart Heisler. The outcome was a successful collaboration that resulted in a documentary that, by the standards of its time, provided a forward-looking, nonstereotypical treatment of the black role in American history and life.

At the time of its release in 1944, *The Negro Soldier* seemed destined for use in the training of black servicemen, but before long the social scientists and African-American pressure groups were encouraging its incorporation into the orientation of white soldiers as well. After minor revisions to quiet nervous critics, the film became an important part of the training program of all recruits of all races. This decision represented a victory for the advocates of social engineering, who succeeded in convincing the War Department that the film was a useful tool for instruction in the course of racial brotherhood. After substantial internal debate, in April 1944 the film also entered public distribution, only to be caught up in the ongoing debate between the Army and the Hollywood War Activities Committee (WAC). Due to WAC concerns, a debate over charges of special pleading, and quibbling about timing of release and the film's length, *The Negro Soldier* failed to match the attendance record achieved by the three *Why We Fight* films that reached civilian audiences.

Despite the modest attendance figures, the film was, in fact, an important landmark in the depiction of African-Americans on screen. Its significance was reflected in the enthusiasm for the picture shown by black organizations such as the NAACP, which actively campaigned for its widespread distribution. As Thomas Cripps and David Culbert have noted, the film was a "watershed in the use of film to promote racial tolerance."[5] It is, therefore, important that it be examined against the background of the motion picture industry's development in the twentieth century. Moreover, as a prime example of social engineering in operation, this film, like *Prelude to War*, merits serious consideration as evidence of the motion picture's function in a society at total war.

As you study *The Negro Soldier*, it will be possible for you to observe the changing image of African-Americans during the wartime years. Think about the reasons for including the themes emphasized in the Capra unit's portrayal of black citizens, their history, and their place in the war effort. In this regard, it should be helpful for you to review the images projected by *The Birth of a Nation* in 1915, casting them side by side with the depictions of African-Americans in the context of World War II. Be aware of the filmmakers' intentions and their connection with the ideas stressed by the social scientists of the wartime era. Evaluate the theory of social engineering, as it was reflected in the work of Capra and his production team. How was the effort to act on this concept evident in *The Negro Soldier*?

The goals may have been those of modern social science, but the instruments employed to achieve them in both pictures were the tools of the Hollywood artists and technicians who populated the Capra team. These two films afford you an opportunity to analyze the techniques and practices used by Capra and the many craftsmen he attracted to government service. Look for overriding themes and cinematic ploys to underscore key concepts. How do the filmmakers use contrast, lighting, sound, music, repetition, and symbolic imagery? As you study the films' artistic qualities, pay close attention to the way in which they employ emotional appeals, historical references, religious sentiments, glorification of individualism, popular unity, and community values in their description of the "free world." Observe the way in which documentary and staged sequences are integrated into a single narrative for maximum effect. How do you think audiences might have perceived those blended images? What aspects of the film suggest the assumption of inevitable success and confident hopes for a democratic future?

The examination of War Department propaganda films enables students and historians to recapture the spirit of social unity that prevailed in wartime America. With a keen eye to the sense of urgency in these pictures, you will be able to experience anew the firm commitment as well as the anxiety of what was arguably the American people's greatest shared national experience of the twentieth century. Moreover, a critical approach to the goals and methods of the planners and craftsmen responsible for these powerful instruments of persuasion will give meaning to the concept of social engineering as it was applied by the social scientists, government bureaucrats, and creative artists of the early 1940s. These wartime documentaries once again provide you with a window into the past, sometimes clear, sometimes blurry, but always open to the critical analyst of the film as historical document.

Thinking About Primary Sources

Because of the government's central role in their production, the paper trail of the *Why We Fight* films and the Army film unit's other productions is extensive. It will therefore be possible for you to trace the historical development of these films, including the important debates surrounding their public distribution, in careful detail. It is wise to review the primary sources in preparation for the screening of the films under consideration.

The place to begin an examination of *Prelude to War* should be the directive from Generals George Marshall and Frederick Osborn outlining the objectives of the *Why We Fight* series. When you view the film, keep these goals firmly in mind and decide whether they were achieved. Pay particular attention to the techniques used by the filmmakers in pursuit of these goals. Think about the term "propaganda" and the regimes Americans in the 1930s and 1940s typically associated with extensive use of such persuasive materials and practices. As you do so, determine whether that term has positive or negative connotations. Within the context of American military and social objectives during the war years, assess the uses of propaganda by both civilian and military authorities in the United States.

Your analysis of intent and outcome should draw you into a deeper study of the armed services' objectives in the employment of motion picture propaganda. Review the documents that address the public distribution of both *Prelude to War* and *The Negro Soldier* for clues to the purposes served by public exposure to the messages projected by the two films. As you compare film content and images with the War Department's and War Activities Committee's views of their potential impact, assess the effort to achieve stated goals.

Bearing in mind the historical context in which the films were produced and distributed, search the documentary record for evidence that will help you to better understand the close, yet tense, relationship between the United States government and the motion picture industry between 1942 and 1945. Pay careful attention to the War Activities Committee and its efforts to support the war effort. To what extent did cooperation between Washington and Hollywood prevail? What were the limits of collaboration? As you explore these ties, be aware of the sometimes tense relations between government agencies, including interservice competition and conflicting interests. Focus especially on the complex interaction among the military establishment, the Office of War Information/Bureau of Motion Pictures, and the Hollywood War Activities Committee. Consider the importance of interagency rivalries as influences on the execution of administration public-information policies and the shaping of public opinion on the war. How do the documents shed light on these issues?

Historical Perspective

By 1944, the Army had established itself as an important purveyor of propaganda aimed at not only service personnel, but also the general public. A fierce battle raged between 1942 and 1944 over the wisdom of the military venture into the realm of filmmaking, especially motion picture production for a nonmilitary audience. In many of these struggles, the army was victorious, in that their productions often reached the civilian audience under the auspices of a sometimes reluctant Hollywood War Activities Committee. The War Department's bold initiative reflected its belief that Hollywood had not done all it could to communicate the noble purposes for which Americans sacrificed on the battlefields of the world. Consequently, the Capra film unit, relying on artists and technicians experienced in Hollywood production, filled the void with its hard-hitting and persuasive documentary films.

For its part, a nervous motion picture industry resisted government intervention in its field of expertise, always insisting that it could do the job more professionally than the military. At the same time, Hollywood cooperated in the distribution of the government productions as part of its own commitment to the war effort. Though sometimes slow to promote the Army product, the War Activities Committee was forced to accept that responsibility, which it carried out with mixed results. Although they were critically praised, both films failed to perform as well at the box office as their sponsors had hoped they might, an outcome that led to debate over the seriousness of the WAC effort on their behalf. Yet they influenced the "selling of the war" in that Hollywood was inspired to improve its product. In 1943, a dissatisfied Lowell Mellett arranged a Hollywood showing of *Prelude to War* for an assemblage of producers and directors, who pledged to redouble their efforts to treat the war more seriously and creatively. While tensions between the BMP and industry leaders continued to simmer, there is some evidence that feature films won greater approval from the agency after mid-1943.

On another front, the Army launched its own psychological study of the first four films in the series in order to assess their impact on the service audience. The results were not encouraging. Since the data revealed a high level of agreement with the films' messages before the screenings, only a modest amount of opinion change could be observed following the showings. These disappointing results, which were confirmed by later studies, seemed to cast doubt on the future of social engineering in a wartime context. Nonetheless, there was at least one way in which the *Why We Fight* series made a contribution to the military's thinking with regard to the practice of warfare. *Prelude to War*, *The Negro Soldier*, and the other Army documentaries revealed a new concern for morale and the psychology of war. These films demonstrated military consideration of the whole person and underscored the benefits of a full orientation program. The entire project laid the groundwork for the armed services' future preoccupation with psychology and sociology as factors in the promotion of high morale.

Because of its pathbreaking departure from long-held racial stereotypes, *The Negro Soldier* also stands as a film of special historical significance. Not only did this film imply a future commitment to equality in the armed forces, but the way in which black organizations grasped its potential for advancing the cause pointed to a future insistence on real social change. Grasping the potential of film imagery to alter public perceptions of African-Americans, the NAACP and other black groups soon increased their efforts to monitor and improve the images projected on the screen. Film historians have shown that the wartime film experience may be linked with the proliferation of socially conscious "message films" in the postwar era. In short, *The Negro Soldier* was a halting first step on a path that would lead African-Americans to demand that the government and the American people make good on the democratic promise of World War II.[6] In this sense, the Army's film program unintentionally contributed to the internal forces that led to its own democratization in the immediate postwar period. Moreover, it documented the need for national unity and a concern for military morale that were the products of the war between the "slave" and "free" worlds.

The Capra films' treatment of the war's origins also sent a message of internationalism and engagement. The lesson they taught was the futility of isolationism in the modern world. The moral tale they told stressed the indivisibility of freedom, the unity of humankind, and the sharp contrast between good and evil in human relations. Whether the lessons of racial tolerance and individual responsibility were absorbed by the American public is a debatable question. Although *Prelude to War* and *The Negro Soldier* oversimplified complex problems, they called Americans to a higher purpose in messages inspired by the wartime emergency. Their importance as primary sources lies in their value as documents of that moment of solidarity experienced by the wartime generation.

Endnotes

1. Richard W. Steele, *Propaganda in an Open Society: The Roosevelt Administration and the Media, 1933–1941* (Westport, Conn.: Greenwood Press, 1985), 172.
2. Frank Capra, *The Name Above the Title* (New York: Macmillan, 1971), 327.
3. Capra, xiii.
4. David Culbert, "'Why We Fight': Social Engineering for a Democratic Society at War," in K. R. M. Short, ed., *Film and Propaganda in World War II* (Knoxville, Tenn.: University of Tennessee Press, 1983), 173; Thomas Cripps and Culbert, "*The Negro Soldier* (1944): Film Propaganda in Black and White," in Rollins, ed., *Hollywood as History*, 116–117.
5. Cripps and Culbert, 130.
6. Cripps and Culbert, 130–133.

THE PRIMARY SOURCES

The documents provide important historical context for understanding the relationship between Washington and Hollywood during the war years. First, the army's instructions to Frank Capra, found in a directive from the Army Morale Branch's Frederick Osborne and Chief of Staff George C. Marshall, outline the objectives of the projected film series. After the release of *Prelude to War*, the armed forces embraced the idea of public distribution, as did the State Department and Treasury Department. In a memorandum to Gardner Cowles, John R. Fleming of the Office of War Information (OWI) summarizes the consensus view (not shared within the Bureau of Motion Pictures) that widespread dissemination would serve the war effort. The following document, a letter from OWI Director Elmer Davis to Undersecretary of War Robert P. Patterson, outlines OWI's concerns over public distribution of *Prelude to War*. BMP Chief Lowell Mellett adds his dissent against wide public distribution. Finally, a Hollywood War Activities Committee memorandum encourages theater owners to provide maximum exposure for *The Negro Soldier*.

THE ARMY STATES ITS OBJECTIVES FOR THE *WHY WE FIGHT* SERIES

Directive
Frederick Osborn and George Marshall
to Frank Capra

1. To create a will to win by:
   a. making clear the enemy's ruthless objectives.
   b. promoting confidence in the ability of our armed forces to win.
   c. showing clearly that we are fighting for the existence of our country and all our freedoms.
   d. showing clearly how we would lose our freedom if we lost the war.
   e. exposing the myth of enemy invincibility.
   f. making it clear that we carry the torch of freedom.
2. To create a desire to insure against a recurrence of World Wars by:

   a. explaining and exposing aggression and conquest.
   b. necessity for better understanding between nations and peoples.
   c. necessity for outlawing conquest and exploitations by the few.
   d. necessity for eliminating economic evils.
   e. The Four Freedoms.
   f. promoting democratic principles.

SOURCE: Directive, Frederick Osborn and George Marshall to Frank Capra, March 4, 1942, Washington, D.C., National Archives, Record Group 208, Records of OWI, Frank Capra File.

AN INTERDEPARTMENTAL ANALYSIS OF *PRELUDE TO WAR* PREPARES THE WAY FOR WIDESPREAD CIVILIAN DISTRIBUTION

Review of Prelude to War
John R. Fleming to Gardner Cowles

Gardner Cowles, Jr.
John R. Fleming

On the movie "PRELUDE TO WAR"

At your request, the Committee representing the Departments of State, War and Navy and the Office of War Information reviewed the War Department picture, "PRELUDE TO WAR" and discussed its suitability for public showing.

The opinion of the Committee may be summarized as follows:

1. The picture is unusually effective, the best thing of this sort any of us have seen. We believe, therefore, that it should be made available to the public.
2. If possible, some changes should be made, but if it is a question of showing the film as it now stands or not showing it, the Committee would vote for showing it as it stands.

3. The Committee suggests that it would be highly desirable to give the film a test preview before an average audience with provision for sampling the opinion of the audience immediately thereafter. The Committee is strongly of the opinion that this would be useful in order to determine what changes, if any, need to be made in the picture. . . .

The major change suggested by the Committee concerns the ending of the film. As the picture now stands, there isn't sufficient indication that the free people of the world are now actively engaged in preparing retribution for the Axis. Nor is there adequate demonstration in the picture that the United States does not face this enemy alone.

If other changes are possible, the Committee recommends attention to these details: the use of the two hemispheres at the beginning and at the end of the film inadvertently suggests that the Western hemisphere is unalloyed virtue and the Eastern hemisphere unrelieved evil; during the Manchurian sequence the narrator's remark "The Manchurian incident is the reason you are going to war today"

ought to be modified to something like, "The Manchurian incident was the first shot in this war"; the sequence showing babies piled up on a platform seemed a little too thick for credibility. These details, it seems to us, could be modified and made acceptable rather easily.

Major Werner of the Bureau of Public Relations, War Department, asked that a letter from him be made a part of the Committee report. A copy is attached.

The members of the Committee are:

John M. Begg, State Department
Michael J. McDermott, State Department
Ferdinand Kuhn, Treasury Department
Ensign Donald W. Duke, Navy Department
Major Al Warner, War Department
John R. Fleming, Office of War Information

SOURCE: John R. Fleming to Gardner Cowles Jr., December 26, 1942, Lowell Mellett Papers, Hyde Park, Franklin D. Roosevelt Library, Box 8.

THE OFFICE OF WAR INFORMATION'S DIRECTOR EXPLAINS THE AGENCY'S RESERVATIONS ABOUT PUBLIC DISTRIBUTION OF *PRELUDE TO WAR*

Comments
Elmer Davis

March 25, 1943

The Honorable
Robert. P. Patterson
Under Secretary of War
Washington, D.C.

Dear Bob:

Sorry I have delayed so long in replying to your letter of March 19th, but I wanted to see the next two pictures in the army series, since they come into this discussion too.

First as to PRELUDE TO WAR. The letter from our office submitting it to the War Activities Committee of the industry went off yesterday. It would have gone sooner except that we sent it over to the

War Department for approval of its phasing, so that there could be no doubt that we were really trying to sell the picture; and some delay was thereby entailed. Meanwhile, some of the changes recommended by an interdepartmental committee (on which OWI has only one member out of five) have not yet been made, and I gather from your letter that the War Department does not want to make them. I think you are mistaken in assuming that those still remaining would be either difficult or expensive; and we must insist that they be made.

Let me recapitulate briefly the history of this affair. We were assured by the War Department that this series was intended solely for training purposes, and would not be publicly shown. Relying on this statement, we assured the motion-picture industry, as part of an arrangement by which they make a short documentary for the government every two weeks, that the government was not going to produce feature pictures for general distribution. Obviously the public interest is paramount, and if these pictures, generally shown, would serve a useful purpose, they ought to be shown; but you will see that the army has put us in the position of breaking a promise which we made in reliance on your promises. This does not make our dealings with the industry any easier, and may somewhat affect the industry's attitude toward this series. They will distribute them, I am sure, but probably on a somewhat different basis from the Zanuck North African Film....

. . . As for *PRELUDE TO WAR* and its six successors, we are willing to let the public see them all if they are all good enough, and if they are pruned of details which in our opinion and that of the Interdepartmental Committee are unsuitable for public information. But we dislike to be put into a position where the army gets all the credit and the OWI takes all the heat.

Cordially,

Elmer Davis
Director

SOURCE: Elmer Davis to Robert P. Patterson, March 25, 1943, Mellett Papers, Box 8.

LOWELL MELLETT EXPRESSES THE BUREAU OF MOTION PICTURES' REASONS FOR LIMITED DISTRIBUTION OF ARMY PRODUCTIONS

Memorandum
Lowell Mellett

March 26, 1943.

Memorandum to Mr. Elmer Davis
From: Lowell Mellett

To supplement the information contained in your letter to the Under Secretary of War concerning the distribution of the series of pictures made by the Army under the title of WHY WE FIGHT, I would like to register these facts:

1. Motion picture producers are no more obliged to make at their own expense pictures to aid the war effort than newspapers are obligated to produce articles for that purpose. Motion picture distributors are no more obligated in this respect than are the Press Associations. Motion picture theaters are no more obligated in the matter than the newspapers are to print such material. All the government can obtain in this field is voluntary cooperation. We have obtained this cooperation to an extraordinary degree, due, in my opinion, through dealing with consistent honesty with the motion picture industry. . . .

2. As the result of considerable experience in dealing with the motion picture industry, it was possible more than a year ago to put in effect a system of distribution and exhibition that seemed calculated to meet the government's greatest needs without transgressing on the freedom of the motion picture industry and without disturbing unduly its operation as a business. . . .

3. When the motion picture unit of the Morale Division of the Army (now the Special Service Division) was organized, I explained this set-up to Colonel Frank Capra, who had been placed in charge by General Osborn. I explained that if that unit contemplated any pictures for use outside the Army or found itself later making any pictures that it considered suitable for public presentation, our office should be advised. I explained that we would wish to know in order that duplication might be avoided and in order that we could know what we might have to offer for distribution during the months ahead. I was assured emphatically, and this assurance was repeated on several occasions by Colonel Capra and Colonel Munson during a long period of months, that nothing

was contemplated of that kind and nothing being made of that kind.

My long dealings with the motion picture industry had made it clear to me that the extraordinary cooperation it was giving the government rested in considerable part on its acceptance of my assurance that the government would refrain from competing with the industry in the field of full-length picture. . . .

4. When the first WHY WE FIGHT series was completed and palpable efforts began to obtain its public showing, I discussed the matter with General Osborn. He denied indignantly that there was any desire on his part to obtain public showing, which denial I accepted fully. The pressure for public showing continued however, and in due course came to the attention of yourself and Mr. Cowles. I explained my situation to you and it was agreed that an interdepartmental committee, including full representation of the armed services, be set up to view the picture and decide whether it should be offered to the industry for distribution. . . .

The matter is now before the War Activities Committee of the Motion Picture Industry for consideration. What its decision in the matter will be, I do not know. I am only hopeful that nothing is done that will wreck or seriously impair our present extremely successful operation, an operation more useful to the armed services themselves than any single picture or series of pictures could possibly be.

SOURCE: Lowell Mellett to Elmer Davis, March 26, 1943, Mellett Papers, Box 8.

THE HOLLYWOOD WAR ACTIVITIES COMMITTEE PROMOTES *THE NEGRO SOLDIER*

Letter to Exhibitors
S. H. Fabian, Chairman

WAR ACTIVITES COMMITTEE
Motion Picture Industry
Theatres Division
1501 Broadway, New York 18, N.Y,

April 4, 1944

To All Exhibitors:

Release of 40 Minute Film
THE NEGRO SOLDIER

At the request of the War Department, Transmitted through OWI, the War Activities Committee—Motion Picture Industry has arranged to handle release of THE NEGRO SOLDIER to such theatres as may find it possible to include it in their programs. This film, produced by Col. Frank Capra, portrays the contribution to American history of our Negro citizens and their participation in the present war as members of the armed forces.

A limited number of prints provided by the War Department are available gratis to all exhibitors desiring to play it. Commencing April 10th these may be secured through the chairman of the Distributors Division of WAC in the exchange here listed:

Albany – Para.	Milwaukee – MGM
Atlanta – Fox	Minneapolis – MGM
Boston – Para.	New Haven – Para.
Buffalo – Para.	New Orleans – Fox
Charlotte – Fox	New York – MGM
Chicago – MGM	Oklahoma City – Col.
Cincinnati – U.A.	Omaha – Univ.
Cleveland – U.A.	Philadelphia – RKO
Dallas – Col.	Pittsburgh – RKO
Denver – RKO	Portland – Warners
Des Moines – Univ.	St. Louis – Univ.
Detroit – U.A.	Salt Lake City – RKO
Indianapolis – Rep.	San Francisco – Warners
Kansas City – Univ.	Seattle – Warners
Los Angeles – Warners	Washington – RKO
Memphis – Col.	

It is hoped that a substantial percentage of exhibitors may find it possible to include this gratis film in their programs. Inquiries from a number of exhibitors catering to Negro patronage indicate their special interest in this picture. Available prints may be used also for any special exhibition which you find it possible to arrange through interested individuals and groups in your community.

Sincerely yours,
S. H. Fabian
Chairman

SOURCE: War Activities Committee, "To All Exhibitors," April 4, 1944, in United Artists Collection, Box 107.

Follow-Up Problems

1. Compare the images of African-Americans in the two films. How would you explain the differences? How do both relate to the standard established in *The Birth of a Nation*?

2. What do the primary sources reveal about the objectives of the War Department, the Office of War Information's Bureau of Motion Pictures, and the Hollywood War Activities Committee? How did the distribution of these films reveal the ways in which governmental agencies cooperated and competed in their attempts to contribute to a successful outcome of the war effort?

3. How would you define propaganda? Is there such a thing as good and bad propaganda? If so, what is the distinction?

4. What were the primary objectives of the *Why We Fight* series? Do you believe that the Capra production team accomplished those goals? Using *Prelude to War* as evidence, show how the series failed or succeeded.

5. What were the key themes to emerge in the films you have viewed? How effective were these movies in clarifying the issues of the war for soldiers and civilians? What were the most important cinematic techniques and methods employed to drive home those themes to the audience?

6. Define the term "social engineering" as it was used by the social scientists of the early 1940s, and explain how it relates to the United States Army's film program.

Further Reading

Capra, Frank. *The Name Above the Title*. New York: Macmillan, 1971.

Culbert, David. "Social Engineering for a Democratic Society at War." in K. R. M. Short, ed. *Film and Radio Propaganda in World War II*. Knoxville, Tenn.: University of Tennessee Press, 1983, 173–191.

Culbert, David, and Thomas Cripps, "*The Negro Soldier* (1944): Film Propaganda in Black and White." In Peter C. Rollins, ed. *Hollywood as Historian: American Film in a Cultural Context*. Lexington, Ky.: University Press of Kentucky, 1998, 109–133.

Doherty, Thomas. *Projections of War: Hollywood, American Culture, and World War II*. New York: Columbia University Press, 1993.

Koppes, Clayton, and Gregory Black. *Hollywood Goes to War: How Politics, Profits, and Propaganda Shaped World War II Movies*. New York: Free Press, 1987.

Murphy, William T. "The Method of 'Why We Fight'." *Journal of Popular Film* I (1972): 185–196.

Steele, Richard W. "The Greatest Gangster Movie Ever Filmed: *Prelude to War*," *Prologue: The Journal of the National Archives* (Winter 1979), 221–235.

Filmography

Battle of Britain (U.S. Army, 1943).

Battle of Russia (U.S. Army, 1943).

War Comes to America (U.S. Army, 1945).

The Celluloid Documents

The Negro Soldier (U.S. Army, 1944).

Prelude to War (U.S. Army, 1943).

Chapter

Social Unity in a Nation at War:
Since You Went Away (1944) and
Women's Mobilization for Victory

While the government propaganda messages delivered in *Prelude to War* and the other *Why We Fight* films were a part of the serviceman's experience, most Americans on the home front were not influenced by those powerful documentaries. For the vast majority of citizens, the war, while of immediate and vital concern, was an adventure that was lived out in the United States. Much more significant than government propaganda films in both shaping and reflecting the hopes, attitudes, and beliefs of the American population were the motion pictures produced in Hollywood for the domestic audience. As Walter Wanger had observed on the eve of American intervention, the movie industry was prepared to assume new responsibility in the effort to maintain public morale in a democratic society at war.

While the Roosevelt administration fully understood the potential impact of feature films on public attitudes and support of the war, the President and his advisors moved slowly towards the establishment of a public information agency. Once the Office of War Information was finally established in mid-1942, its Bureau of Motion Pictures, under Lowell Mellett's active leadership, worked to solidify a close working relationship with Hollywood by encouraging collaboration while avoiding censorship. As a result, the industry remained relatively free to pursue its own objectives within the context of regular consultation and substantial voluntary compliance with government guidelines.

As a consequence of Hollywood's independence, the increased motion picture output of the wartime era was marked by sometimes shallow treatment of the issues of the war. As Clayton Koppes and Gregory Black have argued, Hollywood managed to serve its financial interests, usually without forcing Americans to confront the unpleasant realities of the wartime world. Industry leaders usually elevated entertainment value and diversion over hard confrontation with social issues and unpleasant realities. For its part, OWI offered criticism and suggestions to filmmakers but typically contented itself with the affirmation of democratic values on screen. A prime example of the home front melodrama that fulfilled the function of reassurance was *Since You Went Away* (1944), a sentimental treatment of the war's impact on the American home. Perhaps the clearest example of the wartime domestic drama, this film reveals a great deal about the hopes and fears of Americans coping with the disruptions forced on them by the great national experience that was World War II.

The Historical Background

Not long after American entry into the war, MGM scored a major critical and financial success with its sweeping portrayal of the British home front, *Mrs. Miniver* (1942). A tribute to a gallant ally, this film was one of the most successful domestic dramas of the wartime era. Welcomed as an important friendly gesture by the British Ministry of Information, the film also found favor with American audiences already interested in the experiences of women as part of the war effort.[1] Indeed, it was to be expected that in an increasingly manless society, women's films would gain favor with an American movie audience composed disproportionately of women and children. This tribute to heroic people's warfare garnered six Oscars, including Best Picture of 1942, and was probably the most popular film of the troubled year in which it was released.

It remained for the dynamic producer David O. Selznick to launch an enterprise that would do for the embattled American home what *Mrs. Miniver* had done for its British counterpart. No stranger to the epic film, David Selznick had already scored a major financial success with *Gone With the Wind* in 1939. Fueled by his widely acclaimed account of the Civil War, he now turned his attention to the great national experience of his own time, the drama of world war and its impact on the home front. Sketched from a screenplay written by the producer himself and directed by John Cromwell, *Since You Went Away* was Selznick's personal project from the outset. Based on Margaret Wilder's *Ladies Home Journal* story, Selznick's script focused on one year (1943) in the life of one American family coping with the trials of wartime survival. Sentimental though it was, the film caught the imagination of a viewing public that was then living out the domestic crises it saw portrayed on-screen.[2] While Selznick's female characters captured the main features of traditional womanhood, their brave and responsible reactions to wartime problems also marked them as model citizens and producers in a society disrupted by the conflict.

To this day, this film remains the classic expression of life on the wartime home front. From the early stages of production, OWI monitored its progress. In most instances, the government watchdogs found the film's themes and their expression to be in tune with the agency's guidelines. Selznick worked closely with OWI throughout the production process and, despite personal differences with BMP, his work drew little criticism. His decision to use the experience of one family as a representation of the national ordeal may have shielded him from some of the political sniping that sometimes accompanied efforts to make grand political statements on film. Moreover, the idealism of his central characters underscored the messages OWI desperately wanted communicated to the American public. Not the least of the agency's concerns was a keen interest in women's role in the war. The OWI reviewing staff, composed largely of female analysts, frequently recommended that studios do more to depict women in active producing roles as willing participants in the wartime labor force. The government reviewers attempted to spur the motion picture industry on to highlight women in new nontraditional roles. Convinced that a new era of female labor force participation had dawned, they worked to alert movie producers and other industry leaders to the importance of modern representations of women on the screen. In *Since You Went Away*, OWI was rewarded with a sensitive and engaging treatment of family commitment to the cause of the "people's war."

Analyzing the Film

The first segment of the film faithfully fulfills OWI objectives by reminding the audience of the many sacrifices imposed upon American families and individuals by the war crisis, from housing and food shortages to volunteer work and victory gardens. The emphasis is on doing without and improvising solutions to problems that do not seem so severe in comparison to the larger issue of the war's successful outcome. At a later stage in the narrative, the overriding theme is driven home in a scene in which Mrs. Hilton's daughter, Jane, is criticized by her mother's society-conscious friend, Mrs. Hawkins, for volunteering as a nurse's aide and mixing indiscriminately with young wounded men. In a double assault on lack of patriotic commitment, Jane and her mother blister Mrs. Hawkins for her crass insensitivity to personal sacrifice as well as "all the unpatriotic things [she had] done."

As the narrative progresses, the audience is permitted to experience the sense of personal loss felt by Jane, whose young fiancé is killed in action. Equally moving is the news that Mrs. Hilton's husband, Tim, has been reported missing in action. The pain of death and permanent separation is mingled with the exhilaration of hope regained in response to the news that Tim is safe. In both circumstances, *Since You Went Away* offered anxious wartime audiences models of behavior suitable for a society at war. So pointed was this message that some critics attacked the film for manipulating the audience's emotions in a film in which the resolution of conflict was unrealistic, given the wartime context. As Koppes and Black have observed, this is one reason the film succeeded; precisely because it was not realistic. In its sentimentality and emphasis on popular hopes for the future, the film reinforced the American dream held sacred by many viewers in middle America.[3] Recognizing a possible problem, some OWI staffers encouraged Hollywood to address the unpleasant realities of war more forthrightly by dealing with the hard facts of death, injury, and uncertainty; but the general consensus remained positive.

Although *Since You Went Away* may not have heeded the OWI suggestion that the motion picture industry help prepare Americans for the possibility of loss and permanent separation, the agency generally approved of Selznick's work. From enthusiasm for its inspired story to endorsement of its depiction of American life, the BMP thought the picture especially valuable for overseas exhibition. Moreover, it complimented Selznick for his "splendid cooperation" during the production process. The vote of confidence is not surprising in view of the film's idealism and in spite of its sentimentalism; in fact, it stands as a textbook example of the truce between OWI and Hollywood that enabled the movie industry to endorse democracy while denying reality. And despite its artistic limitations and time-bound topic, it stands as a valuable artifact that documents the needs of the American public in the midst of its war for survival. *Since You Went Away* provides evidence not only of government-business cooperation, but also of Hollywood's effort to reassure the American public that as World War II moved towards its conclusion, all was well in the United States and with the American family.

As you view the film, therefore, you should explore its content for evidence of the filmmakers' analysis of the greatest dangers to wartime morale. Try to determine what the issues addressed reveal about the challenges faced by Americans on the home front, as well as proposed solutions to those problems. Similarly, think about the socially explosive question of gender relations as treated by Selznick and his collaborators. As you examine the way in which women are portrayed in *Since You Went Away*, watch for the messages communicated to the audience. Do you detect any contradictions concerning women's roles in American society? Observe the ways in which potential conflicts are resolved in the film, and relate that outcome to the needs of American audiences in the mid-1940s. As you pursue this analysis, you will note that the film contains important evidence of the dramatic social changes prompted by the demands of total war.

Not the least of these disruptions was the significant change in the roles of women made necessary by the exit of their husbands, brothers, and children from the labor force as well as the home. Six million women entered the labor market between 1941 and 1945, a shift that was to have a long-term influence on self-images as well as postwar gender relations. In what way was the new labor force involvement integrated into the film? Note also the war's impact on family structure. The assumption of responsibility for family leadership had a transforming impact on the female population, as more and more women became heads of families out of necessity. What did the changes experienced by the Hilton women reveal about the life experience of Americans of the wartime generation? When you view *Since You Went Away*, try to understand the problems besetting the Hilton household in the wider context of the adjustments occurring throughout the United States as men went to war.

You should also be aware of women's varied responses to the opportunities presented by war work. Like Anne Hilton, many women entered the workforce in response to the call of patriotic duty. What they found was the excitement of work beyond the home, new economic opportunity, new social contacts, and the empowerment that stemmed from a new, more positive self-image. It is also true that economic discrimination and resentment from male colleagues awaited them in the workplace. Notice the relative absence of images that address the downside of participation in the new workforce. The film also raises but does not answer the question of Anne's plans for the postwar era. Think about the unspoken message in the film with regard to the Hilton family's postwar division of labor, with particular reference to the fate of the war job Anne has taken for the duration. What decision is she likely to make with regard to her presence in the labor force? Note that the question Anne faced was one that many American women confronted as the war came to an end. Are there any aspects of the film's narrative or dramatic structure that allow you to make a judgment about what is to come?

Thinking About Primary Sources

In many respects, *Since You Went Away* was a film tailor-made for wartime moviegoers, many of whom were struggling with the absence of family members. Explore the documents for evidence of a link between the film's subject matter and the gendered composition of the audience. As Selznick planned for the movie's promotion and the exploitation of its unique features, it is obvious that he understood the unique appeal this film would have to a public with a temporary deficit in the male population. Examine the primary sources for indications of the appeal Selznick hoped to make in marketing his film. In addition, as you reflect on the film's depiction of women and their capabilities, try to relate those ideas to the studio's assumptions concerning audience preferences. What do these characterizations have to do with the issue of morale on the home front?

While gender is a central question in any analysis of this film, it is also important to think about the film in a class context. Many scholars have noted that the Hilton household is really more affluent than the average middle-class home in wartime America. In this regard, the Hilton family resembles the Miniver family portrayed in the MGM home front drama. Why do you think Selznick decided to set his film in an upper-middle-class context? What does this setting reveal about the social function of the motion picture, especially in time of national crisis? Link this aspect of the film to the issue of realism (or its absence) in the films of World War II, especially the home front melodramas.

As you consider this issue, think about the reviewer's reaction to the picture. Notice the most important themes identified by the film critic, and reflect upon his evaluation of Selznick's home front melodrama. Be alert to the ways in which the wartime context is evident in his view of the film. Identify the audience whose interests were likely to be served by this picture. What was the reviewer's assessment of *Since You Went Away*'s box office potential? What aspects of the film did he see as influences on the anticipated audience response?

In order to place the film squarely within its historical context, your analysis of *Since You Went Away* must take into consideration Selznick's relationship with OWI and BMP. As you review the documents, be alert to any hints with regard to the government view of this film in the context of the overall war effort. As you review the government information manual, assess the extent to which the picture met the specifications set out by Washington as guidelines for the patriotic filmmaker. Probe the film dialogue for evidence that approved ideas found their way into the picture. As you analyze the messages projected in *Since You Went Away*, it should not be difficult to sense the urgency and spot the propaganda present in the mass media of World War II America.

Historical Perspective

The evidence from the box office suggests that *Since You Went Away* was among the most successful films of 1944, at least in financial terms. The positive public reception of the film suggests that despite (or perhaps because of) its sentimentality, this movie met the needs of the moviegoing public in its own time. Meanwhile, the response from reviewers reveals that despite reservations over its lack of realism, the film was widely regarded as a quality film that contributed in a substantial way to the war effort. Most reviewers were forced to admit that the film worked for its audience. As the *Time* review indicates, there was an air of authenticity in the characters introduced, not to mention the element of harsh reality reflected in the broken bodies and even the death of one of the film's central figures. In this respect, at least, *Since You Went Away* did not completely deny one of the unavoidable realities of a war that was to leave almost half a million American servicemen dead. The picture contains an unusual blend of sentiment and honesty in its depiction of the home front of a nation mobilized for war. You must decide which themes dominate the film, as you attempt to employ the historian's tools of analysis.

While the picture satisfied the needs of the generation in which it was produced and first viewed, it is equally valuable to students of the past. As several critics acknowledged, *Since You Went Away* was destined to become what one called the "definitive home front movie" of World War II. With all of its flaws, the picture still captures many aspects of life in the United States at a time of great peril and social anxiety, but does so without losing the spirit of unity that could be found side by side with doubt and uncertainty. Moreover, in still another way, the film was remarkable in its honesty. As historian Joyce Baker has observed, while most American home front films had made women secondary characters in the dramatic presentation of World War II, *Since You Went Away* places them at stage center, thus mirroring the reality lived by many American families at the time. Baker therefore regards this film as a notable exception to the tendency to marginalize women on-screen.[4] Instead, Selznick and Cromwell crafted a story that without disturbing the most treasured dimensions of women's traditional roles, quietly but effectively gave visual expression to a reality experienced by many women and endorsed by most. This film is unusual in that it chose to include women in a story that had been told largely through the eyes and experience of the men who were called upon to take up arms.

OWI saw the value in correcting that imbalance. In 1943, the agency was engaged in its own effort to highlight women's wartime contributions by sponsoring a "women at work" month. At this time, an MGM executive wrote to BMP official Nelson Poynter to express concern over the possibility that women's home front activities would be ignored. MGM, which had already hit the jackpot with *Mrs. Miniver*, had an American home front film in the planning stage and may have hoped for government cooperation. While the MGM project was never completed, Selznick's epic filled the bill, thereby addressing the problem raised. As we have observed, Ulrich Bell applauded the story, and following the film's release, the BMP took pains to thank Selznick for his "splendid cooperation."[5] All concerned were pleased at the prospect of a quality Hollywood production that so successfully fulfilled the goals of OWI.

As a morale booster, *Since You Went Away* appears to have served admirably. It also provides modern students with a clear expression of the wartime generation's assumptions with regard to gender and the sexual division of labor. Never losing its focus on the home and family, the picture underscores the expectations of the wartime generation by placing Anne Hilton in both the public and private spheres in what seems a temporary arrangement of roles. As the guardian of the home, Anne's future is implied throughout the film. Her short-term sacrifice mirrored that of many American women who were pressed into service during the war. While the evidence indicates that many women did not go quietly back to the home at war's end, Selznick's film contained little to suggest any doubt about the plans of the Hilton family. To moviegoers in 1944, Anne and Tim both fought for a return to normal gender roles and the traditional home. The task of the student and historian is to consider the relationship between the film's popularity and the preferences of the audience exposed to its messages at the time of its release. Just as *Since You Went Away* articulated the innermost fears and hopes of wartime consumers, it also provides modern scholars with a window into the past, through which they may observe the social impact of total war, the penetrating influence of the motion picture on the popular consciousness, and the deeper meaning of the social assumptions and aspirations of the American people in the hour of national crisis.

Endnotes

1. *Mrs. Miniver's* focus on women's issues is discussed in M. Joyce Baker, *Images of Women in Film: The War Years, 1941–1945* (Ann Arbor, Mich.: UMI Research Press, 1980), 31–44.
2. Clayton R. Koppes and Gregory D. Black, *Hollywood Goes to War: How Politics, Profits, and Propaganda Shaped World War II Movies* (New York: Free Press, 1987), 154–155.
3. Koppes and Black, 161.
4. Baker, 95–96.
5. Koppes and Black, p. 160.

THE PRIMARY SOURCES

The primary sources focus on the government's expectations of its Hollywood allies, as well as the wartime experiences of American women. The OWI information manual highlights the movie industry's mission in 1942. The oral history provided by Della Hahne reveals the real life challenges faced by women on the home front. The studio's success in reaching the target audience is confirmed in the *Time* review, which emphasizes the film's authenticity.

OWI OUTLINES HOLLYWOOD'S WARTIME RESPONSIBILITIES

Government Information Manual
for the Motion Picture Industry
Office of War Information

Today the burden rests squarely on the individual to take the initiative. Horse sense is all it takes to figure out what needs to be done and to do it. The time has come for Mr. Civilian to stop expecting miracles from Washington, to stop waiting for The Government to appear at his door and tell him what to do.

A large share of the burden rests on the motion picture industry. Hollywood, speaking directly to Mr.

Civilian from the screen, can challenge his frequently-expressed desire to join in the war effort— can give direction to his patriotic zeal to "do something" to help.

Motion pictures can show Mr. Civilian *what* he can do to help. *Far more important*, they can create the *determination* to pitch in. They can make the seriousness of America's plight a startling reality in millions of minds that still rebel at disturbing their own placid habits. They can crack the shell of public apathy whenever it exists.

Motion pictures are better equipped than any other source of information, than any Government agency or spokesman, to create the emotional enthusiasm and the sense of individual responsibility which, combined, make for unceasing "war-mindedness".

. . .

It is possible to legislate into existence the kind of initiative and cooperative spirit that is ordinarily called civic-mindedness, and is now called war-mindedness.

By every means possible, motion pictures must help to develop an overwhelming war-mindedness in each and every civilian. We must make this feeling of personal involvement in the war so immediate and so acute that every instance of waste, of failure to make a sacrifice that is indicated, will be followed by a sense of guilt. The backslider must be made to feel the full weight of public condemnation.

. . .

Why We Must Go Without

Mr. Civilian, still able today to buy almost everything he wants—as well as what he needs—is not yet convinced that he must start going without now.

These are the four points to be emphasized and re-emphasized on the screen at every opportunity:

(1) *The shortage of production capacity.* Industry cannot supply both the armed forces and ordinary civilian demands.

(2) *The shortage of raw materials.* Production is always ahead of supply. War needs come first. Consumer goods must be curtailed.

(3) *The shortage of transportation facilities.* Trains, planes, ships and trucks are loaded to capac-

ity now. Shipments of civilian goods must not interfere with the transportation of troops and war materials.

(4) *The danger of inflation.* Consumer goods have decreased while income has risen. Buying must be curtailed or we will have inflation, with all its attendant evils.

Until just a few short months ago there was plenty of everything for civilian use. Living in a fabulous land of plenty, we were the most wasteful people in the world. The market was wide open to anyone with the money to spend. We were encouraged to throw away the old and buy the new.

Today there are still large inventories of consumer goods on hand. But with more money than ever in the hands of prospective buyers, these inventories can be exhausted in a relatively short time. With few exceptions they will not be replaced.

We all know why. Industry, workers and civilians have gone to war. The number one job is to supply our armed forces and the armed forces of our Allies. Everything else is secondary.

. . .

In the ordinary scenes, dialogue and bits of business that make up the bulk of film footage, characters should be shown as *aware* of their responsibility to the war effort. They should be shown doing he small things that must be done . . . making the small sacrifices that have to be made . . . naturally, convincingly and without heroics.

Remember this: The *ways* in which people can help are important. The *determination* to do everything possible to help the war effort, to do nothing to hinder the war effort, is ten times as important.

Motion pictures are doing a great job—in supplying war information to the American public and in keeping morale up to a fighting pitch. Let's not let Mr. Civilian forget for a moment that this is his war—that he can win it with eternal vigilance and self-sacrifice or lose it with indifference and petty selfishness.

Discomfort or defeat!

SOURCE: "Government Information Manual for the Motion Picture Industry," 1942, National Archives, Record Group 208, Records of the Office of War Information, Series 285.

"The Good War"
Studs Terkel

While my conscience told me the war was a terrible thing, bloodshed and misery, there was excitement in the air. I had just left college and was working as a substitute teacher. Life was fairly dull. Suddenly, single women were of tremendous importance. It was hammered at us through the newspapers and magazines and on the radio. We were needed at USO, to dance with the soldiers.

A young woman had a chance to meet hundreds of men in the course of one or two weeks, more than she would in her entire lifetime, because of the war. Life became a series of weekend dates.

I became a nurse's aide, working in the hospital. Six or eight weeks of Red Cross training. The uniform made us special.

I had a brother three years younger than I. He was a cadet at the Santa Ana Air Base. Your cadet got to wear these great hats, with the grommets taken out. Marvelous uniform.

I met my future husband. I really didn't care that much for him, but the pressure was so great. My brother said, "What do you mean you don't like Glenn? You're going to marry him, aren't you?" The first time it would occur to me that I would marry anybody. The pressure to marry a soldier was so great that after a while I didn't question it. I have to marry sometime and I might as well marry him.

That women married soldiers and sent them overseas happy was hammered at us. We had plays on the radio, short stories in magazines, and the movies, which were a tremendous influence in our lives. The central theme was the girl meets the soldier, and after a weekend of acquaintanceship they get married and overcome all difficulties. Then off to war he went. Remember Judy Garland and Robert Walker in *The Clock?*

I knew Glenn six weekends, not weeks. They began on Saturday afternoon. We'd go out in herds and stay up all night. There was very little sleeping around. We were still at the tail-end of a moral gener-

ation. Openly living together was not condoned. An illegitimate child was a horrendous handicap. It was almost the ruination of your life. I'm amazed and delighted the way it's accepted now, that a girl isn't a social outcast any more.

The OWI, Office of War Information, did a thorough job of convincing us our cause was unquestionably right. We were stopping Hitler, and you look back at it and you had to stop him. We were saving the world. We were allied with Russia, which was great at that time. Germany had started World War One and now it had started World War Two, and Germany would be wiped off the face of the map. A few years later, when we started to arm Germany, I was so shocked. I'd been sold a bill of goods—I couldn't believe it. I remember sitting on the back porch here, I picked up the paper, and I read that our sworn enemy was now our ally. The disillusionment was so great, that was the beginning of distrusting my own government.

. . .

We didn't fly. It was always a train. A lot of times you stood in the vestibule and you hoped to Christ you could find someplace to put your suitcase and sit down. No place to sleep, sit up maybe three, four nights. The trains were filthy, crowded.

You'd go live with your husband, far from home. In the town, provision was made for the service wife. They needed all the womanpower they could get. You'd work in a factory or a restaurant. In some towns, your husband had a regular day off. They would allow you to have that day off. The townspeople were accommodating because they needed us. But you never got the feeling that you were welcome. It was an armed truce.

. . .

I felt one step above a camp follower. In some cases, I was asked to produce my marriage license.

Most cases, you paid your rent in advance. Lot of times you were told, leave your door open if, say, one of your husband's friends came over. We were looked down upon. Yet they got very rich on the soldiers. . . .

When it started out, this was the greatest thing since the Crusades. The patriotic fervor was such at the beginning that if "The Star-Spangled Banner" came on the radio, everybody in the room would stand up at attention. As the war dragged on and on and on, we read of the selfish actions of guys in power. We read stories of the generals, like MacArthur taking food right out of the guys' mouths when he was in the Philippines, to feed his own family. Our enthusiasm waned and we became cynical and very tired and sick of the bloodshed and killing. It was a completely different thing than the way it started. At least, this is the way I felt.

We had a catchphrase: The War Against Fascism. I remember a Bing Crosby movie. I think he's a cabdriver and some guy is dictating a letter in the cab to a secretary. Crosby's singing a song. The businessman says, "Will you cut it out?" and Crosby says, "The world would be a better place if we didn't have so many dictators." The catchwords and catchphrases again. This was the war to stop Hitler, stop Mussolini, stop the Axis.

There were some movies we knew were sheer bullshit. There was a George Murphy movie where he gets his draft induction notice. He opens the telegram, an he's in his pajamas and bare feet, and he runs around the house and jumps over the couch and jumps over the chair, screaming and yelling. His landlady says, "What's going on?" "I've been drafted! I've been drafted." Well, the whole audience howled. 'Cause they know you can feed 'em only so much bullshit.

If a guy in a movie was a civilian, he always had to say—what was it? Gene Kelly in *Cover Girl*? I remember this line: "Well, Danny, why aren't you in the army?" "Hell, I was wounded in North Africa, and now all I can do is keep people happy by putting on these shows." They had to explain why the guy wasn't in uniform. Always. There was always a line in the movie: "Well, I was turned down." "Oh, tough luck." There were always soldiers in the audience,

and they would scream. So we recognized a lot of the crap.

. . .

There was *one* good thing came out of it. I had friends whose mothers went to work in factories. For the first time in their lives, they worked outside the home. They realized that they were capable of doing something more than cook a meal. I remember going to Sunday dinner one of the older women invited me to. She and her sister at the dinner table were talking about the best way to keep their drill sharp in the factory. I had never heard anything like this in my life. It was just marvelous. I was tickled.

But even here we were sold a bill of goods. They were hammering away that the woman who went to work did it temporarily to help her man, and when he came back, he took her job and she cheerfully leaped back to the home.

There was a letter column in which some woman wrote to her husband overseas: "this is an exact picture of our dashboard. Do we need a quart of oil?" Showing how dependent we were upon our men. Those of us who read it said, This is pure and simple bullshit. 'Cause if you don't know if you need a quart of oil, drive the damn thing to the station and have the man show you and you'll learn if you need a quart of oil. But they still wanted women to be dependent, helpless.

I think a lot of women said, Screw that noise. 'Cause they had a taste of freedom, they had a taste of making their own money, a taste of spending their own money, making their own decisions. I think the beginning of the women's movement had its seeds right there in World War Two.

SOURCE: "Della Hahne," in Studs Terkel, *The Good War: An oral History of World War II* (New York: Ballantine, 1984), 114–115; 116–117, 119.

A WARTIME ANALYSIS
OF SELZNICK'S WORK FROM *TIME*

Analysis
Time

Since You Went Away (Selznick–United Artists). The duck that hatched a swan was lucky compared to David Oliver Selznick. He hatched *Gone with the Wind* and has been trying to hatch another ever since. Last week he punctuated four pictureless years with *Since You Went Away*, a marathon of home-front genre-filming. Sure enough, it was no *Gone with the Wind*. *The Wind* blew for four solid hours; *Went* goes on for ten minutes short of three. *The Wind* cost $4,000,000 to make; *Went*, a mere $2,400,000. *The Wind* was photographed in some of the most florid Technicolor ever seen; *Went* is in Quaker black and white and Hollywood's pearliest mezzotones. *The Wind* was perhaps the greatest entertainment natural in screen history; *Went*, though its appeal is likely to be broad, is essentially a "woman's picture." But it is obviously, in every foot, the work of one of Hollywood's smartest producers.

Since You Went Away is simply the story of a year (1943) and the things it does to the inmates of "that fortress, the American Home." If the Home is not an average U.S. reality, it is an average U.S. dream.

· · ·

What makes *Since You Went Away* surefire is in part its homely subject matter, which has never before been so earnestly tackled in a film, in part its all-star acting (everybody registers with all his might, down to Lionel Barrymore's few seconds as a preacher and newcomer Guy Madison's brief, effective appearance as a sailor), most of all David Selznick's extremely astute screen play and production.

Selznick has given Claudette Colbert the richest, biggest role of her career. She rewards him consistently with smooth Hollywood formula acting, and sometimes—especially in collaboration with Mr. Cotton—

with flashes of acting that are warmer and more mature. He has brought his newest find, Jennifer (*The Song of Bernadette*) Jones out of the cloister and made her an All-American girl. She rewards him with a nervous, carefully studied, somewhat overintense performance. Selznick placed a big bet on Shirley Temple's comeback and she pays off enchantingly as a dogged, sensitive, practical little girl with a talent for bargaining.

Though idealized, the Selznick characterizations are authentic to a degree seldom achieved in Hollywood. When a high-school graduating class sings *America the Beautiful*, the voices are touchingly inchoate, the singers' faces as stolidly reverent, and the shot of the Lincoln statue which begins the song and the meowing cat which ends it, are a deft, valid blend of showmanship, humor and yard-wide Americanism. The wounded men in *Since You Went Away* really look wounded, for almost the first time in a U.S. fiction war film. There are scores of such evidences of a smart showman's eye, mind and heart. Added up, they give the picture taste, shrewdness, superiority, life. Now and then the idealization runs too far ahead of the normal reality. But by and large the blend of flesh and fantasy is pretty close to Hiltonesque life in the U.S. home.

SOURCE: *Time*, July 17, 1944, 351.

VISUAL IMAGES OF THE WOMEN'S WAR

Soldiers Without Guns
U.S. Army

SOURCE: "Soldiers without Guns," U.S. Army Poster, in Nancy Hewitt, ed., *Women, Families and Communities* (Glenview, Ill.: Scott, Foresman and Company, 1990), p. 193.

Follow-Up Problems

1. Is there any social ethic that dominates this film? To what extent does *Since You Went Away* reflect a domestic ideology?

2. In what way does the film respond to the demands of wartime and a government at war? How are the "issues of the war" addressed? Why did OWI respond to this picture in a generally positive way?

3. Assess the film's presentation of women and the concerns and problems confronting American women on the home front. What are the characteristics of a "women's picture"? Where do you find them expressed in this film?

4. What does the content of *Since You Went Away* reveal about the function of the media during times of crisis? Does the film contain hints to suggest how life in the postwar world would compare with that of the prewar era? Explain.

5. Separate the elements of realism in this film from those that reflect nostalgia, sentimentality, and emotion. Which characteristics are dominant?

6. Identify those aspects of the film's narrative and imagery that clearly mark it as a historical document of its time. What is the relationship of the film to the composition of the wartime moviegoing audience? In what ways does this film reflect public attitudes, concerns, and sensibilities as of 1944, the year of its release?

Further Reading

Baker, M. Joyce. *Images of Women in Film: The War Years, 1941–1945*. Ann Arbor, Mich.: UMI Research Press, 1980.

Basinger, Janine. *A Woman's View: How Hollywood Spoke to Women, 1930–1960*. New York: Alfred Knopf, 1993.

Dick, Bernard F. *The Star-Spangled Screen: The American World War II Film*. Lexington, Ky.: University Press of Kentucky, 1985.

Doherty, Thomas. *Projections of War: Hollywood, American Culture, and World War II*. New York: Columbia University Press, 1993.

Hartmann, Susan. *The Home Front and Beyond: American Women in the 1940s*. New York: Twayne, 1982.

Honey, Maureen. *Creating Rosie the Riveter: Class, Gender, and Propaganda During World War II*. Amherst, Mass.: University of Massachusetts Press, 1984.

Koppes, Clayton, and Gregory Black. *Hollywood Goes to War: How Politics, Profits, and Propaganda Shaped World War II Movies*. New York: Free Press, 1987.

Rosen, Ruth. *Popcorn Venus: Women, Movies, and the American Dream*. New York: Avon Press, 1973.

Schindler, Colin. *Hollywood Goes to War: Films and American Society, 1939–1952*. Boston: Routledge & Kegan Paul, 1979.

Filmography

Mrs. Miniver (MGM, 1942).

Tender Comrade (RKO, 1943).

The Celluloid Document

Since You Went Away (United Artists, 1944).

Chapter 10

Hollywood's Cold War:
The Suppression of
Salt of the Earth (1954)

By the late 1940s, Americans had begun to view their wartime Soviet allies with a mixture of fear and hostility. Gone were the warm feelings of sympathy for the gallant people of the Soviet Union, whose heroic struggle against the invading Nazi hordes had encouraged United States citizens to see them as potential partners in a postwar democratic alliance to keep the peace. As the Soviet Union consolidated its hold on Eastern Europe, Americans watched with increasing concern the evidence of brutality abroad and domestic espionage at home. An increasingly wary American public, uneasy about Soviet advances in Eastern Europe and alarmed by the Truman administration's sharp attacks on domestic Communists and their defenders on the Left, closed ranks behind the federal government loyalty program.

Side by side with Truman's militant anti-communism, other political figures warned of the Red menace at home. Probably the most well-known political anti-Communist of this era was Wisconsin Senator Joseph R. McCarthy, who terrorized government figures, labor leaders, educators, and intellectuals whose activities he saw as part of a vast Communist conspiracy to undermine American society. Equally active in the attack on domestic subversion was the House Committee on Un-American Activities (HUAC), which in 1947 launched an investigation of alleged subversion in the nation's motion picture industry. The HUAC probe drew support from conservatives within the nation's film community, many of whom had long opposed the active leftists who had assumed a high profile in Hollywood politics. Hence, the HUAC inquiry found supporters in the industry, including many producers and some prominent actors, such as Walt Disney, Gary Cooper, and Ronald Reagan. Eager to distance themselves and the movies from charges of Communist sympathies, they cooperated with HUAC by providing information on left-wing activity in Hollywood as well as the names of alleged Communists or fellow travelers.

Their concerns reflected an awareness of a strong liberal community, as well as a radical subculture that inhabited Hollywood in the 1930s and 1940s. The influence of the Left in the film community had peaked during the disruptive studio strikes of 1945 and 1946, when violence flared and liberals refused to cross picket lines in sympathy with the reformist Conference of Studio Unions (CSU). Aligned against CSU were the craft unionists in the International Alliance of Theatrical Stage Employees (IATSE), led by conservative unionist Roy Brewer. The studio strikes, which were part of the nationwide surge of labor militancy in the immediate postwar era, exposed the leftist leanings of many Hollywood figures, especially among screenwriters and actors.

Against this background of labor militancy, HUAC opened its 1947 investigation of alleged Communist infiltration of the motion picture industry. Divided in its loyalties and uncertain of the appropriate response to government scrutiny, the film colony's defenses were fatally weakened on the eve of the hearings that publicized the presence of radicals in the industry. Despite resistance from the Hollywood Left, the forces of conformity overwhelmed the remnants of the progressive coalition and isolated the radical minority. When the "unfriendly" witnesses, many of them Communists or ex-Communists, refused to answer HUAC's questions about their political affiliations on First Amendment grounds, they were badgered and shouted down at the Washington hearings. The noncooperators, soon dubbed the "Hollywood Ten," were eventually prosecuted for contempt of Congress and served jail time for their resistance. The stage was set for the industry's moral collapse.

Not long thereafter, Hollywood producers agreed to impose political conformity on screenwriters and actors by denying employment to radicals and liberals who refused to cooperate with Congressional investigators. While the blacklist they established initially targeted the Hollywood Ten, it very quickly spread to incorporate others who refused to cooperate with HUAC and to "name names" of Communists and other Hollywood leftists. The imposition of the infamous blacklist was but one aspect of a larger fear response to what many Americans believed to be the encroachment of Communism in varied areas of American life and culture.

One response to the new blacklist was a movement towards independent motion picture production in an effort to skirt the policy adopted by the frightened industry leaders. An early expression of this trend was the production of a landmark film, *Salt of the Earth* (1954), which dealt with burning social issues not often addressed on the American screen. Its sponsors, most blacklistees and many Communists, hoped to circumvent the blacklist with the production of feature films that would address issues of social and political significance. Analysis of this motion picture offers modern students a unique opportunity to understand the chilling effect of domestic anticommunism on freedom of the screen in Cold War America.

The Historical Background

While the story of HUAC's abuse of the "unfriendly" witnesses (the Hollywood Ten) is central to a general awareness of the Cold War's stifling influence on the film community, its most significant aspect for your analysis involves its impact on one of the Ten witnesses later fined and jailed for contempt of Congress, screenwriter and director Herbert Biberman. Biberman's experience with the Hollywood blacklist provides the background for a review of the celluloid evidence that is the subject of this chapter. His personal nightmare began with the producers' meeting held in October 1947 at New York's Waldorf-Astoria hotel.

In the wake of the Washington hearings, which brought Hollywood extensive negative publicity, the motion picture industry's resistance to external pressure weakened almost immediately. As a result, in October 1947 Eric Johnston of the Motion Picture Producers Association announced at the Waldorf meeting that the studios would deny employment to any Communist or "member of any party or group which advocates the overthrow of the government of the United States by force or any illegal or unconstitutional method."[1] With this statement, management essentially gave in to the demands of the industry's anti-communist critics and laid the groundwork for a sweeping purge of Communists and other dissenters whose ideas or political associations might expose Hollywood to further scrutiny.

Side by side with the attack on the Hollywood Left, the mainstream labor movement was engaged in its own family quarrel. The growing influence of anti-communist liberals like the Steelworkers' Philip Murray and the Autoworkers' Walter Reuther meant that the once-militant and politically progressive Congress of Industrial Organizations (CIO) turned on its Left-led unions in order to rid its ranks of Communist and radical unionists. The roots of the split may be traced to the decision by many leftist unionists to break ranks with the Democratic Party to endorse the presidential candidacy of liberal Henry A. Wallace in 1948. It ended in the expulsion of 11 unions from the CIO due to the presence of Communists in their leadership ranks. Some scholars have noted that the CIO purge deprived the organization of its most militant activists and democratic unions.[2] Labor's attack on its left wing may be viewed as part of the social settlement that united corporate leaders and mainstream unionists in a bargain that limited the development of the welfare state and curtailed the gains made by workers under the New Deal.

One of the key targets of the CIO's anti-Communist drive was the International Union of Mine, Mill and Smelter Workers (IUMMSW), which had organized the Mexican-American labor force in the great copper and zinc mines of the Southwest. Here the union had begun to make major inroads into the social and economic discrimination that for a century had affected the large Chicano populations of New Mexico, Arizona, and neighboring states. From this minority community came the dramatic story of the Empire Zinc strike in Hanover, New Mexico, a struggle that was to affect the future of the area's Mexican-American community and, incidentally, provide the basis for a motion picture that challenged the blacklist that had crippled the film community by the early 1950s.

The Empire Zinc strike was important because it not only challenged the historic "Mexican wage," but also raised the issue of standard contracts throughout the Southwestern metals industry. Even more significant was the unusual strategy employed by strikers bound by court injunction to cease mass picketing as a strike tactic. Departing from their male-centered cultural norms, the members of IUMMSW Local 890 decided that women would replace the union members on the picket line. After a long struggle, the union achieved a partial victory, thus validating women's role in the social struggle and challenging the Mexican wage. It also provided a dramatic tale of men and women making their own history against great odds, a story that proved irresistible to blacklisted Communists Herbert Biberman, Paul Jarrico, and Michael Wilson, all of whom were determined to fight the blacklisting system that had crept over Hollywood in the wake of the HUAC investigations.

As the result of a visit to Grant County, New Mexico, screenwriter-producer Paul Jarrico became convinced that the Empire Zinc strike had all the elements of a dramatic story suitable for film treatment. Similarly, after screenwriter Michael Wilson consulted with the men and women of Local 890 in late 1951, he concluded that their struggle should be brought to the screen. Not long thereafter, he began work on a screenplay that told the strikers' story in human terms. The end result was the making of the independently produced feature film, *Salt of the Earth* (1954).[3]

The tool for the completion of this motion picture was a new production company, the Independent Productions Corporation (IPC), founded in 1951 to produce and market socially conscious movies and, by so doing, break the blacklist. The firm planned to employ blacklisted Hollywood artists to make quality films that might compete successfully with the products of the major studios. While its dedication to the production of socially relevant pictures made it unique among Hollywood filmmaking organizations, IPC's primary goal was always to turn a profit and end the blacklist.

The prime movers in the new company were Biberman, Jarrico, and Wilson, all leftists who at one time or another were active Communist Party members. Born in Philadelphia, Biberman had worked in Hollywood since 1935 as a screenwriter and director, primarily on low-budget films. Jarrico, a screenwriter of some reputation, saw IPC as an opportunity to become a successful producer. Finally, Oklahoma-born Michael Wilson was an Academy Award-winning screenwriter who was the most talented of the trio. While Biberman, one of the Hollywood Ten, had served jail time for his beliefs, all three qualified for anti-Communist suspicions as unfriendly witnesses before HUAC. The only well-known professional actors to accept roles in *Salt of the Earth* were Will Geer, a long-standing supporter of leftist causes, and the talented Mexican actress Rosaura Revueltas. As committed radicals, the IPC leaders found the plight of a left-wing union like Mine-Mill an especially attractive subject for a film production. All social activists, they immediately grasped the feminist and racial dimensions of Local 890's story, which seemed a classic tale of working-class struggle in the search for social justice.

Any such film was bound to be controversial, and once production got underway, problems surfaced almost immediately. Not the least of the obstacles was the determined opposition of California Republican Congressman Donald Jackson, an active member of HUAC who attacked the IPC project on the floor of the House of Representatives in February 1953. In response to Jackson's initiative, Roy Brewer of IATSE pledged Hollywood craft union support for an effort to prevent the completion or distribution of *Salt of the Earth*. Millionaire Howard Hughes, the owner of RKO studios, added his advice on the steps to be taken to ensure the suppression of the film. Even government officials offered their recommendations on possible countermeasures.

During the production process the film's enemies interfered with its timely completion. As a result of negative publicity, alarmed New Mexico vigilante groups harassed the IPC crew and attacked the members of Local 890, many of whom served as actors and actresses in the film. And before filming was finished, the Immigration and Naturalization Service arrested and detained Revueltas, thus depriving the filmmakers of their lead actress. After a physical attack on the crew, the IPC group left Grant County to avoid further violence. But these incidents were only the beginning of the attack on *Salt of the Earth*. During the processing of the film, Hollywood companies refused to provide technical services and no union workers were permitted to work on it. As a result, the production phase of IPC's work was extended at great cost to the company. Once the film was completed, IPC found that no distributor would handle it, which forced the company to create its own distribution organization. Equally damaging were the decisions of exhibitors who refused to book *Salt of the Earth* at first class theaters, often because the studios had passed the word that films would not be available in the future to those who dared to screen the outlaw picture. Combined with an IATSE projectionists' boycott, this reluctance to provide films to theaters spelled serious trouble for the struggling filmmakers.

After a modest run at a second-rate location in New York, further obstacles plagued IPC. Only in Silver City, New Mexico, (the locale for the film) and California was there a real opportunity for commercial exhibition. While successful previews were held in Chicago, Detroit, and Denver, the film never gained significant commercial exposure. By 1955, *Salt of the Earth* had been shown in 13 of the estimated 13,000 theaters in the United States. Though foreign distribution was somewhat more successful, *Salt of the Earth* was a financial disaster. The boycott had sealed its fate.

Analyzing the Film

As you begin your analysis of this film, determine what aspects of film content were sufficiently controversial to cause a conspiracy against it. Then go beyond the social, economic, and political issues raised by the film to think about the free speech and constitutional questions that swirled around the determined effort to halt distribution. Explore the reasons for the American Civil Liberties Union's interest in the controversy over freedom of the screen. As you consider these questions, try to relate the *Salt of the Earth* case to other aspects of the struggle for free expression within the Hollywood film community.

Any analysis of the *Salt of the Earth* story must also examine the clear relationship between the film's production and the struggles of the union movement and the Mexican-American community of the Southwest. Consider the resemblance between the film's content and the realities of Local 890's battle with management in the bitter Empire Zinc strike. Note in particular the Chicano community's pride in heritage, as well as women's developing consciousness of oppression. How do these social ideas relate to the themes typically associated with American domestic life in the 1950s? Do the issues raised by the men and women of Local 890 resemble or clash with those beliefs and concepts? Formulate your own interpretation of American racial, economic, and gendered realities and aspirations in this age of conformity.

By subjecting this exceptional motion picture to critical analysis, it will be possible for you to gain a better understanding of the social and political forces that underlay the uneasy consensus of the early Cold War era. Watch for evidence of diversity in the social values found in the United States at this time. Look for a thematic subtext throughout the picture. With a careful eye to the historical context in which *Salt of the Earth* was created, you will be prepared to make an informed judgment on the depth of the Eisenhower consensus and the scope of the conformity that prevailed in Cold War America.

A socially conscious docudrama, *Salt of the Earth* provides a largely faithful screen version of the Empire Zinc strike. It includes the women's early identification of sanitation as an issue to be bargained, which raises the question of initiative on their part. Their assumption of picketing duties and other strike contributions are portrayed with considerable accuracy as well. Especially useful is the reconstruction of the union meeting at which the decision is made to have women assume an enlarged role in the strike. This scene should be analyzed with emphasis on the gendered aspects of the strike and the film's treatment of the labor dispute. In what way are these developments consistent or inconsistent with Hispanic cultural traditions? To what extent do these events and decisions reflect the complexity of gender relations in the 1950s?

After the women have assumed their new, more active role in the strike, the men's resentment and uncertainty over the role reversal are brought out in the drinking scenes and the hunting episode. Of particular interest is the confrontation between Ramón and Esperanza, in which she reproaches him for his threat to strike her as the "old way." What is the significance of this scene? When Ramón returns from the hunt to observe the community's defiance of the sheriff's deputies' attempted eviction of the Quintero family, the triumph of the workers seems complete. Impressed by the gains made through solidarity across racial and gender lines, Ramón thanks Esperanza for her dignity and the example she has provided in the class struggle. To film viewers, successful resistance to the eviction and the apparent acquiescence of company officials translated as victory in the union's battle against the company.

Salt of the Earth's power is evident in its striking rendition of a labor-management conflict based on historical fact. The clash portrayed was a generally truthful account of a longstanding battle between the mining corporations and the workers of the Southwest. Equally important (and largely accurate) were the film's strong themes of racial and sexual tension, which exposed the reality of an intraclass struggle to raise standards for all members of the worker community. The union's triumph over all obstacles in the film, consistent with the Communist ideology of its makers, expressed an unduly optimistic vision of racial, class, and gender harmony, one not always matched by the realities faced by Grant County workers in the 1950s. Why do you think the filmmakers decided to resolve the film's internal conflicts in the way chosen?

The favorable outcome of the strike and the resolution of conflict in the film should strike you as unusual, given the historical context. It is important to understand that in many respects, this film is an atypical feature film that departs from Hollywood conventions. Indeed, one of the movie industry's first responses to the rise of domestic anti-Communism and the HUAC attack was the production of numerous anti-Communist films designed to insulate Hollywood from further assault. Many of these features were forgettable pictures, such as *The Woman on Pier 13* (1950), *The Red Menace* (1949), and the sincere if pedestrian *My Son John* (1952). Occasionally, a film of merit adopted the anti-Communist line, as in Elia Kazan's brilliant *On the Waterfront* (1954), in which the practice of "informing" on one's peers is justified in a thinly veiled reference to the informing before HUAC that had opened so many wounds in Cold War Hollywood. The dominance of the anti-Communist theme in Hollywood films makes *Salt of the Earth*'s pro-labor expression of advanced concepts of race and gender stand out as a striking indication of what might have come of independent production in a free market, had Hollywood been truly free in the blacklist era.

Thinking About Primary Sources

As you review the documents, be aware of the political forces behind the attack on *Salt of the Earth*. Your analysis should focus on the ways in which the motion picture is a primary source that sheds light on the domestic impact of the Cold War and the impact of anti-communism on American cultural life. Think about the film as a reflection of the issues and fears that dominated the public debates of the times in which it was produced and viewed. Try to understand the strength of the political and industry opposition to a film that raised important questions concerning gender equity, racial equality, and economic justice. Give particular attention to the puzzle of mainstream labor criticism of a movie that portrayed unionism and worker culture in a generally positive light. Why did IATSE work to undermine the film?

As you review the celluloid evidence, ask what dimensions of the film's content and argument might have alarmed an audience in 1954. Consider the human conflicts and class differences that *Salt of the Earth* delineates. At the same time, be aware of the links between the film's message and the political ideology embraced by its makers. What were the political and ideological motivations of those who led the attack on the picture? In reviewing the reactions to the film's production, look for the reasoning behind the criticism and concerns expressed. The debate over this film may be examined as a mirror of the sharp political disagreements that divided American citizens during the Red Scare of the Truman and Eisenhower eras.

As you consider the forces and beliefs that motivated *Salt of the Earth*'s critics, extend your analysis to an examination of the means by which the film's opponents tried to undermine the IPC project. What strategies were employed by Congressman Jackson, Howard Hughes, and Roy Brewer in their fight to suppress this picture? As you study the assault on this film, think about its meaning in the context of free speech and civil liberties as respected principles in the American constitutional system. What was the larger significance of the battle to prevent this film from reaching an audience? Do the provisions of the Bill of Rights extend free speech protection to include freedom of the screen? Try to see the struggle in the larger context of the political guarantees held sacred by most Americans. Then ask why those protections failed to shield the promoters of *Salt of the Earth* when they came under fire for what they believed and what they produced.

Historical Perspective

By the late 1950s the strength of Cold War anti-communism had begun to decline. McCarthyism had peaked and Soviet-American relations had improved during the second Eisenhower administration. In the early 1960s the Hollywood blacklist that had isolated Biberman, Jarrico, and Wilson was lifted, and sanity began to return to the film community. Yet the wounds inflicted on the promoters of *Salt of the Earth* had not healed.

Despite the changing political climate, the IPC group did not fare well. Both Jarrico and Wilson experienced self-imposed exile in France, where they were able to practice their craft freely, though the rewards failed to match preblacklist levels. Meanwhile, a frustrated Biberman turned to a career as a land developer in Los Angeles. Hoping to reverse some of his personal losses and gain recognition for his work, in 1956 he filed a lawsuit against the major motion picture studios, IATSE, and the individuals most responsible for the boycott. Like IPC, this legal action failed. While it was not difficult to show that some of the accused had independently interfered with the production and distribution of the film, it was impossible to prove conspiracy among the defendants, who were acquitted.

Other participants in the *Salt of the Earth* project were equally unfortunate. The militant unionist who had organized Local 890, Clinton Jencks, was convicted of false swearing of a non-Communist affidavit required of union leaders under the Taft-Hartley Act. Although his conviction was later overturned by the Supreme Court, he was forced to resign his position with IUMMSW as a result of the charges that he had belonged to the Communist Party. After losing several jobs, he completed a Ph.D. in labor economics and launched an academic career at San Diego State University. Especially affected was Rosaura Revueltas, whose promising film career was destroyed by the *Salt of the Earth* episode. Despite her artistic gifts, she was blacklisted in both Hollywood and Mexico, where she ended her career as a dancing and yoga instructor. It was a harsh penalty for having given a fine performance in a remarkable film.

In New Mexico, Local 890 retained the loyalty of the Chicano community and the miners, who continued to elect Juan Chacón as president until 1963, when he was defeated in a closely contested election. By this time, Mine-Mill was under heavy pressure from the government and the rival United Steelworkers of America, which absorbed IUMMSW in 1967. Elected again in 1973, Chacón worked to promote the militant unionism of the early 1950s, but the environment had changed dramatically and it was difficult to fight both corporate management and the mainstream unionists of USWA.

Salt of the Earth, however, gained a new lease on life when it was rereleased in 1965 for distribution in the educational film market. More in tune with the social and political militancy of the late 1960s, the film found a new audience among Chicano, feminist, and academic audiences. In a sense, the IPC/*Salt of the Earth* group has had the last word. More important for our purposes, the film survives as an enduring document of Cold War America that informs our understanding of the public consciousness and political constraints of the 1950s. You may "read" this film as celluloid evidence of social and cultural damage inflicted by the great postwar Red Scare.

Endnotes

1. The impact of the Cold War in Hollywood and the origins of the blacklist are discussed in Larry Ceplair and Steven Englund, *The Inquisition in Hollywood: Politics in the Film Community, 1930–1960* (Berkeley, Calif.: University of California Press, 1983). See especially pp. 328–331; see also Appendix 6, p. 455, for complete text of the Waldorf Statement.

2. Steve Rosswurm, ed., *The CIO's Left-Led Unions* (New Brunswick, N.J.: Rutgers University Press, 1992), 13–15.

3. The story of the making and suppression of *Salt of the Earth* is recounted in James J. Lorence, *The Suppression of 'Salt of the Earth': How Hollywood, Big Labor, and Politicians Blacklisted a Movie in Cold War America* (Albuquerque, N. Mex.: University of New Mexico Press, 1999). This analysis is based on that account.

THE PRIMARY SOURCES

The primary sources document the collaborative effort to suppress *Salt of the Earth*, starting with California Congressman Donald L. Jackson's speech in the House of Representatives, promising to prevent the marketing of the film. In a letter responding to Jackson's invitation, Hollywood labor activist Roy Brewer pledges his cooperation in the effort to boycott the film. More extensive is a letter to Jackson from Howard Hughes, who provided a blueprint for the film's suppression. Next, a memorandum from *Salt of the Earth* producer Paul Jarrico recounts the many actions taken as part of the conspiracy to prevent the production and distribution of the film.

CONGRESSMAN DONALD L. JACKSON SOUNDS THE ALARM

Red Movie in Making
Donald L. Jackson

The SPEAKER. Under previous order of the House, the gentleman from California [Mr. JACKSON] is recognized for 30 minutes.

Mr. JACKSON . . .

As an illustration of the ceaseless and diabolical attack upon the United States and its free institutions, I bring to the attention of the Congress, and through it to the American people, some facts regarding a picture now being made under Communist auspices in Silver City, N. Mex. The name of this picture is unknown to me at the present time. However, it is being made by a corporation which calls itself the Independent Productions Corp., and the picture itself is being financed by the Communist-dominated United Mine, Mill, and Smelter Workers Union, which union was expelled from the Congress of Industrial Organizations several years ago because of Communist domination.

The Independent Productions Corp. was incorporated in Los Angeles, Calif., on September 4, 1951, with an authorized capital of $52,000. The corporation is represented in legal matters by Ben Margolis, a Los Angeles attorney, who has been identified by several witnesses under oath, as a member of the Communist Party and who, when called by the committee last fall, declined to answer all questions regarding his alleged Communist Party membership and affiliations on the ground that to do so would tend to incriminate him. Mr. Margolis, in his answers to committee questions, however, did not confine himself to merely taking refuge in the fifth amendment to the Constitution of the United States. He gave every evidence during his appearance before the committee, of the contempt that a confirmed Communist holds for everything American. . . .

Officers of the Independent Productions Corp. are as follows: Simon Lazarus, president; Herbert Ganahl, vice president; Kathleen Sims, secretary; Rose Kolker, treasurer; and Robert Gannon, director.

Lazarus holds 180 shares of stock in the corporation and also owns a number of theaters. It is assumed that the theaters owned by Mr. Lazarus will furnish a medium through which this Communist film can be exhibited to American audiences. So much for the corporate structure of the corporation making the picture.

Engaged in the actual making and production of the picture itself are many persons who have been named before the Committee on Un-American Activities as being members of the Communist Party and who, when called before the committee, declined to answer questions on the grounds that to do so might tend to incriminate them. Some of these persons are Herbert Biberman, Gale Sondergaard, and Paul Jarrico. Herbert Biberman is the actual producer of this Communist-inspired film endeavor, while Gale Sondergaard is the coproducer of the picture. Paul Jarrico is a writer working upon the picture. Michael Wilson and Will Geer are two more uncooperative witnesses said to be active in the production of the picture.

During the committee's investigation of Mr. Jarrico, it was determined that he had attempted to persuade a witness appearing before the committee not to cooperate with the committee and to remain in the Communist Party.

Herbert Biberman was one of the leading Communists in the Hollywood motion picture industry. In addition to being a producer of the picture, he is also its director. He, Jarrico, and Sondergaard all declined to answer questions pertaining to Communist membership and activity when they appeared before the committee. Also associated with the making of the picture is one Paul Perlin, a studio worker, identified as a member of the Communist Party, who appeared before the committee on October 6, 1952, and refused to affirm or deny his membership in the Communist Party. Perlin was ousted from the union to which he belonged, the IATSE, for Communist activity. . . .

As I have said, the picture is being financed by the Communist-dominated union known as the International Union of Mine, Mill, and Smelter Workers. The official in charge of the movie project for the union is one Clinton Jencks who, when he appeared before another congressional committee last year, refused to answer questions regarding sabotage of the defense efforts of the United States, taking refuge behind the fifth amendment. . . .

The production of this picture has been condemned by the Hollywood A. F. of L. Film Council, which represents practically all labor organizations in the film industry. The chairman of the council, Mr. Roy M. Brewer, said:

No motion picture made by Communists can be good for America. Hollywood has gotten rid of these people and we want the Government agencies to investigate carefully the picture being made at Silver City, N. Mex.

I should also like to point out that Mr. Walter Pidgeon, president of the Screen Actors Guild, and who has taken an active part in exposing this Communist movie, in an official statement, said:

I cannot stress too strongly that this picture is not being made by Hollywood or any part of the film industry. We are asking the Federal Government to investigate and take whatever steps are necessary.

Mr. Speaker, the investigation of communism appears to be an endless path. Despite the fact that many of the persons engaged in the making of this picture have been exposed as Communists by the Committee on Un-American Activities, they are continuing to function in the never-ending effort of the Communist Party to discredit the United States in the eyes of the world and, after having lost Hollywood as a source of income, and this only recently, have succeeded in acquiring another source of income, perhaps a more lucrative one.

Mr. Speaker, in my remarks, I have endeavored to point out that under the present laws of the United States it is practically impossible to control Communist activity in the United States. I personally feel that the time has come for the American public and its representatives in Government to decide whether we shall permit this heinous effort of the international Communist conspiracy, the Communist Party of the United States, to continue to exist and, through its existence, corrupt the free peoples of the world. I shall do everything in my power to prevent the showing of this Communist-made film in the theaters of America, and I am confident that millions of Americans will join in that effort.

SOURCE: *Congressional Record*, 83rd Cong., 1st Sess., February 24, 1953, Vol. 99, pt. 2, 1421–1422.

ROY BREWER PROMISES LABOR ACTION

Letter
Roy M. Brewer

Los Angeles, Calif., March 18, 1953.

Donald L. Jackson,
House of Representatives,
Washington, D.C.:

The Hollywood AFL Film Council assures you that everything which it can do to prevent the showing of the Mexican picture, Salt of the Earth will be done. However, an investigation discloses that at this time there is no work being done on this picture in Hollywood nor by any Hollywood persons except those who have been involved in one way or another in pro-Communist activities. The best information seems to indicate that the final shots of this picture are to be taken in Mexico and it is probable that processing of film is being done there. The film council will solicit its fellow members in the theaters to assist in the prevention of showing this picture in any American theaters, but the extent to which we can as a union take action in such a matter is limited by reason of the restrictive features in the Taft-Hartley Act which continues to be a burden on loyal American unions. Thank you for your interest.

Sincerely,

Roy M. Brewer,
Chairman, Hollywood AFL Council.

SOURCE: Roy M. Brewer to Donald L. Jackson, March 18, 1953, *Congressional Record*, 83rd Cong., 1st Sess., March 19, 1953, Vol. 99, pt. 2, 2126–2127.

HOWARD HUGHES OUTLINES A BLUEPRINT FOR SUPPRESSION

Response to Donald L. Jackson
Howard Hughes

March 18, 1953

Congressman Donald L. Jackson
House Office Building
Washington, D.C.

Dear Congressman Jackson: In your telegram you asked the question, "Is there any action that industry and labor in motion picture field can take to stop completion and release of picture to prevent showing of film here and abroad?"

My answer is "Yes." There is action which the industry can take to stop completion of this motion picture in the United States. And if the Government will act immediately to prevent the export of the film to some other country where it can be completed, then this picture will not be completed and disseminated throughout the world where the United States will be judged by its content.

According to the newspaper reports, photography of this motion picture has been finished in Silver City, N. Mex.

However, completion of photography of a motion picture is only the first step in production.

Before a motion picture can be completed or shown in theaters, an extensive application of certain technical skills and use of a great deal of specialized equipment is absolutely necessary.

Herbert Biberman, Paul Jarrico, and their associates working on this picture do not possess these skills or equipment.

If the motion picture industry—not only in Hollywood, but throughout the United States—will refuse to apply these skills, will refuse to furnish this equipment, the picture cannot be completed in this country.

Biberman and Jarrico have already met with refusal where the industry was on its toes. The film processing was being done by Pathe Laboratories, until the first news broke from Silver City.

But the minute Pathe learned the facts, this alert laboratory immediately refused to do any further work on this picture, even though it meant refunding cash paid in advance.

Investigation fails to disclose where the laboratory work is being done now. But it is being done somewhere, by someone, and a great deal more laboratory work will have to be done by someone, before the motion picture can be completed.

Biberman, Jarrico, and their associates cannot succeed in their scheme alone. Before they can complete the picture, they must have the help of the following:

1. Film laboratories.
2. Suppliers of film.
3. Musicians and recording technicians necessary to record music.
4. Technicians who make dissolves, fades, etc.
5. Owners and operators of sound rerecording equipment and dubbing rooms.
6. Positive and negative editors and cutters.
7. Laboratories that make release prints.

If the picture industry wants to prevent this motion picture from being completed and spread all over the world as a representative product of the United States, then the industry and particularly that segment of the industry listed above, needs only to do the following:

Be alert to the situation.

Investigate thoroughly each applicant for the use of services or equipment.

Refuse to assist the Bibermans and Jarricos in the making of this picture.

Be on guard against work submitted by dummy corporations or third parties.

Appeal to the Congress and the State Department to act immediately to prevent the export of this film to Mexico or anywhere else.

Sincerely,

Howard Hughes

SOURCE: Howard Hughes to Donald L. Jackson, March 18, 1953, *Congressional Record*, 83rd Cong., First Sess., March 19, 1953, Vol. 99, pt. 2, 2127.

PAUL JARRICO'S CHRONICLE OF EXTERNAL HARASSMENT

"*Salt of the Earth*—Chronology"
Paul Jarrico

Feb. 13, 1953—AFL Film Council issues public attack, carried in trade press in Hollywood and in press and on radio nationally. Roy Brewer quoted widely as council chairman:

". . . Hollywood has gotten rid of these people and we want the government to investigate carefully. . . . Hundreds of Mexicans and Americans of Mexican descent are being told the film is a 'major Hollywood production.' . . . A scene in the film will show a deputy sheriff pistol-whipping a small Mexican child." (Etc. *Hollywood Reporter*, *Daily Variety*, others.)

Feb. 13, 1953—Motion picture industry council issues public attack, carried in trade press and national media.

None of the motion picture companies represented in the MPIC has any connection whatsoever with this picture or the organization or individuals making it. The studios . . . do not recognize this operation or its product as reflecting their own views, interests or policies." (Los Angeles *Times*, Silver City *Daily Press*.)

Feb. 18, 1953—Studio sound refuses to continue processing our sound tape. (Since the sound equipment they rented to us was so geared that no other sound company could normally process the tape recorded on it, this was a special blow. We have hearsay evidence of pressure of Ben Winkler, Head of Studio Sound, not only by Brewer but by Wheeler, Investigator for the Un-American Activities Committee.)

Feb. 10 thru Feb. 22, 1953—Increasing repercussions in the Bayard area of the press and industry attacks. Local theater owners refuse to continue private projection. (McClaughan in Bayard; Ward of the Silco Theater in Silver City.) News representatives converge on us. Airplane "buzzes" our location, interfering with sound recording. Workmen's compensation insurance policy cancelled. (Lou Lagrave, agent.) In Los Angeles during this period or shortly thereafter,

our accountants, Richard M. Rothschild DO., notify us they will no longer handle our business.

Feb. 13 thru Feb. 22, 1953—Misrepresentations in the press continue despite our efforts to set record straight. Front page editorial in Silver City *Daily Press*: "It's Time to Choose Sides." (Feb. 20.) *Time* Magazine repeats "Two Carloads of Negroes" story. (Issue of Feb 23, distributed Feb. 18 or 19, 1953.)

Feb. 22, 1953—Two investigators of the immigration service, Robert Stewart and Robert Schoenenberger, visit Bear Mountain Lodge to question Rosaura Revueltas. Take her passport "for inspection," promising to return it soon. . . .

Feb. 25, 1953—Immigration investigators return with matron, arrest Rosaura Revueltas, take her to El Paso. (Administrative warrant signed by Joseph Minton, District Director of Immigration Service, specifies she will be freed on bond.)

Feb. 26, 1953—Jarrico offers bond, which Minton refuses. Minton offers Revueltas parole on condition she not return to work, which she refuses. (Revueltas housed in hotel rather than jail thru ten day detention and allowed freedom of movement in El Paso, but under 24 hour a day guard.)

Feb. 26, 1953—Jackson asks state, commerce and justice departments whether "there are any legal means currently on the books to bar the export" of "Salt," and asks Attorney General whether "those individuals directly connected with the production of this picture are subject to the provisions of the Alien Agents Registration Legislation, assuming that the picture is found to be of a propaganda nature." (Quoted in *Hollywood Reporter*, Feb. 27, 1953, and other newspapers.)

May 23, 1953—Employ Barton (Bud) Hayes, member of IATSE in Los Angeles, as Chief Editor, though he has had no previous experience in that category. . . .

July 21, 1953—Barton Hayes quits as Chief Editor, telling us that the IATSE has pressured him into resigning. On or about the same day, we receive confidential information that Hayes has told the Executive Board of the Editor's Local of the IATSE that he has worked on "Salt" in order to provide information about our production to the FBI. We are told that he showed his board an FBI identification card to substantiate this claim. On the same day, *Daily Variety* prints the following:

> "AFL reveals it slipped spotters into 'Salt'; moves to stymie pic . . ."

July 28, 1953—Registered letters sent to Pathe Laboratories, Inc., Consolidated Film Industries, Acme Film Laboratories, Inc., General Film Laboratories Corporation, Glen Cleri Sound Co., Sound Services, Inc., Ryder Sound Services, Inc., and RCA Sound System, all in Los Angeles, requesting services on "Salt." Registered letter sent to Roy Brewer asking that IATSE and AFL Film Council repudiate their boycott of "Salt" and withdraw false and malicious statements. Registered letters also sent to Sound Technicians Local and Editors Local of IATSE asking for personnel. (Copies of these letters and registration receipts available as exhibits.)

July 31, 1953 thru Aug. 13, 1953—Consolidated replies it cannot handle our work because IPC is "engaged in a controversy with Pathe." We reply we will "abandon our controversy with Pathe if you will accept our work." Consolidated replies, "We are not interested in marketing our services to you at this time." Pathe writes, "We are unable to accept your business at this time." None of the others addressed send a reply. (Entire correspondence available as exhibits.) . . .

Jan. 25, 1954—Scheduled run of second answer print at Movielab is cancelled. We are told that the IATSE not only refuses to run the film but that it will do no further lab work. This stoppage is apparently ordered by John J. Francavilla, an official of the motion picture laboratory technicians (Local 702, IATSE, New York). During next few days Movielab and its attorney protest to IATSE President Richard F. Walsh, to no avail. Indicated by the following quotation from *The Hollywood Reporter* (in a story dealing with Paul Perlin):

> ". . . Perlin's last work was on the controversial film, 'Salt of the Earth,' which Walsh disclosed has been retitled 'The Earth' and whose negative is now in New York. IATSE members have refused to process the negative and prints, Walsh said." (Will be checked and made available as an exhibit.)

SOURCE: Paul Jarrico, *"Salt of the Earth*—Chronology," May 9, 1955, Herbert Biberman–Gale Sondergaard Papers, Madison, Wis., Historical Society, Box 51.

Follow-Up Problems

1. What constitutional issues are raised by the documents and the film?
2. In what ways did *Salt of the Earth* challenge the values, assumptions, and beliefs of Americans with regard to gender relations?
3. What do historians mean when they refer to the decade of the 1950s as a period of conformity and consensus? To what extent does your analysis of *Salt of the Earth* confirm or challenge that view of American society in 1953–1954?
4. What were the key arguments against *Salt of the Earth* raised by the critics? What is your reaction to their reasoning?
5. In what ways was the suppression of *Salt of the Earth* accomplished?

Further Reading

Biberman, Herbert. *Salt of the Earth: The Story of a Film*. Boston: Beacon Press, 1965.

Buhle, Paul, and Dave Wagner. *Hide in Plain Sight: The Hollywood Blacklistees in Film and Television, 1950–2002*. New York: Palgrave/Macmillan, 2003.

Cargill, Jack. "Empire and Opposition: The 'Salt of the Earth' Strike." In Robert L. Kern, ed., *Labor in New Mexico*, 183–267. Albuquerque, N. Mex.: University of New Mexico Press, 1983.

Ceplair, Larry, and Steven Englund. *The Inquisition in Hollywood: Politics in the Film Community, 1930–1960*. Berkeley, Calif.: University of California Press, 1983.

Kern, Robert L. "Organized Labor: Race, Radicalism, and Gender." In Judith Boyce DeMark, ed., *Essays In Twentieth Century New Mexico History*, 149–168. Albuquerque, N. Mex.: University of New Mexico Press, 1994.

Lorence, James J. *The Suppression of 'Salt of the Earth': How Hollywood, Big Labor, and Politicians Blacklisted a Movie in Cold War America*. Albuquerque, N. Mex.: University of New Mexico Press, 1999.

Miller, Tom. "Salt of the Earth Revisited. " *Cineaste* 13 (1984): 31–36.

Rosenfelt, Deborah Silverton. *Salt of the Earth*. Old Westbury, N.Y.: Feminist Press, 1978.

Filmography

Big Jim McLain (Warner Brothers, 1952).

My Son John (Paramount, 1952).

The Woman on Pier 13 (RKO, 1950).

The Celluloid Document

Salt of the Earth (Independent Productions Corporation, 1954).

Chapter 11

A Cautionary Tale: *Dr. Strangelove* (1964) as a Vision of Nuclear Endgame

At the dawn of the Cold War, American policy makers relied confidently on the nuclear monopoly enjoyed by the United States as a trump card in the Soviet-American diplomatic and political contest of the postwar era. Once the Soviet Union developed its own nuclear arsenal after 1949, however, public anxiety in the United States increased as the possibility of thermonuclear war took on frightening dimensions during the Eisenhower years. Placing its eggs in the nuclear basket, the Eisenhower administration relied on a large arsenal and deterrence theory in its determined effort to counter Soviet advances in an escalating arms race. The idea of deterrence was based on the assumption that a huge nuclear stockpile would discourage any adversary from launching a first strike in view of the overwhelming response (massive retaliation) the United States was capable of delivering.

Side by side with this competitive struggle, there emerged a sharpened public awareness of the increasing danger of a nuclear holocaust. With the development of the more sophisticated and powerful hydrogen bomb after 1954, these fears contributed to the growth of a small but effective nuclear test ban movement in the United States. The intensity of this public concern only increased with the publication of articles and novels such as Neville Shute's *On the Beach* (1957), which dealt with the consequences of all-out nuclear war. During the fearful fifties, Americans built backyard bomb shelters and students participated in classroom "duck and cover" exercises. Meanwhile, civil defense authorities planned for survival following a nuclear event. Cultural historian Paul S. Boyer has observed that in the landmark film, *Dr. Strangelove*, director Stanley Kubrick and his screenwriters "convey all too accurately the weird logic of deterrence theory, the paranoia of the Cold War, and the nuclear jitters of the early 1960s."[1] Against a background of doubt and insecurity, many Americans now viewed the arms race with a greater sense of urgency, even alarm. Close examination of *Dr. Strangelove* will reveal the depth of popular concern over the threat of nuclear destruction in an age of anxiety.

The Historical Background

After a presidential campaign stressing an alleged missile gap that endangered American national security, John F. Kennedy took office in 1961 with renewed determination to confront the Soviet Union in an ideological battle that would dominate his short administration. Public fears of nuclear disaster further increased in the wake of a danger-ous clash over the placement of Soviet missiles in Cuba in 1962. Despite his success in resolving the Cuban missile crisis, Kennedy emerged from the confrontation sobered by what seemed a narrow escape from nuclear engagement. It had been a truly close call.

The result of his new awareness of the risks in a program of deterrence and the con-flicts it might promote was the president's new emphasis on peaceful resolution of great power differences. The first clear outcome of Kennedy's sensitivity to the nuclear danger was the landmark Nuclear Test Ban Treaty of 1963, which bound the United States and the Soviet Union to halt atmospheric and underwater testing of nuclear weapons. This more mature approach to the dangers of nuclear competition and the flaws of deterrence theory marked a new stage in the history of the Cold War, one in which contending lead-ers and populations were to engage in both active competition and peaceful coexistence.

At this moment of cooperation in international relations, a striking film treatment of the nuclear arms race and the idea of deterrence appeared to document the danger only recently avoided. During the Eisenhower era, Hollywood had reinforced administration policy with several films, such as *Bombers B-52* (1957) and *Strategic Air Command* (1955), extolling the strengths of the nuclear air defense system. These films celebrated the "pro-fessional warrior" in pictures often completed with the active support of the armed forces. In 1964, however, producer-director Stanley Kubrick used satire and black humor to chal-lenge the rationality of the military and strategic thought that had dominated the thinking of the Eisenhower and Kennedy administrations since 1954. *Dr. Strangelove* pinpointed the weak link in the most sophisticated system of military preparedness and watchful deterrence, namely, the human element. Through nightmare comedy, Kubrick's film sug-gested the unthinkable—that human error might unleash a chain of events that could lead to a nuclear holocaust.

Based on Peter George's novel *Two Hours to Doom* (published later in the United States as *Red Alert*), the film not only raised questions about the theories that supported the nuclear buildup of the postwar years, but also contained characters similar to histori-cal figures identifiable by the audience. Moreover, Kubrick was very successful in recreat-ing the sites and backdrops for the action. As a result of his careful research, the on-screen description of the nuclear stockpile and the B-52 delivery system is fairly accu-rate. The film's reference to the "doomsday gap" reminded moviegoers of the "missile gap" debate during the election of 1960. The film's closeness to reality was also evident in the bitterness of the official response: the Air Force insisted that an irreversible order to launch a nuclear attack was impossible. Yet millions of filmgoers were not reassured as they followed Kubrick's account of an unintentional approach to the brink of disaster.

By 1964, Stanley Kubrick had already achieved the status of major director. Kubrick's previous work had questioned the accepted view of social evolution inherent in the liberal beliefs of the 1960s. In 1957, for example, his brilliant antiwar drama, *Paths of Glory*, featured French soldiers who threatened mutiny rather than sacrifice themselves in the mechanized destruction that was World War I. As Charles Maland has noted, his cinematic work revealed a strong interest in the "gap between man's scientific and tech-nological skill and his social, political, and moral ineptitude."[2] It is this problem that is confronted directly in *Dr. Strangelove*. The film was the end product of Kubrick's own research on the nuclear arms race, which inspired him to attempt a cinematic exploration of Cold War assumptions that placed him outside the prevailing worldview of his era.

Working with George's novel as his basic text, he arrived at the conclusion that comedy was the only way to approach the contradictions of the nuclear age. The result was the release in 1964 of the wickedly amusing, yet horrifying, antinuclear farce, *Dr. Strangelove or: How I Learned to Stop Worrying and Love the Bomb*.

Analyzing the Film

An American expatriate living in England, Kubrick had read deeply in deterrence theory, including the work of the RAND Corporation's nuclear strategist Herman Kahn. As a consequence, he had become convinced that unauthorized behavior might lead to an accidental bombing. It is this assumption that provides the premise on which *Dr. Strangelove* is based. As a result of a misguided attack order by the mentally unbalanced anti-Communist General Jack D. Ripper (Sterling Hayden), American military and diplomatic policy makers are thrown into a frantic struggle to prevent a nuclear holocaust. When American president Merkin Muffley (Peter Sellers) learns that the Soviets have a "doomsday machine" capable of destroying the world, he is forced to order the destruction of American bombers in order to save the planet. Advised by former Nazi scientist Dr. Strangelove (Sellers) and military attaché General Buck Turgidson (George C. Scott), Muffley fails to prevent the delivery of one nuclear weapon, which triggers the catastrophe all had attempted to avoid. While viewers observe an artistic arrangement of mushroom clouds, recording artist Vera Lynn sings "We'll Meet Again," a tune reminiscent of World War II sacrifice, which was starkly out of step with the disaster unfolding on screen. As you think about deterrence theory carried to such absurd lengths, ask what made it possible for audiences to consider the awful possibility of technology gone wrong in the atomic age. Black humor had reached a point of climax at which terror and amusement were so blended as to produce shock, and then relief. How did this outcome influence audiences' consciousness of the risk inherent in prevailing nuclear strategy?

Released in January 1964, *Dr. Strangelove* was a breakthrough in several ways relevant to the social and political context in which it was first seen. The film clearly rejected Cold War assumptions with regard to the rationality of the nuclear arms race, the doctrine of massive retaliation, and the entire structure of deterrence theory that had guided policy makers in the fifties and sixties. Indeed, in a broader cultural context, this movie hinted at the more sweeping breakdown of accepted social values that was to characterize the chaotic fragmentation of the 1960s. Finally, it clearly documented the fear and anxiety of Americans who lived in the shadow of Hiroshima and who, having approached the brink of nuclear confrontation, looked for new courses of diplomatic and political action designed to reduce international tensions. In this sense, *Dr. Strangelove* marks the beginning of a new, less confrontational stage in the history of the Cold War.

As you study this film, think of yourself as an American citizen in early 1964, with emphasis on your awareness of the recently resolved Cuban missile crisis of October 1962. Now immerse yourself in the social and political environment of that era, conscious of the heated debate over the missile gap and the importance of massive retaliation as a deterrent to any first strike in a potential nuclear confrontation. Think about the terms "deterrence," "massive retaliation," and "mutually assured destruction" (the certainty of total annihilation as the outcome of nuclear combat) so that you understand the strategic theories that made the events portrayed on the screen seem possible. Discuss with your classroom colleagues the growth of the nuclear arms race in the 1950s and 1960s as well as the military hardware and delivery systems actually in place in 1964. By familiarizing yourself with the mindset of this historical era, you will be better able to make sense of the Cold War irrationality exhibited by the characters in the movie.

A closely related issue to be considered is the film's treatment of the relationship between the civilian and military leadership of the United States. Think about this question in a historical and constitutional framework. Compare the movie's depiction of this relationship and the reality of the discussions that had taken place during the Cuban missile crisis of 1962. Examine the words of both Ripper and Turgidson against the background of American constitutional traditions. Because Kubrick worried about openly attacking the United States Air Force, the film treads a careful path in its handling of American assumptions concerning warfare and the issue of authority.

Dr. Strangelove is especially effective in the use of humor in character development to explore the boundaries of the difficult interaction between civilian and military leaders. Once you have seen *Dr. Strangelove* for the first time, try to sort out the various characters in the film and relate them to the political and military figures upon whom these characterizations were based. Pay particular attention to the historical analogues to President Muffley (the failed Democratic presidential candidate of the 1950s, Adlai Stevenson), Dr. Strangelove (a combination of political intellectuals Henry Kissinger, Edward Teller, and Wernher von Braun), and General Jack D. Ripper (an easily recognized General Curtis LeMay).[3] Based on the actual historical record, was there was any validity to the on-screen interpretations given these characters?

It is also important that you understand the uses of humor to expose human shortcomings. Think about the meaning of the term "satire" and watch for its presence in the film. Be aware of the sports metaphors used, especially in the war room scenes. Consider Kubrick's intentions in presenting nuclear warfare in terms of competitive sports. How is irony used to drive home the filmmakers' point concerning the absurdity of the Cold War? Focus on the billboards at the army base, Muffley's response to the wrestling diplomats in the war room, and other playful use of language. Note that Kubrick allows viewers to laugh at ideas and policies that were terribly close to reality.

Perhaps the harshest reality of all lay in the gap between scientific advances and the human capacity for managing technology. This film addresses the issue of scientific knowledge out of control, highlighted by the failure of an elaborate structure of safeguards due to human failings. Consider the doomsday machine and the breakdown of deterrence as a result of secrecy that prevented the adversary from understanding the consequences of its use. Place the inability to control the march of technology within the context of the debates of the 1960s over massive retaliation and mutually assured destruction. What does the film imply about the widely held assumption that science and technology represented a potential solution to all of the problems that plagued struggling humanity? How do the helpless men in the war room compare with the fatalistic soldiers in *All Quiet on the Western Front*, who were caught up in the new technology of their own era? Focus on Kubrick's awareness of the dilemma created by man's reverence for scientific achievement.

Kubrick's analysis of triumphant science contained a heavy dose of machismo, as evidenced by the numerous sexual references that appear in a film that on the surface, at least, has little to do with gender relations. Note that the film is filled with sexual imagery, including several explicit references to sexual activity. Consider the initial refueling scene, the messages written on the missiles, the dialogue between Turgidson and his beautiful secretary, or even Ripper's concern over "bodily fluids" and the danger posed by fluoridation, which forced him to "deny his essence" to women. In what way are these sexual references connected to Cold War military language and the rhetoric of mortal combat? Explain why these images and references appear so prominently in *Dr. Strangelove*.

You are viewing this film within the context of a post-Cold War environment, which has replaced the cultural context and political environment of the 1960s. You must decide whether the issues it addresses have relevance for modern audiences, in view of the new world order confronting modern leaders. Are there linkages between the fears of the postwar decades and the new uncertainties of your own time? Use this film to perfect your understanding of American cultural anxieties in the sixties, but also to link the issues of that era with the insecurities that trouble us in the age of international terrorism.

Thinking About Primary Sources

The documents in this chapter place heavy emphasis on the political realities of the historical era recreated by the film. Use the words of Kennedy Defense Secretary Robert McNamara to inform your understanding of the deterrence theory widely accepted in the 1960s. Connect McNamara's basic assumptions with the political and military ideas evident in the situation portrayed in *Dr. Strangelove*. Given the prevailing strategic thought of this historical era, do you believe that the events played out on-screen would have seemed possible to an audience at the time?

As you work to understand the logic of deterrence as represented on-screen, note that the rush toward nuclear preparedness was not universally applauded. How did SANE (the Committee for a Sane Nuclear Policy) perceive the prospects for rational control of an ever-expanding nuclear arsenal? Examine journalist I. F. Stone's comments on the outcome of the Cuban missile crisis and its meaning for his generation. Compare the insights of Stone and SANE as evidence of dissenting opinion on the nuclear buildup of the 1950s and 1960s. Their words provide evidence of public anxiety at the time the film was released.

These concerns spilled over into the making and reception of this film. As you read Terry Southern's account of the original conception and development of the project, try to understand why Kubrick chose to approach such a serious topic through the medium of humor. Why did Columbia Pictures react to the movie as it did? Account for Columbia's perspective on the film and its attitude on promotional activity. Link these views with *New York Times* reviewer Bosley Crowther's ambivalent evaluation of the film. Determine what these responses reveal about the thinking of the American public at the time of the picture's release in 1964. When you view the film, use the print sources and the themes you observe to enrich your understanding of the anxieties felt by a viewing public that lived in the shadow of the bomb.

Historical Perspective

As revealed in the accompanying documents, the immediate critical response to *Dr. Strangelove* was decidedly mixed. From the ambivalence in Crowther's conflicted review to Columbia Studios' determined effort to distance itself from Kubrick's nightmare comedy, there was great uncertainty about the public response to a film that clearly broke with the Cold War consensus of its times. While critics debated the film's meaning, American conservatives and the armed forces were enraged at the suggestion that such a colossal military blunder could take place. Some argued that it was intentionally antimilitary, anti-American, or even pro-Communist. Others missed the message in what was first and foremost a warning against nuclear disaster. It is no wonder that the studio retreated from the political implications of a film it preferred to bill as merely good fun.

Despite the missed messages and apprehensive responses, Kubrick's achievement was eventually recognized by both scholars and peers. The Library of Congress has included *Dr. Strangelove* among the 50 greatest American films ever made, celluloid treasures that have been placed in the National Film Registry of film classics to be preserved as culturally and historically significant works of art. Similar recognition has been extended by the American Film Institute, which ranks the picture among the 100 finest films ever produced in the United States.

While *Dr. Strangelove* is aesthetically important, scholars and students of history will examine this film as a valuable historical document that provides them with insight into the deepest fears and doubts of an American public conditioned by a generation of Cold War rhetoric and shaken by the near miss associated with the missiles of October 1962. For in the final analysis, *Dr. Strangelove* was a deadly serious cautionary tale warning not only that nuclear holocaust was possible, but also that it must never happen. In this context, think about the ironic meaning of the subtitle. What did Kubrick believe humanity must indeed worry about? What were viewers to think about the bomb and government intentions concerning its use? In the moment of maturity that produced the Nuclear Test Ban Treaty of 1963, Americans started to turn away from the brink and towards a new emphasis on arms control and detente; and a nightmare comedy on the screen marked the new vision, thus providing future generations with a glimpse of that historic departure.

Endnotes

1. Paul S. Boyer, "Dr. Strangelove," in Mark C. Carnes, ed., *Past Imperfect: History According to the Movies* (New York: Henry Holt & Co., 1996), 266.
2. Charles Maland, "*Dr. Strangelove* (1964): Nightmare Comedy and the Ideology of Liberal Consensus," in Peter Rollins, ed., *Hollywood as Historian: American Film in a Cultural Context* (Lexington, Ky.: University Press of Kentucky, 2nd ed., 1998) 194.
3. Boyer, 267–268.

THE PRIMARY SOURCES

The primary sources focus on the historical context in which *Dr. Strangelove* was conceived, produced, and viewed. The public statement made by the Committee for a Sane Nuclear Policy in 1957 calls for the suspension of all nuclear testing. In contrast, Kennedy Defense Secretary Robert McNamara's speech in 1962 makes the case for a strategy of deterrence. Following the Cuban missile crisis, dissenting journalist I. F. Stone uses his newsletter to reflect on the dangers of nuclear confrontation. In a personal memoir, screenwriter Terry Southern recalls Stanley Kubrick's decision to employ humor to address the possibility of accidental nuclear war. Finally, in a *New York Times* review, film critic Bosley Crowther expresses ambivalence over *Dr. Strangelove* and the implications of its outcome.

SANE Launches the Debate over Nuclear Proliferation
Statement
Committee for a SANE Nuclear Policy

First, As It Concerns the Peace, America Can Say:

That we pledge ourselves to the cause of peace with justice on earth, and that there is no sacrifice that we are not prepared to make, nothing we will not do to create such a just peace for all peoples;

That we are prepared to support the concept of a United Nations with adequate authority under law to prevent aggression, adequate authority to compel and enforce disarmament, adequate authority to settle disputes among nations according to principles of justice.

Next, As it Concerns Nuclear Weapons, America Can Say:

That the earth is too small for intercontinental ballistic missiles and nuclear bombs, and that the first order of business for the world is to bring both under control;

That the development of satellites or rocket stations and the exploration of outer space must be carried on in the interest of the entire human community through a pooling of world science.

As it Concerns Nuclear Testing, America Can Say:

That because of the grave unanswered questions with respect to nuclear test explosions—especially as it concerns the contamination of air and water and food, and the injury to man himself—we are calling upon all nations to suspend such explosions at once;

That while the abolition of testing will not by itself solve the problem of peace or the problem of armaments, it enables the world to eliminate immediately at least one real specific danger. Also, that the abolition of testing gives us a place to begin on the larger question or armaments control, for the problems in monitoring such tests are relatively uncomplicated.

As is Concerns Our Connections to the Rest of Mankind, America Can Say:

That none of the differences separating the governments of the world are as important as the membership of all peoples in the human family;

That the big challenge of the age is to develop the concept of a higher loyalty—loyalty by man to the human community;

That the greatest era of human history on earth is within reach of all mankind, that there is no area that cannot be made fertile or habitable, no disease that cannot be fought, no scarcity that cannot be conquered;

That all that is required for this is to re-direct our energies, re-discover our moral strength, re-define our purposes.

SIGNED

Michael Amrine
Science Writer

Cleveland Amory
Author, "The Proper Bostonians"

Roger N. Baldwin
Dr. John C. Bennett
Dean of the Faculty, Union Theological Seminary

Dr. Harrison Brown
Professor of Geochemistry, California Institute of Technology

Harry A. Bullis
Chairman of the Board, General Mills Corporation

Norman Cousins
Editor, The Saturday Review

The Rev. Henry Hitt Crane
Detroit

Dr. Paul Doty
Chairman, Federation of American Scientists

The Rev. George B. Ford
Pastor, Corpus Christi Church

The Rev. Harry Emerson Fosdick
Pastor, Emeritus, Riverside Church, New York

Clark Eichelberger
Director, American Association for the United Nations

Harold Fey
Editor, The Christian Century

Dr. Erich Fromm
Psychoanalyst, Author

Robert Gilmore
Executive Secretary, American Friends Service Committee, New York

The Right Rev. Walter M. Gray
Bishop, Episcopal Diocese of Connecticut

Clinton Golden
Labor Official

Oscar Hammerstein II
Playwright

The Rev. Donald Harrington
Minister, Community Church, New York

Leland Hazard
Vice-President, General Counsel, Pittsburgh Plate Glass Co.

John Hersey
Author, "Hiroshima" and "The Wall"

Brigadier General Hugh B. Hester

Dr. Homer Jack
Minister, Evanston, Illinois

James Jones
Author, "From Here to Eternity"

Rabbi Edward E. Klein
Stephen Wise Free Synagogue, New York

*Dr. Stanley Livingston
Department of Physics, Massachusetts Institute of Technology

Dr. Kirtley F. Mather
Professor of Geology, Emeritus, Harvard University

*Lenore G. Marshall
Author of "Other Knowledge"

*Lawrence S. Mayers, Jr.
President L & C Mayers Co., Inc.

The Rev. Robert J. McCracken
Minister, Riverside Church, New York

Lewis Mumford
Author, "The Condition of Man"

Robert R. Nathan
National Chairman, Americans for Democratic Action

Dr. William F. Neuman
Associate Professor of Biochemistry, University of Rochester

Elliot Nichols
Civic Leader

James G. Patton
President, National Farmers Union

*Clarence Pickett
Executive Secretary Emeritus, American Friends Service Committee

*Josephine W. Pomerance
*Dr. Charles C. Price
Chairman, Department of Chemistry, University of Pennsylvania

Eleanor Roosevelt

Elmo Roper
Marketing Consultant and Public Opinion Analyst

Philip Schiff
Washington Representative, National Jewish Welfare Board

James T. Shotwell
President Emeritus, Carnegie Endowment for International Peace

Dr. Pitirim A. Sorokin
Professor of Sociology, Emeritus, Harvard University

*Norman Thomas
*Dr. Paul J. Tillich
University Professor, Harvard University

Dean Howard Thurman
Marsh Chapel, Boston University

*Dr. Hugh Wolfe
Chairman, Department of Physics, Cooper Union, New York

Jerry Voorhis
Executive Director, Cooperative League of America

(The signers of this statement are acting in their individual capacity and not as representatives of organizations or as members of the National Committee for a Sane Nuclear Policy. Names preceded by an asterisk indicate members of the organizing committee.)

NATIONAL COMMITTEE FOR A SANE
NUCLEAR POLICY
02 East 44th Street   New York 16, N.Y.

Source: Committee for a SANE Nuclear Policy, *New York Times*, November 15, 1957, in Thomas R. Frazier, ed., *The Many Sides of America: 1945–Present* (Fort Worth, Tex.: Harcourt Brace College Publishers, 1996), 58, 60.

SECRETARY OF DEFENSE ROBERT MCNAMARA
EXPLAINS ASSURED DESTRUCTION

Mutual Deterrence
Robert McNamara

In a complex and uncertain world, the gravest problem that an American Secretary of Defense must face is that of planning, preparation and policy against the possibility of thermonuclear war. It is a prospect that most of mankind understandably would prefer not to contemplate. For technology has now circumscribed us all with a horizon of horror that could dwarf any catastrophe that has befallen man in his more than a million years on earth.

Man has lived now for more than twenty years in what we have come to call the Atomic Age. What we sometimes overlook is that every future age of man will be an atomic age, and if man is to have a future at all, it will have to be one overshadowed with the permanent possibility of thermonuclear holocaust. About that fact there is no longer any doubt. Our freedom in this question consists only in facing the matter rationally and realistically and discussing actions to minimize the danger.

No sane citizen, political leader or nation wants thermonuclear war. But merely not wanting it is not enough. We must understand the differences among actions which increase its risks, those which reduce them and those which, while costly, have little influence one way or another. But there is a great difficulty in the way of constructive and profitable debate over the issues, and that is the exceptional complexity of nuclear strategy. Unless these complexities are well understood rational discussion and decision-making are impossible.

One must begin with precise definitions. The cornerstone of our strategic policy continues to be to deter nuclear attack upon the United States or its allies. We do this by maintaining a highly reliable ability to inflict unacceptable damage upon any single aggressor or combination of aggressors at any time during the course of a strategic nuclear exchange, even after absorbing a surprise first strike. This can be defined as our assured-destruction capability.

. . .

Clearly, first-strike capability is an important strategic concept. The United States must not and will not permit itself ever to get into a position in which another nation, or combination of nations, would possess a first-strike capability against it. Such a position not only would constitute an intolerable threat to our security, but it obviously would remove our ability to deter nuclear aggression.

We are not in that position today, and there is no foreseeable danger of our ever getting into that position. Our strategic offensive forces are immense: 1,000 Minuteman missile launchers, carefully protected below ground; 41 Polaris submarines carrying 656 missile launchers, with the majority hidden beneath the seas at all times; and about 600 long-range bombers, approximately 40 percent of which are kept always in a high state of alert.

Our alert forces alone can carry more than 2,200 weapons, each averaging more than the explosive equivalent of one megaton of TNT. Four hundred of these delivered on the Soviet Union would be sufficient to destroy over one-third of her population and one-half of her industry. All these flexible and highly reliable forces are equipped with devices that ensure their penetration of Soviet defenses.

Now what about the Soviet Union? Does it today possess a powerful nuclear arsenal? The answer is that it does. Does it possess a first-strike capability against the United States? That answer is that it does not. Can the Soviet Union in the foreseeable future acquire such a first-strike capability against the United States? The answer is that it cannot. It cannot because we are determined to remain fully alert and we will never permit our own assured-destruction capability to drop to a point at which a Soviet first-strike capability is even remotely feasible.

Is the Soviet Union seriously attempting to acquire a first-strike capability against the United States? Although this is a question we cannot answer with absolute certainty, we believe the answer is no. In any event, the question itself is—in a sense—

irrelevant: for the United States will maintain and, where necessary strengthen its retaliatory forces so that, whatever the Soviet Union's intentions or actions, we will continue to have an assured-destruction capability vis a vis their society.

SOURCE: Robert McNamara, "Mutual Deterrence" Speech, 1962, http://www.atomicarchive.com/Docs/Deterrence.shtml, A. J. Software and Multimedia, 1998–2003.

JOURNALIST I. F. STONE READS THE LESSONS OF THE CUBAN MISSILE CRISIS

I. F. Stone's Weekly
I. F. Stone

Last week was the world's first thermonuclear crisis. It will not be the last. This issue of the *Weekly* might never have been written. You who read it might have been one of the lucky few, huddled half-mad with anxiety about missing loved ones, in the ruins of New York or Washington. Mr. Kennedy's gamble paid off. But what if it had failed? Unless we can achieve a fundamental change of behaviour among nations, the Cuban confrontation is only a preview.

SOURCE: *I. F. Stone's Weekly* 10, no. 40 (Nov. 5, 1962), in Frazier, 86, 89.

TERRY SOUTHERN RECALLS THE ORIGINS OF *DR. STRANGELOVE*

Notes
Terry Southern

"It's big Stan Kubrick on the line from Old Smoke."

I had once jokingly referred to Kubrick, whom I had never met but greatly admired, as "big Stan Kubrick" because I liked the ring and lilt of it. "Get big Stan Kubrick on the line in Old Smoke," I had said, "I'm ready with my incisive critique of *Killer's Kiss*." And my wife, not one to be bested, had taken it up.

"Big Stan Kubrick," she repeated, "on the line from Old Smoke."

"Don't fool around," I said. I knew I would soon be on the hump with Mr. Snow Shovel and I was in no mood for her brand of tomfoolery.

"I'm not fooling around," she said. "It's him all right, or at least his assistant."

I won't attempt to reconstruct the conversation; suffice to say that he told me he was going to make a film about "our failure to understand the dangers of nuclear war." He said that he had thought of the story as a "straightforward melodrama" until this morning, when he "woke up and realized that nuclear war was too outrageous, too fantastic to be treated in any conventional manner." He said he could only see it now as "some kind of hideous joke." He told me that he had read a book of mine which contained, as he put it, "certain indications" that I might be able to help him with his script.

. . .

It was a time when the Cold War was at its most intense. As part of the American defense strategy, bombing missions were flown daily toward targets deep inside the Soviet Union, each B-52 carrying a nuclear bomb more powerful than those used on Hiroshima and Nagasaki combined. Bombers were instructed to continue their missions unless they received the recall code at their "fail-safe" points.

In my Knightsbridge rooms, I carefully read *Red Alert*, a book written by an ex-RAF intelligence officer named Peter George that had prompted Stanley's original interest. Perhaps the best thing about the book was the fact that the national security regulations in England, concerning what could and could not be published, were extremely lax by American standards. George had been able to reveal details concerning the "fail-safe" aspect *of* nuclear deterrence (for example, the so-called black box and the CRM Discriminator)—revelations that, in spy-crazy U.S.A. of the Cold War era, would have been downright treasonous. Thus the entire complicated technology of nuclear deterrence in *Dr. Strangelove* was based on a bedrock of authenticity that gave the film what must have been its greatest strength: credibility.

. . .

It soon became apparent that no one in the company wished to be associated with the film, as if they were pretending that it had somehow spontaneously come into existence. Kubrick was hopping. "It's like they think it was some kind of fucking conception," he exclaimed with the ultrarighteous indignation of someone caught in an unsuccessful bribery attempt. It was difficult to contain him. "Bad form!" he kept shouting, "Can you imagine *Mo Rothman* saying that? His secretary must have taught him that phrase!"

In the months that followed, the studio continued to distance itself from the film. Even when *Strangelove* received the infrequent good review, it dismissed the critic as a pinko nutcase and on at least one occasion the Columbia Pictures publicity department *defended* the company against the film by saying it was definitely not "anti-U.S. military," but "just a zany novelty flick which did not reflect the views of the corporation in any way." This party line persisted, I believe, until about five years ago, when the Library of Congress announced that the film had been selected as one of the fifty greatest American films of all time—in a ceremony at which I noted Rothman in prominent attendance. Who said satire was "something that closed Wednesday in Philadelphia"?

SOURCE: "Strangelove Outtake: Notes from the War Room," Terry Southern, Memoir, from Jean Stein, *Grand Street.* http://www.terrysouthern.com/texts/t_strange.htm

Review of *Dr. Strangelove*
Bosley Crowther

Stanley Kubrick's new film called "Dr. Strangelove or: How I Learned to Stop Worrying and Love the Bomb," is beyond any question the most shattering sick joke I've ever come across. And I say that with full recollection of some of the grim ones I've heard from Mort Sahl, some of the cartoons I've seen by Charles Addams and some of the stuff I've read in Mad Magazine.

For this brazenly jesting speculation of what might happen within the Pentagon and within the most responsible council of the President of the United States if some maniac Air Force general should suddenly order a nuclear attack on the Soviet Union is at the same time one of the cleverest and most inclusive satiric thrusts at the awkwardness and folly of the military that have ever been on the screen. It opened yesterday at the Victoria and the Baronet.

My reaction to it is quite divided, because there is so much about it that is grand, so much that is brilliant and amusing, and much that is grave and dangerous.

On the one hand, it cuts right to the soft pulp of the kind of military mind that is lost from all sense of reality in a maze of technical talk, and it shows up this type of mentality for the foolish and frightening thing it is.

In a top-level Air Force general, played by George C. Scott with a snarling and rasping volubility that makes your blood run cold, Mr. Kubrick presents us with a joker whose thinking is so involved with programs and cautions and suspicions that he is practically tied in knots.

It is he who is most completely baffled, bewildered and paralyzed when word comes through to Washington that a general in the Strategic Air Command has sent a wing of bombers off to drop bombs and that the planes cannot be recalled. It is he who has to answer to the President for this awesome "accident" when the President gathers his council in the War Room at the Pentagon. And it is he who looks the most unstable and dubious in the causes of peace when it begins to appear that the Russians have a retaliatory "doomsday device."

Some of the conversations in that War Room are hilarious, shooting bright shafts of satire through mounds of ineptitude. There is, best of all, a conversation between the President and an unseen Soviet Premier at the other end of a telephone line that is a titanic garble of nuttiness and platitudes.

Funny, too, in a mad way, is the behavior of the crew in one of the planes of the airborne alert force ordered to drop the bomb. The commander is a Texan who puts on a cowboy hat when he knows the mission is committed—Slim Pickens plays this role. He and Keenan Wynn as a foggy colonel are the funniest individuals in the film.

As I say, there are parts of this satire that are almost beyond compare.

On the other hand, I am troubled by the feeling which runs all through the film, of discredit and even contempt for our whole defense establishment, up to and even including the hypothetical Commander in Chief.

It is all right to show the general who starts this wild foray as a Communist-hating madman, convinced that a "Red conspiracy" is fluoridating our water in order to pollute our precious body fluids. That is pointed satire, and Sterling Hayden plays the role with just the right blend of wackiness and meanness to give the character significance.

But when virtually everybody turns up stupid or insane—or, what is worse, psychopathic—I want to know what this picture proves. The President, played by Peter Sellers with a shiny bald head, is a dolt, whining and unavailing with the nation in a life-or-death spot. But worse yet, his technical expert, Dr. Strangelove, whom Mr. Sellers also plays, is a devious and noxious ex-German whose mechanical arm insists on making the Nazi salute.

And, oddly enough, the only character who seems to have much common sense is a British flying officer, whom Mr. Sellers—yes, he again—plays.

The ultimate touch of goulish humor is when we see the bomb actually going off, dropped on some point in Russia, and a jazzy sound track comes in with a cheerful melodic rendition of "We'll Meet Again Some Sunny Day." Somehow, to me, it isn't funny. It is malefic and sick.

SOURCE: Bosley Crowther, "Dr. Strangelove," The New York Times, January 31, 1964.

Follow-Up Problems

1. A central theme in Dr. Strangelove revolves around the issue of the human relationship with the science and technology that have revolutionized modern life. How does the film address the question of maintaining control over the machinery and technological systems that resulted from the climax of the scientific revolution?

2. Is Dr. Strangelove a document unique to the period in which it was first produced and viewed? In what ways does the film address issues relevant to the political and diplomatic problems faced in the modern world?

3. Examine the key characters in Dr. Strangelove in comparison with some of the actual historical figures involved in scientific research and governmental policy making in the 1950s and 1960s. To what extent does the film represent their perspectives accurately?

4. What is the meaning of the term "satire"? What is the meaning of the film's title?

5. Film scholar Charles Maland has argued that Dr. Strangelove represents a "new sensibility" found in the post–missile crisis American public. What did he mean?

6. Discuss Kubrick's portrayal of the "professional warriors" of the military in the 1960s. How do you think the military and civilian-military relationships depicted in Dr. Strangelove would compare with those of films made in the 1940s and 1950s?

7. Why are there so many sexual references in the film? In what way does this movie reflect the "macho" nature of nuclear brinksmanship?

Further Reading

Boyer, Paul S. *By the Bomb's Early Light: American Thought and Culture at the Dawn of the Cold War*. Chapel Hill, N.C.: University of North Carolina Press, 1994.
_____. "*Dr. Strangelove*." In Mark C. Carnes, ed., *Past Imperfect: History According to the Movies*. New York: Henry Holt & Co., 1996, 266–269.

Lowery, J. Vincent. "*Dr. Strangelove*: Or How I Learned to Stop Worrying and Teach the Film in the Classroom." *OAH Magazine of History* 16 (summer 2002): 32–37.

Maland, Charles. "*Dr. Strangelove* (1964): Nightmare Comedy and the Ideology of Liberal Consensus." In Peter Rollins, ed., *Hollywood as Historian: American Film in a Cultural Context*. Lexington, Ky.: University Press of Kentucky, 2nd ed., 1998, 190–210.

Renaker, John. *Dr. Strangelove and the Hideous Epoch: Deterrence in the Nuclear Age*. Claremont, Calif.: Regina Books, 2000.

Suid, Lawrence. "The Pentagon and Hollywood: *Dr. Strangelove or: How I Learned to Stop Worrying and Love the Bomb (1964)*." In John E. O'Connor and Martin A. Jackson, eds., *American History/American Film Interpreting the Hollywood Image*. New York: Frederick Ungar, 1979, 219–236.

Filmography

Fail Safe (Columbia, 1964).

On the Beach (MGM, 1959).

Seven Days in May (Warner Brothers, 1964).

The Celluloid Document

Dr. Strangelove or: How I Learned to Stop Worrying and Love the Bomb (Columbia, 1964).

Chapter 12

The Alienation Films of the 1960s: *Alice's Restaurant* (1969), *The Graduate* (1967), and Social Fragmentation

If *Dr. Strangelove* heralded a break from the social and political consensus of the postwar era, the film fare of the late 1960s formally recorded the collapse of traditional values. No film marked the social fragmentation of this decade more clearly than Arthur Penn's adaptation of Arlo Guthrie's musical assault on conformity, *Alice's Restaurant* (1969). By the end of the sixties, American society was deeply divided by the combined impact of the civil rights movement, the black power struggle, and a bitterly contested war in Vietnam. As this eventful decade came to a close, several antiestablishment "youth films" raised a challenge to a mainstream culture that had alienated a substantial number of young Americans. One of the most successful of these was the Penn-Guthrie production, which mocked the values held dear by middle-class America. Equally revealing was the Mike Nichols production of *The Graduate* (1967), which attacked middle-class consumer culture with devastating effect. Analysis of *Alice's Restaurant,* with a comparative look at *The Graduate* for another celluloid critique of 1960s values, will provide insight into the experience of distinct segments of the youth culture, while exposing the underside of the affluent but morally deficient society they objected to.

The Historical Background

During the chaotic 1960s, most Americans watched in disbelief as armies of young men and women made common cause with the old Left to pursue liberal goals ranging from the University of California, Berkeley, free speech movement to the rapidly growing civil rights movement, which demanded a more just and democratic society based on full racial equality. The freedom rides, sit-ins, voter registration drives, and pressure for civil rights legislation inspired great hopes but also led to a "revolution of rising expectations." Consequently, in the mid-1960s, black Muslims and African-American nationalists gained in popularity, especially among young urban blacks, by embracing their heritage and calling for the exercise of a new "black power" that included black control of the black community. Simultaneously, the nation's cities were disrupted by a series of long, hot summers during which the African-American community seemed to turn on itself to destroy social order.

The disorder in urban communities was matched by increasing bloodshed in Vietnam, where a succession of presidential administrations sent hundreds of thousands of young Americans to fight a war that, in the eyes of many observers, lacked legitimacy and moral justification. As the American commitment deepened, opposition to the war escalated after 1966, when college-educated youths combined with an increasingly middle-class peace movement to question American foreign policy and military interventionism. These protests reached a climax in 1968 with the chaos at the Democratic National Convention in Chicago, where violence against protesters disillusioned many young people who had engaged in the political process and alienated the voting public from the incumbent Democratic liberals who had governed since 1960.

It is clear that the majority of college-aged youth chose not to engage directly in the social and political struggles of their era, though many shared the goals of the activists. Nonetheless, a vocal and active minority of students spoke out against mainstream politics, impersonal universities, racial inequities, and a war that most opposed. Led by such organizations as Students for a Democratic Society (SDS) and Student Non-Violent Coordinating Committee (SNCC), this active minority engaged in protests and political organizing, which they believed would bring the dawn of a new, more just society. While the political activists drew most of the media attention, it is important to note that a much larger body of middle-class young people became increasingly skeptical of the acquisitive values of their upwardly mobile parents' generation and resentful of the impersonal colleges and universities through which they passed as they prepared to take a number in the corporate world. Both activists and bystanders shared an interest in building a world free of the racism and neoimperialism they saw at home and abroad.

While campus political activists mobilized for social change, a much smaller group of students rejected the political system and the consumer culture. By the mid-sixties, these less-activist youths began to question the validity of a society based on competitive capitalism. The social dropouts, sometimes branded "hippies" by unsympathetic critics, leaned in a more communitarian direction and despised most aspects of the consumer society that threatened to engulf them. Instead, they developed a counterculture that valued love, peace, and a cooperative lifestyle but renounced the activism that drove the young political activists who worked to purify the system. Participants in the counterculture envisioned their own brand of community, a cooperative society that would replace an American social system that they believed empty and corrupt.

It was this hippie counterculture that is featured in Arlo Guthrie's musical lyrics, which were incorporated into "Alice's Restaurant," a "talking blues" hit song that openly ridiculed the dominant culture of sixties America. Arlo Guthrie was the son of legendary radical folksinger and labor activist, Woody Guthrie, who had worked in the 1930s and 1940s to promote social justice first for Dust Bowl refugees and later for workers and unionists in all parts of the United States. Arlo's song, which became a huge hit, was a direct descendant of his father's style, though the topical material was based on the issues and social tensions of the 1960s. Arthur Penn's cinematic treatment of *Alice's Restaurant*, in turn, closely followed the narrative from the popular tune, which had become a smash hit in 1968.

This film was not the only movie to explore the idea of alienation in the 1960s. The widespread questioning of American institutions that occurred in this period was found in several motion pictures released in the late 1960s, all of which addressed rebellion in one way or another. In *The Graduate* (1967), for example, young Benjamin Braddock (Dustin Hoffman) rejects the middle-class values of his affluent family and friends. Ben's disdain for a career in "plastics" echoes his generation's contempt for the world of his parents and their contemporaries. The first of several alienation films, this picture expressed the disillusionment felt within a wide spectrum of the youth culture that rejected the crass materialism of their society.[1]

By the time Arthur Penn became interested in a film based on the Guthrie hit, he had already explored violence in America in a cinematic study of two Depression-era outlaws, *Bonnie and Clyde* (1967), which had exposed the raw brutality of Vietnam-era America. Hence, when Penn launched the *Alice's Restaurant* project, he was no stranger to the alienation film. He was also familiar with the disillusionment behind the generational tension that had made Guthrie's record such a success. Penn recalls that the first time he heard the song, his response was: "that's a movie." Fired by the conviction that such a picture could capture the historical moment by portraying the counterculture of the sixties, he set about the process of beefing up the thin story line that carried the song.

Analyzing the Film

The film and its musical source tell the tale of a communal experiment in Great Barrington, Massachusetts, where a young hippie (Arlo) establishes temporary residence with the commune's symbolic parents, Ray and Alice. After a climactic Thanksgiving Day feast, the youths illegally dump an impressive load of garbage and are arrested, events that later enable Arlo to evade the draft. Throughout the picture, Penn attacks social hypocrites, mindless bureaucrats, the military, and the war. Look for the ways in which this picture addresses the War in Vietnam, the Penn-Guthrie perspective on the war, and the widespread American anxiety over that failed conflict. How is an attitude towards the war evident in the life of the community under construction in Ray and Alice's newly purchased church?

While the picture celebrates the collective lifestyle, it is not an uncritical treatment of communalism. Eventually, after a drug-related death within the commune family, the experiment is abandoned, a result that suggests that this film marks both the apex and the end of the alienation cycle. Bearing in mind the troubled social causes of the 1960s, think about the significance of the movie's bleak conclusion. What does this ambiguity reveal about the outcome of 1960s social experimentalism? Compare this conclusion with the social questions posed by the ending of *The Graduate* as Ben Braddock escapes with his partner, Elayne, to face an uncertain future. Both films may be understood as artifacts of a decade of disruption and youthful alienation, as well as indicators of the social fragmentation soon to follow in the 1970s.

Since the central theme in *Alice's Restaurant* is the idea of community, you might begin your analysis of the film with a thoughtful examination of this term. Note that while individual characters are developed, the film tries to examine the assumption that a communal lifestyle was superior to one that revolved around personal striving. Think about the filmmaker's techniques in exploring the communitarian ethic and determine what his assessment of that ideal turns out to be. As you consider Penn's judgments on this point, note that by 1970, the hippies in San Francisco's Haight-Ashbury community had fallen victim to drugs, violence, and community intolerance. Similarly, some of the cultural radicals who had retreated to rural communes had come to understand that self-sufficiency was not an easy road to follow.

The film's conclusion and the outcome of the communal experiment raise the question of the filmmaker's intent, as well as the audience response. While contemporary viewers greeted the movie as an endorsement of the counterculture and the communal lifestyle, thoughtful analysis some two generations later confirms that the film is ambiguous on the "hippie" ideology.[2] Ask yourself what the film reveals about the pursuit of alternative lifestyles. Was Penn embracing communalism or questioning its wisdom? How does his treatment of life choices compare with those explored by Nichols in *The Graduate*? The answer to these questions may be related to the nature of the motion picture business and the purposes for which films are made.

While questions of social ideology may be addressed, you must also view these films as social documents that provide you with access to the styles, dress, and values of the period in which they were produced. Consider, for example, attitudes concerning sex and the key characters' definitions of sexuality as they are represented on-screen. Focus on Alice, Ray, Shelley, Arlo, and the teenaged groupie in *Alice's Restaurant* as you look for clues to the changing social and moral values of the 1960s. Turning to *The Graduate*, what is the significance of Ben's relationship with the seductive Mrs. Robinson (Anne Bancroft)? Think about women, women's roles, the sexual revolution, and intergenerational relationships. Finally, reflect on the premium placed by each film's characters on personal freedom and the right to pursue it. Try to identify other social or cultural ideas expressed in these films.

Thinking About Primary Sources

As you review the documents, you will note that Penn chose to film *Alice's Restaurant* on location at the scene of the original events depicted in the song and film. The crew and cast found themselves stranded in Pittsfield, Stockbridge, and Great Barrington, Massachusetts for much of their work. Equally significant was the decision to use a large number of nonprofessional actors, including some of the townspeople. Try to decide why this plan was adopted, and evaluate the results. Note that the filmmakers expressed some anxiety about the potential consequences of on-location shooting, and use the primary sources to determine the source of their concern. Then link these anxieties to the state of urban-rural/small town relationships and intergenerational tensions in a historical period marked by social and political conflict. The uneasy relationship revealed in the documents underscores the value of the film as a primary source for the study of the anxious 1960s and the crisis of authority that accompanied the period's social conflict and youthful rebellion.

One of the clearest indicators of the social dislocations of the sixties was certainly the way in which music recorded the changes then underway. Penn's entire film project, after all, rested on the transformation of musical lyrics to cinematic narrative, weak though it might have been. For Nichols, the words of the Simon and Garfunkel sound track reinforce the alienation displayed by Ben Braddock at every turn. As you experience these films, consider the use of music to enhance the total effect of the action on-screen. Think about these sounds and words, and be aware of the meaning of music to any rising generation of young people, including your own. In *Alice's Restaurant*, what was the impact and meaning of "Amazing Grace" in the larger context of the film's story line? In what way does Joni Mitchell's rendition of "Songs to Aging Children" reinforce the narrative? Likewise, as you follow Ben's personal quest for identity, ask how "The Sounds of Silence" and "Mrs. Robinson" underscore the key theme of *The Graduate*.

Parallel to the exploration of family and community, Penn's film highlights some critical political issues confronting the American public in 1969. As you think about the concrete problems introduced by Penn in *Alice's Restaurant*, use the documents to help form an opinion about the important political points made. Based on the reviews, what issue seems to dominate the film and the critics' response? What techniques were used by the filmmaker to make his political viewpoint on that problem clear? In contrast, *The Graduate* is more subtle in its political perspective. How does it differ from *Alice's Restaurant* with regard to the place of politics in the narrative? How would you account for this difference?

It will be obvious that in these pictures humor was the clearest vehicle for delivering important messages to movie audiences. Track the use of humor to drive home more serious points. At what points are Penn and Nichols most effective? As you think about the reviews, notice that while narrative structure often relies on ridicule, there is also a deadly serious side to each story. Identify these elements of sober reflection in both the outcomes for the central characters, as well as the end result for the families involved, whether surrogate or real. As you pause to consider the outcomes, compare the experiences of Arlo, his friends, Ben, and Elayne to the lives of most American young people, including the life choices they made. What were Penn and Nichols saying with their conclusions?

As you contemplate the films' outcomes, return to the organizing principle of the motion picture as primary source. Be aware of the fact that by 1970, the civil rights movement was in a state of disarray, without a clear national leader. It is also true that by this time, President Richard Nixon was working to promote "law and order," while implementing a "Southern strategy" of stalling on civil rights to rebuild the Republican Party on a Southern conservative base. Finally, recall that as the nation entered the 1970s, the Vietnam War raged while the Nixon administration carried out a program of Vietnamization that delayed the American exit from Vietnam until 1973. The moviegoers who saw *Alice's Restaurant* in 1969 and 1970 had witnessed the collapse of 1960s liberalism; and as they watched, they were experiencing the disillusionment that accompanied the decline of idealism. This film documents the mixed emotions of a nation entering a period of identity politics and social fragmentation.

Historical Perspective

When *Alice's Restaurant* was released in 1969, the critical response was sharply divided. Ironically, it was not a great box office success with the youth audience it aimed to reach. Its broad success with the general public may be related to the widespread interest in the central issue of the Vietnam War, which helped build a more mainstream audience for what was essentially a film of youthful rebellion. The picture is, in fact, a left-wing political statement criticizing the war and therefore aligning itself with a growing body of opinion in the United States in 1969. *The Graduate*, while less overtly political, was even more successful, both financially and critically. In several ways, both films advance a mainstream liberal interpretation of sixties culture that emphasized public dissatisfaction with regimentation, cold inhumanity, social inequities, and a war that by this time, seemed misguided at best and immoral at worst. In the last analysis, then, the underlying themes of *Alice's Restaurant* went beyond the interests of the counterculture that it depicted, while *The Graduate* more accurately captured the spirit of alienated middle-class youth in an age of anxiety.

While *Alice's Restaurant* is a revealing historical document, it was something less than an artistic triumph at the time of its release. Not only was the story line thin, but its featured actor was less an actor than a traveling musician; after all, Arlo Guthrie was not acting so much as he was merely playing himself and re-creating the sometimes uninspiring story of his personal journey towards maturity. This is hardly the stuff of which great drama is composed. Although it introduced a few talented newcomers, such as Pat Quinn and James Broderick as Alice and Ray, *Alice's Restaurant* failed to impress the Motion Picture Academy with its offbeat countercultural themes. Only Arthur Penn was recognized with an Academy Award nomination for his direction, which was instrumental in bringing the issues of Vietnam and home front social tensions to the attention of the moviegoing public. In contrast, *The Graduate* won several Oscars, including Nichols's recognition as best director;[3] and anxiety-ridden Benjamin Braddock entered the domain of American popular culture as the symbol of alienated youth in the 1960s. Film scholar Robert Sklar concludes that this film was one of a very few that, by reaching a new mass audience, "brought movies once again to the center of national attention."[4]

A critical stance on Vietnam, together with its concentration on the deep alienation felt by some young people in the 1960s, makes *Alice's Restaurant* a useful primary source for the study of a divided America. Likewise, *The Graduate* records an even more widely held youthful alienation from the bourgeois values of upwardly mobile middle-class Americans. The collapse of Ray and Alice's substitute family symbolically records the end of the liberal idealism observed by social critics as the decade drew to a close. Penn's picture of the joys and sorrows of the communal experience also reminds modern students of the mixed feelings of many Americans towards the social movements and searching criticisms of the era. Before long, disappointment over unmet goals was to be replaced by a wider and deeper public disillusionment when the Watergate crisis laid bare the cynicism and moral failures recognized by both the activists and the dropouts of the sixties. Each in its own way, *Alice's Restaurant* and *The Graduate* document a social analysis developed by a generation of early skeptics.

Endnotes

1. This analysis is based in part on Michael Ryan and Douglas Kellner, "From Counterculture to Counterrevolution, 1967–1971," *Camera Politica* (Bloomington, Ind.: Indiana University Press, 1988), in Steven Mintz and Randy Roberts, *Hollywood's America: United States History Through Its Films* (St. James, N.Y.: Brandywine Press, Rev., 2001) 268.
2. Ryan and Kellner, 269.
3. Peter Biskind, *Easy Riders, Raging Bulls: How the Sex-Drugs-and-Rock 'n' Roll Generation Saved Hollywood* (New York: Simon & Schuster, 1998), 48, 81.
4. Robert Sklar, *Movie-Made America: A Cultural History of American Movies* (New York: Vintage) Rev. ed., 1994, 301.

THE PRIMARY SOURCES

The primary sources open with a newspaper account of the factual events that provided the basis for both the Arlo Guthrie hit "Alice's Restaurant" and the film of the same name. The next document suggests that the producers and film crew tried to avoid antagonizing local citizens while shooting on location. In August 1968 before production had begun, a New York agent wrote to Penn and Producer Hillard Elkins to warn that the local police in Great Barrington, Massachusetts might react negatively to any provocative behavior on the set. Finally, several reviews place the two films in historical context.

AN ACCOUNT OF THE "CRIME OF THE CENTURY"

Youths Ordered to
Clean Up Rubbish Mess
Unidentified Newspaper

Lee—Because they couldn't find a dump open in Great Barrington, two youths threw a load of refuse down a Stockbridge hillside on Thanksgiving Day.

Saturday, Richard J. Robbins, 19, of Poughkeepsie, N.Y., and Arlo Guthrie, 18, of Howard Beach, N.Y., each paid a fine of $25 in Lee District Court after pleading guilty of illegally disposing of rubbish. Special Justice James. E. Hannon ordered the youths to remove all the rubbish. They did so Saturday afternoon, following a heavy rain.

Police Chief William J. Obanhein of Stockbridge said later the youths found dragging the junk up the hillside much harder than throwing it down. He said he hoped their case would be an example to others who are careless about disposal of rubbish.

The junk included a divan, plus nearly enough bottles, garbage, papers and boxes to fill their Volkswagen bus.

"The stuff would take up at least half of a good-sized pickup truck," Chief Obanhein said.

The rubbish was thrown into the Nelson Foote Sr. property on Prospect Street, a residential section of Stockbridge consisting largely of estates on the hill across from Indian Hill School.

Chief Obanhein told the court he spent "a very disagreeable two hours" looking through the rubbish before finding a clue to who had thrown it there. He finally found a scrap of paper bearing the name of a Great Barrington man. Subsequent investigation indicated Robbins and Guthrie had been visiting the Great Barrington man and had agreed to cart away the rubbish for him. They told the court that, when they found the Barrington dump closed, they drove around and then disposed of the junk by tossing it over the Stockbridge hillside.

SOURCE: "Youths Ordered to Clean Up Rubbish Mess," Unidentified Newspaper Clipping, n.d., in *This Is the Arlo Guthrie Songbook* (New York: 1969), 39.

THE PRODUCERS ARE WARNED OF
POSSIBLE LOCAL RESISTANCE TO *ALICE'S RESTAURANT*

Letter
Robert H. Montgomery Jr.

Mr. Arthur Penn
1860 Broadway
New York, New York

Messrs, Hillard Elkins and Joseph Manduke
19-1/2 east 62nd Street
New York, New York

Dear Arthur, Hilly and Joe:

I want to pass on to you a bit of information that comes to me by reason of my representation of Max Raab and "END OF THE ROAD", now filming in

Great Barrington, Mass. I have Max's permission to pass this information along to you.

In the last two weeks, the unit in Great Barrington has been having some trouble with two Great Barrington police officers named Zucco and Gardella. According to Steve Kesten (and you really should talk to him directly about this), these two men are fairly antagonistic to strangers, and particularly to strangers with hair. When they see Arlo, they are going to get very up tight indeed.

The situation is so bad in Great Barrington at the moment between these two cops and the END OF

THE ROAD unit, and Steve is so worried about it, that we are about to engage local counsel to "represent" us there. The representation of the local counsel will hopefully be more in the nature of public relations than legal representation.

Now, I don't want to upset you unduly about this situation but I do think that you should talk to Steve about it if you have not already done so. It might be worth going to the town selectmen at this point and saying that you have heard of this situation and that you want assurance that there will be no such incidents of xenophobia before you commit to shooting the film there. Or is it too late to do that at this point?

With best wishes,

Sincerely,

[Bob]

Robert H. Montgomery, Jr.

RHM/jl

P.S. Since dictating this letter, I have talked to Hilly and he tells me that he is quite aware of this situation and that steps are being taken now to avert any disasters. However, I am sending you this letter anyway.

SOURCE: Robert H. Montgomery Jr. to Arthur Penn, Joe Manduke, and Hillard Elkins, August 19, 1968, Hillard Elkins Papers, Madison, Wis., Wisconsin Center for Film and Theater Research, Wisconsin Historical Society, Box 6.

MIXED REVIEWS REFLECT HISTORICAL CONTEXT

Review in the *New York Times*
Vincent Canby

ONE of the definitions of grace is "the power of disposition to endure with patience the trials of the earthly state." Such grace is the leitmotif of Arlo Guthrie's best-selling recording "The Alice's Restaurant Massacree," the long, cheerful, "talking blues" number in which Woody Guthrie's folk-singing son recounts in a wry, surreal monologue his actual confrontations with the law of Stockbridge, Mass., and the draft board of New York City.

Grace is also manifest throughout the movie called "Alice's Restaurant," which Arthur Penn, the director of "The Miracle Worker" and "Bonnie and Clyde," has made with Arlo Guthrie starring as Arlo Guthrie and with the ballad as a frame. It's hardly an accident that the old evangelical hymn "Amazing Grace" ("How sweet the sound/That saved a wretch like me"), keeps cropping up in this film—at a tent meeting, during church services or in a line of dialogue. The film itself is a hymn to the amazing grace of some of the most beautiful, funny and affectionate wretches you're ever likely to meet in a movie.

"Alice's Restaurant," which opened yesterday at the Festival and the Murray Hill Theaters, seems—on its surface—to be about Arlo's growing up, his short, disastrous college career, his relationships with his parents, and his friendships, particularly with Alice and Ray Brock, a young couple who live in a deconsecrated Stockbridge church, run a restaurant and act as surrogate parents to a colony of hippies.

On a more profound level, it's about the America of the nineteen-sixties, which is like a dog being wagged by a tail pronounced "VEETnam," about the continuity between generations (as well as the gap), about the mindlessness of authoritarian systems, which it treats with gentle satire, about the responsibilities of love, which can be terribly painful, about the ceremonies of death—about almost everything, in fact, except Alice's Restaurant.

Penn, who collaborated on the screenplay with Venable Herndon, has made a sort of folk movie—wise, fantastic, technically superb (especially the color photography by Michael Nebbia), sometimes wildly funny, sometimes touching in ways that are most agreeable because they are completely unforeseen. He mixes up real people who play themselves (Arlo, Stockbridge Police Chief William Obanhein, Pete Seeger), real people played by actors, including Pat Quinn and James Broderick, who play the Brocks, and composites of real-life characters played by both actors and real-life people. . . .

In "Alice's Restaurant," Penn has made a very loving movie, but the loving is not verbalized; it is sung and seen, in sequence after sequence. It is there when Arlo visits Woody, the "old citizen up the road," now mute and dying in a hospital bed while Pete Seeger stands in the corner and plunks out the older Guthrie's "The Pastures of Plenty." It is there in Arlo's funny encounter with a sniffly teeny-bopper (Shelley Plimpton) who wants to make it with Arlo because she's sure he'll be an album some day, "like the Raspberry Wristwatch."

There is an extraordinarily cinematic funeral during a quiet New England snowfall, while Joni Mitchell sings "Songs to Aging Children." It may be self-conscious but it's also very beautiful. Not unexpectedly, the movie's flashiest and funniest sequence is Penn's visualization of "The Alice's Restaurant Massacree," Arlo's arrest and imprisonment for "litterin'," followed by his Army physical exam, which becomes hilarious nightmare of things like spilled urine specimens and the filling out of incomprehensible forms.

Through it all, Arlo maintains amazing grace, which provides both the theme and the continuity for a very original movie whose structural weaknesses couldn't bother me less. With a film as interesting and fine as "Alice's Restaurant," structural weaknesses, seen in proper perspective, simply become cinematic complexities to be cherished.

SOURCE: *The New York Times*, n.d., 1969, Elkins Papers, Box 6.

Review in *Newsweek*
Paul D. Zimmerman

In his droll, fanciful "talking blues," Arlo Guthrie goes on to recount how he was arrested for littering, locked in the Stockbridge, Mass., jail and convicted by a blind judge ("a typical case of American blind justice"), and how this conviction eventually disqualified him for the draft. In the song's mixture of whimsy and anger, moral outrage and absurdist humor, thousands of disaffected and disillusioned young people recognized themselves and their own responses to American life. "Alice's Restaurant" sold 700,000 copies and, a year after it appeared, the slender seraphic son of the dust-bowl balladeer of the 1930s, Woody Guthrie, was canonized at the 1967 Newport Folk Festival as the new folk hero of America's alienated young.

Now, five years after the great garbage arrest, "Alice's Restaurant" has become a brilliantly successful—and significant—movie. Director Arthur Penn, who established himself as a major American director with "Bonnie and Clyde," heard in Arlo's ballad something beyond satire. He heard the voice of a significant part of an entire generation, singing the painful absurdity of living in a world inhospitable to their Aquarian dream of peace, freedom and brotherhood.

A resident of Stockbridge, Penn and his family had eaten at Alice's Restaurant; they knew the town and police commissioner William Obanhein, the man who arrested Arlo. They lived not far from the deconsecrated Episcopal church where Alice and Ray Brock, former teachers at the progressive Stockbridge School, had become surrogate parents to a community of intelligent, confused middle-class kids—the same kids who would troop to the Woodstock Music Festival by the hundreds of thousands, America's wandering army of the young—unimpressed by affluence, opposed totally to the war in Vietnam, horrified by the prospect of middle-class life and desperate to find an alternative.

Penn's film version of "Alice's Restaurant" focuses on the attempt of Alice and Ray and their adopted kids to find a way out, to start a new life. In treating thoughtfully—and wittily—the themes of youthful alienation and adult confusion, "Alice's Restaurant" is the best of a number of remarkable new films which seem to question many of the traditional assumptions of establishment America. . . .

Dissent: These movies—made, financed or distributed by the film establishment, welcomed by the critics, and astonishingly successful—testify to an increasing prevalence of dissent and skepticism about ideas that Hollywood wouldn't have dreamed of questioning, attacking or satirizing even a couple of years ago. "Films today have to be anti-establishment," says the 47-year-old Penn. "In fact, how can you make an establishment picture today that says anything? What could that picture be?"

Certainly, "Alice's Restaurant" has confirmed the feeling of Penn and producer Hillard Elkins that there is a vast constituency for the new irreverent movie. "Alice," which cost some $2 million, has already earned back a staggering one-half million dollars in its first month. It has been booked into two houses in New York to accommodate the hordes of kids willing to put $3 on the line to see Arlo Guthrie play himself. Arlo Guthrie is not the greatest singer of his generation—"I sing as bad as Woody" is the way he puts it—and he is not the finest songwriter of his generation. And, far from being the finest actor of his generation, he cannot really act well at all. But, with his muted wit and his eloquently understated rage, his freewheeling life style, he is not so much a spokesman or leader as an embodiment of what has almost instantly been labeled the Woodstock generation. . . .

Penn brings the perspective of middle age to his vision of Arlo Guthrie's world. "One of the things these kids are trying to do," says Penn, "is to go back to a first premise. They have been saturated with the well-being of the affluent society and find it very unpleasant. They want to get out of the rat race-credentials, grades, upward mobility—the whole thing. They're getting back to the first principles of using their hands. These kids are fighting up from the mat."

Indictment: Penn does not see them as a lost generation. "They're not simply dropping out," he says of the Stockbridge kids who have taken jobs as carpenters, artisans, construction workers. "They're using their anger at the world—their disillusionment—in a very constructive way. Their response to Vietnam and the ugliness around them has been to say 'OK, let's make something beautiful.' This kind of life style isn't viable beyond a stage, perhaps, and it's dependent on the affluence around them. But these kids belong to America. . . ."

"Alice's Restaurant" ends with the world in pieces. Arlo leaves, heading in no particular direction. Alice stands alone before the church—neither young nor old. Ray's dream of utopia is shattered. American culture and the youth counterculture hang suspended in precarious balance. Perhaps, with the affluence that comes from his music, Arlo will be able to realize his pastoral dream of independence in a green place, an American dream rooted in Thoreau, Emerson and Whitman. Perhaps the young man with the cloud of a terminal disease over his head will escape both fate and society. But what about the other kids who sooner or later will have to capitulate to the demands of economics, and what about the Alices and Rays, the young men and women in their late 20s and early 30s who are searching too for a new life? And what about America in 1969, split between Arlo's generation and a straight world fearful of its own sons and defensive about its own values? "Alice's Restaurant" and Arlo Guthrie ask these questions and the rest of us must inevitably answer.

SOURCE: *Newsweek*, Sept. 29, 1969, Elkins Papers, Box 6.

Review in the *Boston Globe*
Marjory Adams, *Globe* Staff

When Arlo Guthrie was arrested in Stockbridge, Mass., for "littering," and thus escaped Army induction as an enemy of society (minor crime), there could have been no idea in his mind that this would lead to his becoming the star of a film. But he wrote the ballad, "Alice's Restaurant Massacree" about his

hangout in Stockbridge and the singer with the long, glossy curls turned into a hippie hero. . . .

My apologies to the Messrs. Herndon and Penn—but I think they were so influenced by Guthrie's real life adventures that they forgot to write a convincing script. What the picture has turned into is a collection of Guthrie adventures. Some of them are hilarious—the experiences in an induction center would be funny in any film. Some of them are tedious and take up too much footage—let the audience discover this for themselves. There are scenes which have been dragged in and obviously shortened to keep the picture down to 111 minutes.

Most of these should have been eliminated altogether. They don't add to the value of the production and give it a rather mish-mash quality.

"Alice's Restaurant" has been aimed to get the hippies off Cambridge Common and Boston's Charles St. and into the theater, I suggest.

As for the musical numbers—and how could you have a hippie film without rock and folk music—the numbers include "Songs to Aging Children," sung by Joni Mitchell; and Guthrie's "Car Song" and "Pastures of Plenty." Guthrie has composed original music for the film, which is an important contribution.

One of the better values is the photography by Michael Nebbia, and the outdoor sequences are excellent. The picture should be a sell-out in Stockbridge for the scenic beauty alone.

Of course, an LSD trip or a couple of Mary-Janes may keep an addict happy for a longer period than a two-hour movie, but why not try a film for a change of pace?

SOURCE: *The Boston Globe*, n.d., Elkins Papers, Box 6.

Second Sight
Richard Schickel

I am beginning to think that the most pernicious phrase of our age is that well-known battle cry "Never trust anyone over thirty." Personally, I couldn't care less if our junior citizens don't trust me, because I don't trust them either. But I notice a growing tendency among my fellow fuds—especially the artists and the intellectuals—to try to ingratiate themselves with their adolescent critics by agreeing with them, and that disturbs me. There is something undignified—not to say masochistic—about one's deciding not to trust his own generation. In effect he is declaring that he does not trust himself, and I submit that the quality that best characterizes our time is not the revolt of our youth but the supine acquiescence of so many elders in that revolt. I regard this not only as disloyal to our own not totally dishonorable histories but unhelpful to the kids themselves, who need a strong-minded, but not rigid, older generation against which to test themselves.

The occasion for these geriatric musings is *The Graduate*, a film which starts out to satirize the alienated spirit of modern youth, does so with uncommon brilliance for its first half, but ends up selling out to the very spirit its creators intended to make fun of. Its protagonist, Benjamin Braddock (Dustin Hoffman),

is introduced as the archetype of youthful angst, a sensitive lad whose collegiate triumphs in academics, athletics and campus activities fill his parents with delicious pride and fill him with an equally delicious disgust. By rights, his passage into the world of bourgeois striving should be smooth, but he loathes the whole idea of getting and spending. The more the adults around him urge him to take his first brisk strides toward success the deeper he sinks into a swoon of despair, the style of which is borrowed from certain nineteenth-century Russian novelists—a style that could not contrast more comically with the setting of upper-middle-class Los Angeles, preoccupied with sports cars, swimming pools and other sunlit status symbols, the awfulness of which director Mike Nichols catches with such wicked assurance.

Poor Ben. It is basic sex that undoes his enjoyable ennui. A determined young man can resist almost anything, but if his first seducer is an older woman (the wife of his father's partner, no less), he doesn't have a chance. His attempts to keep his cool when subjected to the consuming heat Anne Bancroft generates are hilariously pathetic, and the way he zigs when she zags will put you in mind of the best skits Mr. Nichols used to do with Elaine May.

Mr. Hoffman is the master of an infinite variety of soulful stares, half-finished thoughts and phrases, and of a wonderfully wheezy expulsion of breath that occurs whenever he is up-tight, which is most of the time. His sureness of insight is delivered with such technical precision that I have no hesitation calling it the year's most significant screen debut. Would that everyone connected with the film shared his sense of where he is and where he is going.

But once the May–September affair is established, things start to go wrong. Ben falls in love with his mistress's daughter (the lovely Katharine Ross), understandably upsetting her mom and causing a slightly sour stench to start pervading the comedy. We pass over the line separating farce from potential tragedy as Nichols and the scriptwriters, Calder Willingham and Buck Henry, try to compensate by subtly shifting their attitude toward Ben.

From anti- or at least non-hero, he suddenly starts to emerge as a romantic hero of the unhyphenated variety. Oh, he still fumbles and mumbles and trips all over himself, but the emotional distance from which we previously viewed him—a distance absolutely essential for satire—suddenly disappears. We find ourselves asked to stand shoulder to sympathetic shoulder with him as he attempts to rescue his (young) lady love from living death—marriage to a square.

The movie is less shrewd. Sentiment replaces even-handed toughness, and there is an attempt to force our acknowledgement of Ben's final superiority over environment and elders. He is likable enough, and they are indeed ghastly. But he is also desperately self-absorbed and shamelessly spoiled. And while he is seen to strike the poses of exquisite sensitivity and sensibility, nothing in his talk or actions seems to substantiate his right to criticize, withdraw or revolt from the society in which he has yet to take a man's place. The failure of Nichols and company to insist on this proof strikes me as a fatal defect in artistic, not to mention social, responsibility.

We are distracted from this shortcoming by a succession of gags that ill suit the darkening mood of the film's last half and which, unlike the preceding humor, have no organic connection with character or situation. The true tensions generated by the generation gap are thus avoided and, along with them, the deepest comic possibilities as well. It's a shame—they were halfway to something wonderful when they skidded on a patch of greasy kid stuff.

SOURCE: "The Graduate," Jan. 19, 1968, in Richard Schickel, *Second Sight: Notes on Some Movies, 1965–1970* (New York: Simon & Schuster, 1972), 160–162.

Follow-Up Problems

1. How do these films document the generational differences of the 1960s, and what solutions to that conflict are advanced? Relate these ideas to the political and social problems that lie behind this gap. Compare the two pictures as "coming of age" narratives.

2. As you link the themes in *Alice's Restaurant* to the policy debates of the 1960s, what do you see as the central issue explored? How is this point addressed on-screen?

3. What is the meaning of "community"? What evidence of a communal ethic appears in *Alice's Restaurant*? How would you compare these ideas with the world view and personal concerns of Benjamin Braddock in *The Graduate*?

4. Some scholars argue that *Alice's Restaurant* marks the end not only of a decade, but also of an important period in American popular culture. In what ways may this generalization be validated or rejected?

5. How is music used to reinforce the themes that dominate each film? Analyze the lyrics to "Alice's Restaurant" and "The Sounds of Silence." Explain their meaning in connection with the "feel" of the movies. As you think about the important social and policy issues debated in the 1960s, consider the great popularity of the song "Alice's Restaurant" among young Americans in 1968. Why do you think this song was so successful?

6. Compare *Alice's Restaurant* and *The Graduate* as depictions of the predominant youth culture of the 1960s. Which do you see as most representative of 1960s youth? Why?

Further Reading

Biskind, Peter. *Easy Riders, Raging Bulls: How the Sex-Drugs-and-Rock 'n' Roll Generation Saved Hollywood*. New York: Simon & Schuster, 1998.

Davis, Ronald L. *Celluloid Mirrors: Hollywood and American Society Since 1945*. Fort Worth, Tex.: Harcourt Brace & Co., 1997.

James, David. *Allegories of Cinema: American Film in the Sixties*. Princeton, N.J: Princeton University Press, 1989.

Man, Glenn. *Radical Visions: American Film Renaissance, 1967–1976*. Westport, Conn.: Greenwood Press, 1994.

May, Lary *Big Tomorrow: Hollywood and the Politics of the American Way*. Chicago: University of Chicago Press, 2000.

Mordden, Ethan. *Medium Cool: The Movies of the 1960s*. New York: Alfred A. Knopf, 1990.

Murray, Lawrence L. "Hollywood, Nihilism, and the Youth Culture of the Sixties: *Bonnie and Clyde* (1967)." In O'Connor, John E., and Martin A. Jackson. *American History/American Film: Interpreting the Hollywood Image*. New York: Frederick Ungar Publishing Co., 1979, 237–256.

Filmography

Easy Rider (Columbia, 1969).

Getting Straight (Columbia, 1970).

The Celluloid Documents

Alice's Restaurant (MGM, 1969).

The Graduate (MGM, 1967).

Chapter 13

Worker Solidarity and Human Dignity: *Norma Rae* (1979) and Southern Labor Activism

Throughout the twentieth century, organized labor struggled to bring unionism to the workers of the South, who made up the least privileged and most exploited regional labor force in the United States. As the bitter labor conflicts of the 1930s showed, labor's failure in the South did not always reflect a lack of interest on the part of working people in the potential benefits of organization. In 1933 and 1934, Southern laborers had flocked to the union banner in response to the new policies and encouragement of the Roosevelt administration. During the nationwide textile strike of 1934, textile workers challenged management in an effort to raise living standards through union organization. As a result of brutal management tactics, racial differences, and internal divisions within the workforce, the "uprising of 34" was suppressed and labor in the South suffered a major setback from which it has never fully recovered. With the collapse of the CIO's "Operation Dixie" in the immediate postwar era, the fate of unionism in the South seemed assured. Against the odds, however, union-minded workers continued to challenge management in the staunchly antilabor textile industry. In the 1970s, the film *Norma Rae* told the story of these efforts in the nonunion city of Roanoke Rapids, North Carolina. The result was a strong statement in labor's cause.

The Historical Background

Despite many handicaps, the Textile Workers Union of America (TWUA) and later the Amalgamated Clothing and Textile Workers Union (ACTWU) persisted in the effort to improve the lives of Southern textile workers by bringing them into the union family. Faced with the accumulated abuses of two generations, including harsh working conditions, long hours, and the hated "stretchout" with its uncompensated productivity increases, the newly diverse Southern labor force of the 1970s again considered the benefits of organization. In response, management used clever tactics to fight this new drive among workers who remained divided on the basis of both race and gender.

No Southern firm was more hostile to organized labor than the huge J. P. Stevens & Co., which employed 3000 workers in its seven plants in Roanoke Rapids, North Carolina. Here the company pushed its labor force to the limit, confident that it could hold off unionism as it had so many times in the past. Fear of unemployment, dependence on company housing, the influence of racial divisions, and an awareness of management's disciplinary methods had caused workers to accept low wages and harsh working conditions rather than challenge corporate power. In the early 1970s the company's position seemed strong.

Into this environment came the aggressive ACTWU organizer Eli Zivkovich, a West Virginia miner who worked against great odds to bring local workers into the union. One of several local union backers who aided in this drive was Crystal Lee*, who soon emerged as the central figure among those who were ready to break with the nonunion past. After an extended struggle, during which she lost her job at the Stevens plant, the union won a narrow victory in a result that shook the textile industry in North Carolina. What followed was a 6-year effort to secure a union contract, which the company stubbornly resisted. So dramatic was Crystal Lee's story that journalist Henry P. Leifermann chronicled her experience in a book-length account, *Crystal Lee: A Woman of Inheritance* (1975). Almost immediately, film producers Tamara Asseyeu and Alex Rose bought the rights to the story, which became the literary source for their cinematic characterization of Crystal Lee in *Norma Rae* (1979).[1]

This motion picture was not only a dramatic account of the union struggle for existence in Roanoke Rapids, but also a compelling tale of personal growth and self-realization. During the course of the film, viewers are able to observe the flowering of Norma Rae's sense of independence and worth as her consciousness of self is raised. Crystal Lee's full development as a strong woman occurred in the unsettled 1970s, a time when feminism was on the rise. Both the struggle over the Equal Rights Amendment and the *Roe v. Wade* decision (1973) raised public awareness of women's issues and mobilized a new generation of female activists. The events portrayed in the film are therefore consistent with one of the most important historical themes of the decade in which it appeared. The feminist themes appealed directly to both Asseyeu and Rose, who were themselves women deeply interested in producing socially conscious films. Moreover, the potential appeal of the topic promised to attract an increasingly politically aware female audience.

Historian Robert Toplin has noted that while *Norma Rae*'s sharp development of feminist ideas reflected the interests of its female producers, the powerful working-class themes were largely the contribution of director Martin Ritt. The liberal activist Ritt brought to the project a long history of emphasis on blue-collar topics in his previous work, which had included such films as *The Molly Maguires* (1970), *Sounder* (1972), and *The Great White Hope* (1970). Blacklisted in the 1950s, by the 1970s Ritt was committed to filmmaking that focused on social issues, which meant that Crystal Lee's story dealt with his longstanding interests. The result of Ritt's involvement was the brilliant expression of the spirit of union solidarity projected in *Norma Rae*,[2] one of the few Hollywood films to place organized labor in a clearly positive light. While feminist themes fill the film, the central message lies in its depiction of the successful union campaign. The impression left in the minds of most viewers was almost certainly the image of the defiant Norma Rae (Sally Field) standing atop a table brandishing the large sign displaying the hand-lettered message: "UNION."

---

*While she had three different surnames from separate marriages, Crystal Lee will be used throughout the text portion of this chapter.

While Ritt and his screenwriters, Irving Ravetch and Harriet Frank Jr., crafted a script that told the story from the union's perspective, they did confront the realities of labor organizing in the difficult Southern field. The picture frankly acknowledges worker resistance to collective action, which was itself a reflection of the South's painful labor history. Norma Rae encounters stiff resistance not only from the lowest of the working poor, but also from those favored workers who saw their meager existence as the result of company benevolence. Racial suspicions are openly dealt with, as are the pressures exerted by middle management on those who refused to toe the company line.[3] In addition, Norma Rae's healthy sexuality is presented against the background of grinding poverty that intensified the need for some release of the tensions resulting from hard living. Given the presence of such hardship, the appeal of unionism could be understood by even the least sympathetic viewer. The film's social realism makes the outcome, including the final vote for the union, entirely plausible, as it surely was in Roanoke Rapids.

While the J. P. Stevens campaign ended in union recognition, the future was not kind to the ACTWU. The company continued its fight and resisted the union's effort to negotiate a contract for 6 long years. Some scholars suggest that the film's appearance in 1979 may have influenced the company's decision to settle in 1980, though evidence is scarce. While labor and management finally arrived at an agreement, it is equally true that Crystal Lee lost her position at Roanoke Rapids and never returned to work for J. P. Stevens. Following the organizing campaign, she found other employment and eventually went to work for the union. The final blow to workers came in 2003, when the increase of foreign competition forced the plant's closure, which left the workforce reeling in an era of job contraction.

Despite the long-term outcome, *Norma Rae* had energized a new generation of textile workers, many of whom responded to the modern drive by the Union of Needle Trades, Industrial, and Textile Employees (UNITE), which has again begun to make a few gains in the Southern textile field, still a difficult region for American labor unions. The movie remains one of the strongest pro-union statements ever made in an American film, possibly Hollywood's finest. By remaining true to the original story and actual historical events, the picture succeeds in communicating a message of working-class dignity, personal integrity, and women's initiative. In so doing, it mirrors some of the critical economic and social themes of the historical era of which it is a product.

Analyzing the Film

You may analyze *Norma Rae* on several levels, starting with the way in which working-class Americans are represented. As you think about the working families portrayed on-screen, explore their responses to the union's organizational efforts. Note their reactions to Norma Rae's activities and account for the attitudes expressed. Your examination of working-class values and the factors that influence the workers in the film should take into consideration the origins and importance of divisions among the various elements in the workforce. Why was union organization so difficult for Norma Rae?

Your assessment of the working-class attitudes expressed in the film should lead you to think about a larger question posed by the filmmakers. What was the significance of regional identity as an influence on attitudes concerning labor and labor relations? The film raises the question of Southern uniqueness and self-conscious awareness of a separate regional identity, which may have influenced the response to the union's organizational initiatives. Do you think that the South is in some way different or distinct from the rest of the United States and therefore immune to the historical forces that have driven national social and economic life, including patterns of labor relations? Try to determine what might be different about the South, including social life and work experience, that affects attitudes concerning collective action.

As you consider these issues, pay special attention to the ethnic and racial composition of the Southern labor force as a factor in shaping attitudes towards organization. In what way was the historical segmentation of the Southern workforce employed as a management practice designed to influence worker consciousness of self-interest? Examine the interplay of individualism and community in the character of the Southern worker. How would you explain mutual suspicions among potential class allies? As you proceed with this analysis, think about the roots of class awareness and the prerequisites to class formation, asking whether these preconditions had been met among the workers of the American South.

Your analysis of class and race should also raise the question of sexual identity and gender roles as they appear in *Norma Rae*. As you study Norma Rae's character, observe the ways in which she challenges society's assumptions with regard to female roles. Think about sexual relationships, beliefs about sex, economic roles, and assumptions concerning appropriate female behavior. As you follow her increasing involvement in union organizing, contrast her activism with her father's and husband's outlooks on life, particularly in the workplace. What makes her different from her peers? Explain her behavior patterns, which seem to defy the social values and community mores accepted by most of her fellow workers. How are these behavioral tendencies related to the ideas circulating among feminists in the activist 1970s? How would you explain their appearance in a region apparently remote from the mainstream of liberal thought? Account for Norma Rae's choices, sacrifices, and initiatives, as well as her ultimate success (at least as far as the union campaign is concerned).

The outcome of this particular labor struggle was favorable for the union, and the film is clear in its sympathy for the workers and their organization. Review Chapter 10 and think about the themes that dominated *Salt of the Earth* (1954). Compare and contrast *Norma Rae* with the blacklisted film produced by the Independent Productions Corporation. Can you identify any themes that link the prounion statements of the two historical periods? Why do you think these ideas seemed reasonable in the 1970s but unacceptable in the 1950s? Assess the two films as expressions of modern conceptions of gender equity and social justice.

Norma Rae was an important breakthrough film for its time, in that it sent a strong prounion, worker-friendly message to theater audiences. Although changes are made in Crystal Lee's story, the film remains a fairly close account of actual events, which makes it a valuable document of not only 1970s feminism, but also the economic strivings of forgotten people, the poor whites and African-Americans of countless Southern mill towns, where unions worked to change the power structure and tip the balance in the struggle between local elites and powerless workers seeking dignity and self-respect.[4] In the early twenty-first century, unions have fallen on hard times both in the American South and in the nation at large. Yet the fight goes on in many out-of-the-way locations, where UNITE continues to fight for a newly diverse labor force seeking a place in the sun for workers at the bottom of the economic pyramid. For these seekers of social and economic justice,

Norma Rae provides inspiration, together with a reminder of the American worker's unrealized potential.

Thinking About Primary Sources

Because *Norma Rae* is based on historical events, the documents offer an opportunity to compare the actual facts with the cinematic representation of history. As you consider the accuracy of the filmmaker's account, ask whether the film may be studied as a truthful re-creation of actions taken and decisions made by men and women of previous generations. Do you think it is essential that films be absolutely faithful to the facts in such cases? As you compare the film and the newspaper account of Crystal Lee's personal experience, assess the picture as an account of historical events. Look for the similarities and differences in the celluloid and journalistic treatments of the experiences portrayed on-screen. While there may have been discrepancies between actual events and the filmmaker's representation of a historical situation, it is true that the spirit and social consciousness that penetrate this film bear substantial resemblance to the historical experience of those who lived the story played out on-screen. Where do reality, life, and art intermingle?

The filmmaker's success in representing historical reality is evident in organized labor's willingness to employ *Norma Rae* and Crystal Lee as weapons in the ongoing work of a struggling union movement. As you examine the press account of Crystal Lee's personal experience, try to determine what the union meant to the real-life counterpart of the picture's heroine. What does the union leaflet reveal about the labor movement's recognition of the film's power as an organizing weapon? Notice how the entire unionization effort transformed the life of the central character in the film. How does the on-screen account compare with the lived experience of the person whose life it portrays? In what way do the documents help clarify the effect of collective action on those who took up the union cause in Roanoke Rapids?

While the modern union movement has embraced this film and incorporated the picture into its organizational work, the film had an impact outside the world of work. It was widely acclaimed as an artistic triumph that developed important themes relevant to the social trends of the historical period in which it appeared. Use the reviewers' accounts to identify the dramatic and human themes that made *Norma Rae* both a box office and artistic success. In view of its release in a period of increased union difficulty, why do you think is was so widely accepted among movie audiences? If it did not reflect the experience of many union activists, other aspects of Norma Rae's experience appear to have struck a responsive chord for audiences of the late 1970s. Why was the picture critically acclaimed and enthusiastically received as a film of merit?

Beyond the reviewers' reactions, *Norma Rae* must also be examined for the way in which it valued the lives of working people. As the press accounts indicate, this film is set largely in a working-class world and the action occurs largely in the workplace itself. As you view the film and review the documents, think about the way in which the world of the worker is represented in this film: the sounds, sights, and experiences of the men and women who provide labor in an industrial economy. Use the primary sources and the film itself to open discussion of the ways in which human dignity, sexual identity, and racial pride can be maintained against the pressures exerted by an impersonal economic system.

In view of the union's challenge to widely held social assumptions, how was it possible to develop the union solidarity that is evident as the film reaches its conclusion?

Historical Perspective

The initial critical response to *Norma Rae* was overwhelmingly positive. Within the modern labor and women's movements, it has been embraced as a statement of resistance to the economic and social trends of the postmodern era. At the time of its release, the picture was widely regarded as a bold and realistic expression of honest social concern. It received several Academy Awards, including one for best actress to the impressive and sensitive Sally Field, whose career was rescued from her earlier casting as the frivolous "Flying Nun." Not surprisingly, it also remains a favorite of American labor activists, who still employ the film as an organizing tool and instrument of labor education. In your opinion, does the film speak to the current generation? Why or why not?

Despite union recognition for the real workers of Roanoke Rapids, the negotiation of a union contract was a long and difficult process. The tension-ridden labor-management relationship in this locale mirrored the serious obstacles to unionization evident in the 1970s, when the American labor movement was embarking on a period of bitter struggle that continues to this day. It is possible to observe in the J. P. Stevens story, as told in the barely fictional *Norma Rae*, some of the problems and management techniques soon to plague American unions in the late twentieth century as their membership shrank in the face of government indifference and employer assertiveness. Thoughtful analysis reveals that the problems of the Southern worker were to become the problems of union labor nationwide in the shift from an industrial to a service economy in the 1990s. At the dawn of a new century, a shocked but militant American labor movement looks again to the unorganized worker for future growth. Today, minority and low-wage workers constitute the new target of unions forced by necessity to renew their commitment to the "have-nots" of the modern labor force. For them, the story of Crystal Lee, as told in *Norma Rae*, has been an inspiration and a call to the social conscience of an earlier era in which unions made a difference for Southern workers in a weakened position. Yet that vision is clouded by an economic future dominated by the new global economy in which great corporations join in the race to the bottom of the world wage scale.

For modern students, *Norma Rae* opens the door to a clearer understanding of American social and economic history in the 1970s. Thanks to the collaboration of the left-wing activist Martin Ritt and two socially committed female producers, it is possible to revisit a historical period when feminism was fresh and militant. The character of Norma Rae sends a strong message of women's social engagement in economic struggles to revolutionize their status and opportunities. Equally bold is the film's endorsement of collective action as a force for social change. *Norma Rae* provides a snapshot of active labor in the pre-Reagan era, an image of collectivism against which the student may evaluate the strident individualism so evident in twenty-first century America.

Endnotes

1. Robert Brent Toplin, *History by Hollywood: The Use and Abuse of the American Past* (Urbana, Ill.: University of Illinois Press, 1996), 205–206.

2. Paul Buhle and Dave Wagner, *Hide in Plain Sight: The Hollywood Blacklistees in Film and Television, 1950–2002* (New York: Palgrave-Macmillan, 2003), 197.

3. Tom Zaniello, *Working Stiffs, Union Maids, Reds, and Riffraff* (Ithaca, N.Y.: ILR Press, 1996), 177–178.

4. Toplin, 296, 219–220.

THE PRIMARY SOURCES

The first document in this set, a newspaper account of Crystal Lee's personal story, reveals that unionism changed her life in a significant way. As a follow-up, two critical reviews from 1979 assess the film *Norma Rae*. Finally, an ACTWU leaflet demonstrates the value of Crystal Lee's story and the film as organizing weapons.

CRYSTAL LEE SUTTON ASSERTS THE NEED FOR UNION ORGANIZATION

The Need for Union Organization
Megan Rosenfeld, *The Washington Post*

Some of Crystal Lee Sutton's life and times were dramatized in "Norma Rae," but after the victorious election that ends the movie, the real-life scene was that she had to find a job. The first one she got after she was fired from J.P. Stevens in Roanoke Rapids, N.C., was at a fast-food fried chicken stand in another town. It was the worst job she ever had. This was after she'd been fired from J.P. Stevens for "insubordination," and after her story had been written up and was about to be dramatized on celluloid as "Norma Rae."

. . .

The best job she ever had, in fact was at J.P. Stevens, where she folded towels into boxed gifts sets for $2.65 an hour.

Her job now is, essentially, giving interviews. She is paid as an organizer for the Amalgamated Clothing and Textile Workers Union (ACTWU), the union that won the right to represent the workers at the Roanoke Rapids plant on Aug. 28, 1974. After she was fired by J.P. Stevens—she says it was for copying down from the company bulletin board a letter she describes as anti-union and racist; the company says it was for "insubordination"—she was reinstated by a court order in 1977 and awarded $13, 436 in back wages. She went back to work for two days just to "prove a point."

For the last four years the ACTWU has organized a boycott against J.P. Stevens products, an anniversary they are celebrating this week by bringing Crystal Lee Sutton to Washington and showing "Norma Rae" on Capitol Hill. A spokesman for J.P. Stevens said the company's sales and profits last year were "record highs," a claim the boycott organizers question.

That battle of the union (originally it was the Textile Workers Union of America, which merged with the 500,000-member ACTWU in 1976) and the company has become one of the epic sagas of union-versus-management history—one fought more with the modern tools of public relations than old-fashioned fists. It's been going on since 1963, through the courts and the National Labor Relations Board and the living rooms and meeting halls of the South, and there is no end in sight.

"Norma Rae" is probably one of the most powerful tools the labor movement will ever have. Its moving saga of simple good and bad, of plain people winning against the bad-guy establishment, has inspired thousands and certainly clinched a career uplift for actress Sally Field, who will always be remembered for holding up that UNION sign.

. . .

She grew up in Roanoke Rapids, a town divided clearly into workers and managers, as she recalls it.

"All my life, textile workers were looked down on. The doctors and lawyers and managers didn't want their children to associate with us. They always had new clothes, they were the smartest. They were the cheerleaders, and the majorettes—anything outstanding, it came from your higher class of people."

Crystal Lee Sutton is a simple, straightforward woman. She has long hair that she hasn't cut for 15 years. At 39, she no longer wears makeup, and her clothes are often something she has made herself. Her celebrity, which is increasing now that she is on the union payroll and being built up as a labor heroine, has helped insure that her children do not suffer from the classism she was so conscious of.

. . .

So she went to a meeting of the fledgling union, which was being organized by 55-year-old Eli Zivkovich, a former coal miner from West Virginia who was transformed in the movie "Norma Rae" into a zippy young intellectual type from New York. In the climactic scene of the movie, after Norma Rae has been fired, she stalks back into the plant, writes the word UNION on a piece of paper and stands on a table to show it to all her co-workers above the din of the machines and is then carried out by police. That really happened.

What didn't really happen is that everyone lived happily ever after once the union won the election. For one thing, there is still no contract signed between J.P. Stevens and the ACTWU in Roanoke Rapids.

For another thing, Cookie and Crystal Lee split up. "Before, I was working second shift, so like in the mornings I could do the laundry, I could clean the house and I could cook dinner before I went to work. But when I got involved with the union, I was working at trying to help Eli organize people. And there was just no way that I could do what I had done before because then I had two jobs. And a lot of times I'd come in with hamburgers instead of having a hot meal on the table. And he thought I had to do the laundry every day. And that started causing trouble. And he didn't want his wife to get involved, because like he told me, 'You're going to get fired.'

He didn't want me to go to the first union meeting because is was held in an all-black church. . . . Every day I'd come home and he'd say, 'Well, you made it through one more day, did you?' So then when I did get fired I was mad as hell. I was mad at the company but then I was mad at him because he said I would get fired."

After their separation in 1976, she found it hard to get a job and believes it was because of her union activities. She moved more than 100 miles away, where her job at the fried-chicken stand was the first of many she subsequently had.

Now she is married to Lewis Sutton, who works at a unionized textile plant. "His dues help to pay my salary," she said with a smile. Her oldest son works in construction and has a 3-month-old baby (his wife just graduated from high school and will soon start work at a "towel place.") Her son Jay sought her help in organizing workers at the hotel where he worked last fall (the election produced a tie vote). Elizabeth, her daughter, is finishing high school—much to Crystal Lee's relief. "She hates school as much as I did."

The movie, which won an Academy Award for Sally Field but not a cent for Crystal Lee Sutton, was based on a book detailing the lives of Southern textile workers. Sutton thinks it is "funny. It made me cry in parts and it made me laugh . . . I just thought if they're going to spend millions of dollars making a movie, I wanted it to be a good educational union movie, not a soap-opera love story like you can see every day on TV."

. . .

For Crystal Lee Sutton, who is "trying to be less emotional as I get older," the union changed her life. She is a believer. Her life, and those of her friends, is far away from the exclusive halls of Capitol Hill, the company board rooms or even the inner circles of union power. She is the kind of person who takes it on the chin when a union official is convicted of corruption, or when the sophisticated outwit the simple.

"I can only talk about what I know," she said. ". . . The textile worker is an important worker. We didn't have any respect. We didn't have decent working conditions. I just decided if it was okay for other people to have unions, I didn't see why we couldn't."

SOURCE: *Washington Post*, June 11, 1980.

TWO CONTEMPORARY EVALUATIONS
OF *NORMA RAE* AS A DEPICTION OF WORKING-CLASS LIFE

Norma Rae, an Old-Fashioned Film
Film Library Quarterly

Norma Rae throws off her married lover and marries Sonny before she ever marches down to Reuben Warshovsky's (Ron Liebman) office for her union card. Nor is she suddenly transformed into a militant by Reuben's presence; in two different scenes, including the opening one, we learn that Norma Rae has a long history in the mill of angrily complaining about working conditions. Her healthy sexual appetites are part and parcel of her essential steeliness, her ability to talk back to her father and the mill supervisor or, most clearly, her quiet but unflinching determination to go ahead with her plans for the union meeting in spite of her pastor's opposition. "I never was a good Girl Scout," she says to Reuben as she signs up with the union, and that's why we like her, right from the start.

Norma Rae's sexuality is not a problem, but Ritt and the screen-writers have an awful time with the men in her life. It is as though in creating a strong, fully realized woman character they could not devise true-to-life male counterparts. There is no real sexual magnetism between Sonny and Norma Rae; their kisses are almost embarrassingly chaste. The film, meanwhile, builds up an enormous emotional bond between Norma Rae and Reuben, although what has been taken by reviewers as sexual attraction between Norma Rae and Reuben is more likely her curiosity about his greater experience and a profound need for him to recognize the validity of her life. The tension which arises between them has little or nothing to do with whether they have sex or not, but rather with the nature of their working relationship. Reuben is utterly self-absorbed and patronizing. He seems to see Norma Rae strictly as an entrée to the factory. He comes down quickly and wrathfully on her when she dares to criticize a male unionist who comes in late; he explains her new leadership role in the most condescending manner possible to a bewildered Sonny; he belittles her traumatic arrest and jail stay. While he says he couldn't have done it without her, he never acknowledges her as an equal.

The virtue of *Norma Rae* is that so much of it takes place at work. We hear the deafening noise of the power looms, we see the lint float through the air, we sense the heat of the windowless rooms. To its credit *Norma Rae* devotes no time to the personalities of the bosses. It shows instead how value is expropriated in the work process itself, watched over by white male supervisors, uniformed in short-sleeved dress shirts and even shorter haircuts. These men embody the racist, the sexist, and the class structure of southern textile mill production, as is made explicit when Norma Rae is fired in the manager's office for copying down a notice designed to exploit racial tensions between workers. Trying to hold her own with a boss who has just ordered her to call her husband so he can "come and fetch" her, the camera shows Norma Rae seated in front of a solid wall of faceless male torsos, ties and zippers.

Norma Rae is an old-fashioned film. It underplays collective action and never develops the secondary characters, many of whom are black. It must include a love story, though it does not make clear who is in love with whom. Ritt works from the auteurist tradition, and he was unable to relinquish any script control to the real Norma Rae.

SOURCE: Edward Benson and Sharon Hartmann Strom, "Crystal Lee, Norma Rae, and All Their Sisters," *Film Library Quarterly* 12 (1979): 22–23.

Textile Mill Organizing
Raleigh News and Observer

In May 1973, Crystal Lee Jordan was fired from her job at the J.P. Stevens & Co. Rosemary plant in Roanoke Rapids. When the police chief came to take her away, he found her standing atop her work table, holding over her head a card marked "UNION" and turning slowly so fellow workers could see.

Soon after that, she took her three children aside to tell them things they'd never known before: that one child's father, her first husband, was dead; that she had never married her second child's father; and that she had had affairs with several other men as well.

That scene and her arrest were recounted in a 1973 *New York Times Magazine* article and a 1975 book ("Crystal Lee: A Woman of Inheritance") by the same author, journalist Henry Leifermann. Martin Ritt (director of "Hud," "Hombre," "Sounder," "Conrack" and "The Front") read Leifermann's account.

"I simply fell in love with that incredible woman," Ritt recently explained to a New York interviewer.

. . .

The movie follows these events so closely, in fact, that McCormick said he was considering filing an invasion-of-privacy lawsuit against the producers on behalf of Crystal Lee Sutton, her former husband Larry "Cookie" Jordan and former union organizer Eli Zifkovitch.

Aside from its legal ramifications, "Norma Rae" marks a number of cinematic firsts. For starters, it presents a union-management struggle without easily identifiable, on-screen villains.

Moviegoers are not accustomed to a union without communists, corruption, racketeering and goons. And, on the other side, they're used to sadistic sweatshop supervisors they can hiss at. But for "Norma Rae," Ritt did not cast a single, stock, reactionary redneck.

Instead, the film's violence is embodied in the choking, backbreaking work routine of the dusty mill itself.

The scream of the machines temporarily deafens one woman. The pressure of a speed-up order causes one man's arm to go numb. A supervisor pauses, urges him to hold out until his next scheduled break, and hurries away. A moment later, the man drops dead.

The supervisor is not the bad guy here—there's someone else rushing around him, watching him, pressing him to get more and more from his workers, faster and faster. We never meet the source of this evil, just as we never see the originator of the company's radically divisive antiunion tactics.

At the core of the movie is Norma Rae herself, who starts out tired of her sex life, dissatisfied with her job as a weaver and unsure of her ambitions. Sally Field has now shed the giggly "Flying Nun" habit that carried her through a decade of lightweight film and television comedy, and her performance as Norma Rae is solid and hearty.

Because the film focuses on Norma Rae and her relationships with her husband (Beau Bridges) and a young, Jewish union organizer (cheerfully and earnestly played by Ron Leibman), we do not see much of the tremendous group effort that must be involved in any union campaign.

Most of the time, Norma Rae seems to be the only mill worker fully committed to the union. And, except for a brief visit from two other union officials, we see only one union organizer handling the entire campaign.

Norma Rae and the union man go skinny-dipping, share a few meals and discuss Dylan Thomas as they fight for their cause. Clearly, as Mrs. Sutton said, union organizing is neither so simple or "that much fun."

While they simplified the story of the union struggle, however, the makers of "Norma Rae" avoided oversimplifying the eloquent story of one woman's own struggle.

SOURCE: Bruce Siceloff, "Moviegoers Get New View of Textile Mill Organizing," *Raleigh News and Observer*, March 18, 1979, AFL-CIO Civil Rights Department, Southeast, Papers, Atlanta, Special Collections, Pullen Library, Georgia State University, Box 1799, Folder 152.

Norma Rae
ACTWU

THE *REAL* 'NORMA RAE' WAS FIGHTING J.P. STEVENS

If you've seen or heard about the widely hailed movie, *Norma Rae*, you know about Sally Field's superb portrayal of a southern cotton mill worker trying to organize a union in the face of vicious, illegal resistance by a powerful textile company.

Norma Rae, as you perhaps did not know, is based on the lives and experience of Crystal Lee Sutton and the textile workers in the South who have been waging a 17-year battle for justice against J.P. Stevens & Co.—the nation's second largest textile firm and one of the most notorious union-busters and labor scofflaws in history.

Crystal Lee Sutton was a major figure in the 1973–74 organizing battle for the seven Roanoke Rapids, N.C. plants of J.P. Stevens ("O.P. Henley" in the movie). Her efforts, as well as those of the other employees, climaxed in an historic first union victory at Stevens in August 1974. Crystal Lee paid a price for her involvement—spending a night in jail, then "blacklisted" throughout the industry.

But the Hollywood "happy ending" even in a film as realistic as *Norma Rae*, was only an encouraging episode in the lives of Crystal and her fellow workers. J.P. Stevens has been found guilty of failure to bargain in good faith with the Roanoke Rapids workers, who still do not have a contract more than five years after the election.

Crystal Lee is here to tell the workers' stories and her experiences as a woman facing horrible conditions in southern textile mills. At Stevens, she witnessed safety and health violations, relatives and friends suffering from Brown Lung, discrimination against women, blacks and the disabled, and special treatment for those who curried favor with the "bosses."

Crystal Lee stood up, spoke out about these abuses, and urged her fellow workers to protect themselves by forming a union. Today she is speaking out across the nation to aid all of the workers in the 81 Stevens plants.

Please join us to hear her story. Compare the real events to the scenes in the movie and learn why your support is vital.

JOIN CRYSTAL LEE SUTTON AND ACTWU—HELP THE J.P. STEVENS WORKERS

- **Don't** Buy Stevens products at local retail stores under the brand names of Utica, Fine Arts, Gulistan, Tastemaker, Meadowbrook, or Forstmana.
- **Do** write or phone local retailers to tell them to stop carrying or advertising J.P. Stevens products.
- Sign a pledge card to volunteer for the campaign.

SEE NORMA RAE AND HEAR "THE REAL NORMA RAE" AT THE LOCAL SHOWING

Time and place on the reverse.

ACTWU, 770 Broadway, New York, N.Y. 10003

SOURCE: "The Real Norma Rae Was Fighting J.P. Stevens," March 1980, AFL-CIO Civil Rights Department, Southeast, Papers, Box 1799, Folder 152.

Follow-Up Problems

1. In what ways were the South and Southern workers different from those in other sections of the United States? In what ways were they similar? How would you account for the attitudes encountered by labor organizers?

2. How did Norma Rae challenge the gender roles accepted by her community? How were these themes related to the social environment at the time of the film's production and release?

3. In what ways did Norma Rae need the union for her own reasons? How were her personal desires and needs fulfilled by Reuben and the organization?

4. What evidence do you find in this film to suggest that racial and/or ethnic biases were a factor to be addressed by Southern union organizers?

5. What is to be learned from this film about the prerequisites for social or political leadership? What techniques are used in promoting union organization in this film? How did Reuben's and Norma Rae's methods differ?

6. In your view, is the primary message in *Norma Rae* a feminist argument or an endorsement of collectivism and unionism? Using illustrations from the film, defend your position.

7. How was union solidarity created among members of the worker community? What resources and techniques were used by employers to contest the drive for unionization? Why were they not successful in preventing the union victory?

Further Reading

Bodnar, John E. *Blue Collar Hollywood: Liberalism, Democracy, and Working People in American Film*. Baltimore: Johns Hopkins University Press, 2003.

Conway, Mimi. *Rise, Gonna Rise: A Portrait of Southern Textile Workers*. New York: Anchor, 1979.

Hall, Jacqueline. "Disorderly Women: Gender and Labor Militancy in the Appalachian South." *Journal of American History* 73 (September 1986): 354–382.

Leifermann, Henry P. *Crystal Lee: A Woman of Inheritance*. New York: Macmillan, 1975.

Lev, Peter. *American Films of the '70s: Conflicting Visions*. Austin, Tex.: University of Texas Press, 2000.

Puette, William J. *Through Jaundiced Eyes: How the Media Viewed Organized Labor*. Ithaca, N.Y.: ILR Press, 1996.

Toplin, Robert Brent. "Norma Rae: 'A Female Rocky.'" Toplin. *History By Hollywood: The Use and Misuse of the American Past*. Urbana, Ill.: University of Illinois Press, 1996.

Zaniello, Tom. *Working Stiffs, Union Maids, Reds, and Riffraff: An Organized Guide to Films About Labor*. Ithaca, N.Y.: ILR Press, 1996.

Filmography

Alice Doesn't Live Here Anymore (Warner Brothers, 1974).

Nine to Five (Twentieth Century Fox, 1980).

Silkwood (Twentieth Century Fox, 1983).

The Celluloid Document

Norma Rae (Twentieth Century Fox, 1979).

Chapter 14

Coming Home (1978):
Vietnam and the Uncertain Future
of American Foreign Policy

During the early years of the Cold War, American foreign policy had made its first priority the effort to checkmate Soviet expansionism in Europe. The result of this European emphasis had been the declaration of the Truman Doctrine and containment policy in 1947. Yet starting with the Chinese Revolution in 1949 and the police action in Korea one year later, American policy makers turned their attention to the growth of Communism and the outbreak of wars of national liberation in the underdeveloped world. From the Truman administration on, the Communist-led Vietnamese revolution had worried diplomatic and political leaders in the United States. The result was a gradual increase in American aid and advice to the government of first Ngo Dinh Diem and later a series of military governments in South Vietnam, all intended to halt the advance of Communism in Southeast Asia. The unfortunate result was the alignment of the United States against the forces of nationalism, which since World War II had been fused with the Communist movement led by the charismatic patriotic leader Ho Chi Minh.

The by-product of the United States' intervention in Vietnam was a burgeoning American military presence in the jungles of Southeast Asia, where the North Vietnamese and their Viet Cong allies fought a spirited and ultimately successful guerrilla war that they perceived as an extension of their long war for independence and self-determination. As American casualties mounted, a domestic antiwar movement grew dramatically, first among the young on college campuses but before long spreading into middle-class groups and even the nation's Congressional leadership. Thus, an ugly and divisive by-product of the Vietnam War was widespread dissatisfaction and outright opposition at home. Following American withdrawal from Vietnam in 1973, deep suspicion of both the executive branch of government and the military haunted the public. This disillusionment was captured by several films related to the Vietnam War, including the very successful *Coming Home,* which caught the imagination of war-weary moviegoers as the 1970s came to an end.

The Historical Background

Faced with widespread domestic dissent, Democratic President Lyndon Johnson chose not to run for reelection in 1968 rather than risk a humiliating defeat. In the bitter electoral contest that followed, Johnson's surrogate, Senator Hubert Humphrey, was narrowly defeated by former Republican Vice President Richard M. Nixon. During the campaign, Nixon claimed to have a secret plan to end the war, which could not be revealed lest the enemy take advantage of this knowledge to strengthen its resistance. Once elected, President Nixon concluded that given the state of public opinion, the war could not be won in time to prevent total political disruption at home. As a result, he launched the "Vietnamization" program, which emphasized gradual American withdrawal and increased responsibility for South Vietnamese forces. A sad by-product of this policy was both the extension of high casualty rates for American troops and uncertainty about the future of the South Vietnamese government. A related problem was the collapse of military discipline within the armed forces and the emergence of a serious problem caring for those Americans who returned physically and emotionally wounded.

While the invasion of Cambodia in 1970 and the return of increased numbers of disillusioned Vietnam veterans gave the antiwar movement a new lease on life, the president was able to undercut opposition to the war by ending the draft and emphasizing the problem of law and order on American streets. Although critics continued to resist Nixon's policies, the Paris Treaty of 1973 defused the war as a foreign-policy issue. After the completion of the Vietnamese revolution with the Communist occupation of Saigon in 1975, Americans experienced a period of amnesia with regard to the war and tried to forget the conflict and the social and political disruption it had created.

Symptomatic of that social distress was the motion picture industry's inattention to Vietnam as a subject for topical films. During the war itself, profit-minded Hollywood producers often avoided Vietnam-related subjects that might remind the public that the war was confusing and divisive. In contrast to the predominance of war-themed films during World War II, the bulk of the movie industry output of the 1960s ignored the conflict that was tearing American society apart. The most prominent exception was John Wayne's distorted account of the Vietnam experience, *The Green Berets* (1968), which did reasonably well at the box office. Attacked mercilessly by the critics, the film depicted a war unrecognizable by most Vietnam veterans and out of step with the stories of failure and frustration that filled the news columns of the daily press. More in tune with the cynicism of the times was the indirect statement on Southeast Asia made by the successful Korean War film *M.A.S.H.* (1970), which expressed disillusionment akin to public attitudes concerning the Vietnam quagmire.

Not until the late 1970s, with the war safely behind them, were most American filmmakers ready to explore Vietnam and its impact on American society and those who had fought and shouldered the burden of defeat. In 1978 and 1979, several thoughtful accounts of the war and its victims reached the screen in the first wave of meaningful cinematic commentary on a war gone wrong. Among the breakthrough films were the combat pictures, all of which captured the complexities and contradictions of American intervention in Vietnam. Of these, none was more powerful than Francis Ford Coppola's dark and brooding nightmare epic, *Apocalypse Now* (1979). At least two productions from this period, *The Deer Hunter* (1978) and *Coming Home* (1978), addressed the impact of the war on the home front and the veterans who returned, physically and emotionally scarred by the combat experience. While these pictures may have distorted some aspects of the conflict, they found an audience ready to grapple with the war's meaning. The reception afforded the two films suggested that the American public, which had been deeply affected by the war and the sometimes devious means by which the United States government had made its commitment and presented the war on the home front, was at last prepared to emerge from the dreamy state that had removed Vietnam from popular discussion. At last, Americans seemed able to examine the past and consider its lessons.[1]

Perhaps no film of this era so captured the veteran's dilemma as *Coming Home*, a sensitive and moving treatment of the returning serviceman's sense of dislocation, as well as the disruptive impact of the Vietnam War on the home front. This film, which was highly critical of American involvement in Vietnam, captured the loss of faith in government that plagued the Vietnam generation and expressed itself in the cultural fragmentation of the 1970s. Focusing on the readjustment problems of one paralyzed veteran, Luke Martin (Jon Voight), the picture crafted a new sympathetic image of the Vietnam veteran as an intelligent, worldly, and independent critic made wise beyond his years by a disastrous war.

At first bitter, then just angry, Luke eventually evolves into a thoughtful commentator on the war. His rehabilitation is eased by a love affair with a young officer's wife, Sally Hyde (Jane Fonda), whose initial shallowness is erased by her experience as a hospital volunteer and the ensuing relationship with Luke following his release. In this way, the film suggested that the pain and bad memories of a frustrating war might be erased by the healing power of love. Although the casting of Fonda in the part raised doubts among veterans (she was an outspoken antiwar activist and had visited North Vietnam during the conflict while Americans were imprisoned in Hanoi), the film was an artistic success that most critics treated as an important statement on the Vietnam War.

Analyzing the Film

Coming Home was an original, creative motion picture that recorded widespread American disillusionment with the crusade against Communism in Southeast Asia. The message is clearly delivered by Luke at the film's conclusion during his speech before an audience of wide-eyed high school students. As you consider his comments, try to identify his key point concerning the moral justification offered for the war. Equally moving was the suicide of Sally's husband (Bruce Dern), who upon his return from Vietnam is unable to reconcile his wartime experiences with the hollow rhetoric of his military and political superiors, much less his wife's unfaithfulness. By the end of the film, few of the major characters have been left unscarred by the wartime experience, though Luke at least has accepted himself and his disability, an outcome that promised that the wounds of war could be healed.

The powerful influence of Vietnam on the film's characters reflected the shattering effect of the war on the pride and self-confidence of the United States, a nation still in rehabilitation four years after the war's end. In *Coming Home*, American audiences were able to survey the human wreckage of foreign policy gone astray but also found hope that reconciliation could be achieved at home. While Luke is physically damaged, he has become emotionally whole. What evidence do you find that he is moving towards reintegration into the fabric of American society? While sentimental in its treatment of Luke's readjustment, the film documented the hopes of an American public not yet recovered from the Watergate-era revelations of dishonesty among political leaders and the humiliation of a war gone wrong. *Coming Home* is a revealing primary source to be examined in your search for a better understanding of American political attitudes on the eve of the Reagan era.

Your analysis of this film should begin with an examination of American public opinion in 1978 with regard to the Vietnam War. Remember that *Coming Home* appeared well before the public discussion of the 1980s that led to a new willingness to embrace Vietnam veterans. Place this film in the context of public demoralization over the outcome of the Vietnamese revolution in 1975. As you study *Coming Home,* try to understand the mixture of confusion and humiliation felt by Americans as they watched the North Vietnamese tanks roll into Saigon. Be equally aware of the widespread uneasiness and disagreement about the impact of the war on those who had fought and returned. What does the treatment received by Luke both in the hospital and after his release reveal about the public response to the Vietnam veteran in the 1970s?

As you think about American attitudes in 1978 concerning Vietnam, ask what the implications of the war were, both short-term and long-term. Consider the image of the American military as it was projected in *Coming Home* and relate that impression to the state of public opinion in the late 1970s. Beyond widely held viewpoints towards the armed forces, you should also think about the course of American foreign policy in the 1980s and 1990s. Your review of public attitudes towards overseas military interventions in this historical period will lead you back to the policy impact of the Vietnam War. Try to understand the much-discussed "Vietnam syndrome" against the background of the issues raised directly or indirectly by this film. Compare the attitudes towards overseas military interventions implied in *Coming Home* with American viewpoints expressed in 1991 and 2003 when the wisdom of two Gulf wars became the subject of public debate.

Your examination of this film should also include an effort to link its lead actress, Jane Fonda, to the sharp public disagreement over American involvement in the Vietnam War. Recall Fonda's role in the antiwar movement of the early 1970s, including her involvement in the Indochina Peace Campaign, and watch for evidence of her views in the film narrative. A member of a well-known political family of socially engaged movie people, she was in a position by 1978 to select those films that best expressed her opinions. Recall that her father, Henry, had played a key role in making the important social protest film *Grapes of Wrath* in the 1930s. The Vietnam War had become the most important political issue of his daughter's era. *Coming Home* was actually the only Vietnam-related picture Fonda made, but in it, she played a role that legitimated radical political action in opposition to a war that had raised serious moral issues. While Sally Hyde's new-found political awareness seemed respectable, the personal involvement with Luke that helped advance her radicalization tended to sanitize the hard public issues the film was raising.[2] As you explore the policy questions that lay beneath the sentimental love story, try to link the film's message with Jane Fonda's personal political life. How did the film justify antiwar activism? In what way did Fonda's very public engagement in political activity relate to the smaller debates that went on in many households and families as Americans tried to come to terms with the Vietnam War and its outcomes?

Thinking About Primary Sources

The question of Jane Fonda's outspoken politics may be approached through careful analysis of the documentary evidence concerning her public life. For an understanding of her stance on the war, review the excerpt from her Radio Hanoi broadcast, which has so enflamed many veterans since the war's end. How does this document help you to understand the content of the film and the motives of those who made it? Your analysis of the linkage between Fonda's personal views and her on-screen work will take you back to her political agenda and use of celebrity to engage in public debate over a controversial issue. Compare her activism with the activities of high-profile media personalities in your own time and assess the legitimacy of their well-publicized actions. Identify similarities and differences in the historical situations as you make your judgment concerning the public lives of well-known entertainment figures, such as Sean Penn and the Dixie Chicks, who have commented publicly on the war in Iraq. As you consider Jane Fonda's political actions, remember that she was part of the younger generation that in the 1960s had broken with the Cold War era's anti-Communist consensus. Think about this film as a reflection of the 1960s generational conflict and a delayed expression of that era's revulsion against the Vietnam War.

While the war is subject to sharp critical analysis in *Coming Home*, it is possible to identify in the picture a new attitude towards veterans who sometimes found themselves in an inhospitable environment. Search the public opinion polls and the words of General Norman Schwartzkopf for insight into public attitudes towards the war and those who fought it. Connect these views with the experiences of Luke Martin as he undergoes rehabilitation and healing. Study Luke's character for clues to changes in the public perception of Vietnam veterans, including those whose injuries had created new and challenging readjustment problems. What evidence does the film offer of the unprecedented psychological traumas sometimes believed to affect the Vietnam veteran? What does it reveal about public attitudes, hospital treatment, and family relationships? Compare the Vietnam veteran's experience with the readjustment problems faced by those who returned from combat in previous and subsequent wars and decide what, if anything, made Vietnam unique.

Careful attention to the themes found in *Coming Home* will enable you to gain insight into the nature of the Vietnam War, the composition and views of those who resisted, the experiences of returning veterans, and the difficulty the American civilian population had in adjusting to a war that destroyed the vision of omnipotence that had underlain the foreign policy of the United States since 1945. Examine the words of Nicholas Lemann for evidence of the war's long-term impact on public attitudes towards authority in the post-Vietnam era. What distinction does he draw between his generation's views and those of his parents' generation? As you examine Lemann's words, reflect on the film as a useful primary source that provides insight into the sweeping impact of the Vietnam war not only on the American public in the 1970s, but also on the next generation, which until the 1990s was haunted by the "Vietnam syndrome." *Coming Home* provides a point of departure for discussion of Vietnam's lessons for American leadership in the post–Cold War world. Think about the Vietnam experience and its implications as you assess the global reach of American military might in what some scholars argue promises to be a new imperial age.

Historical Perspective

Despite Jane Fonda's wartime trip to Hanoi as a member of the Indochina Peace Campaign and the image she had projected in her personal political life, *Coming Home* achieved wide popularity, even more than some of the other breakthrough films of 1978 and 1979. Not only was it a box office smash, but it was a huge critical success. Most reviewers lavished praise on Director Hal Ashby and screenwriter Waldo Salt, as well as Fonda, Voight, and Dern. Its clearly stated perspective on the war penetrated the film, which suggests that the American public was prepared in 1978 to accept the basic argument it advanced. While the picture clearly contained generous amounts of poorly concealed political propaganda mixed with a romantic vision of redemption through the power of love, these flaws were overshadowed by its forthright yet sensitive treatment of handicapped veterans' emotional distress, physical discomforts, family disruptions, and sexual anxieties. In short, it directly addressed some of the serious domestic problems resulting from the Vietnam War. In this respect, it was a film for the times.

The Hollywood establishment agreed with this analysis, as evidenced by the public acclaim bestowed on the film. Nominated for eight Academy Awards, *Coming Home* received Oscars for Best Screenplay, Best Actor in a Leading Role, and Best Actress a in Leading Role. Fonda and Voight also received Golden Globe awards, while the picture received a total of five nominations. The film had been a huge financial winner, and nothing succeeds like success.

While these plaudits spoke eloquently to the picture's triumph as cinematic art, it was equally important as a historical milestone. The frankness of its approach to veterans' rehabilitation won it a place as a valuable historical document that marked the gradual willingness of American film audiences to confront the cost of a war widely regarded in the late seventies as the product of tragically mistaken national interest. Since the 1970s, the movie industry has been more willing to address the Vietnam War and those who fought it in a sympathetic way. While Vietnam veteran Oliver Stone's films were influenced by his own experience and political perspective, Stone's *Platoon* (1986) and *Born on the Fourth of July* (1996) have advanced a more sophisticated understanding of the war and its consequences.[3] More recently, Mel Gibson's *We Were Soldiers* (2002) has embraced not the war, but the sacrifice and heroism of those who fought in the Battle of the Ia Drang Valley, thus offering a distinctly different perspective on the Vietnam experience from that which was evident in the 1970s.

The response to *Coming Home* revealed a viewing public that was willing to read lessons from the recent past. Most Americans had been deeply affected by the "Vietnam syndrome" and were ready to apply the war's lessons to future foreign-policy decisions, as in the case of the Gulf War in 1991, when the specter of Vietnam haunted the Congressional debate over a war resolution. More recently, the lessons of Vietnam have again surfaced in the controversy over the wisdom of the Iraq War of 2003–2004 as well as the question of the Vietnam-era service of both President George W. Bush and Democratic presidential candidate John F. Kerry. Vietnam, it seems, is with us still. By examining *Coming Home* in its immediate historical context, you will be able to grasp the deep soul-searching of the Vietnam generation and the vague uneasiness about the conduct of foreign affairs that gripped the nation in the Carter years. Use the film to gain a more sophisticated understanding of a nation coming to terms with a failed war and a broken foreign policy.

Endnotes

1. The evolution of the Vietnam War film is fully discussed in Michael Anderegg, ed., *Inventing Vietnam: The War in Film and Television* (Philadelphia: Temple University Press, 1991).

2. Anderegg, "Hollywood and Vietnam: John Wayne and Jane Fonda as Discourse," in Anderegg, *Inventing Vietnam*, 21–22.

3. The cinematic work of Oliver Stone has received sophisticated treatment in Robert Brent Toplin, ed., *Oliver Stone's USA: Film, History, and Controversy* (Lawrence, Kans.: University Press of Kansas, 2000).

THE PRIMARY SOURCES

Jane Fonda's political perspective on the Vietnam War is clearly stated in the excerpt from her broadcast from Hanoi during her trip to North Vietnam in 1972. Next, in 1978 reviewer Seth Cagin argued that *Coming Home* must be understood as an element in the ongoing debate over the war. The state of American public opinion on Vietnam is revealed in the excerpts from the Lou Harris poll conducted at the direction of the Carter administration in 1978. Public views of the war and the military in the postwar era are discussed in the memoir of Vietnam veteran General Norman Schwartzkopf. His words reveal the long-term impact of the war on the armed forces. Finally, the war's influence on the thinking of the post-Vietnam generation is documented by the frank comments of journalist and social commentator Nicholas Lemann, editor of *Texas Monthly*, in 1978.

JANE FONDA'S RADIO HANOI BROADCAST

Broadcast
Jane Fonda

This is Jane Fonda. During my two week visit in the Democratic Republic of Vietnam, I've had the opportunity to visit a great many places and speak to a large number of people from all walks of life—workers, peasants, students, artists and dancers, historians, journalists, film actresses, soldiers, militia girls, members of the women's union, writers.

. . .

As I left the United States two weeks ago, Nixon was again telling the American people that he was winding down the war, but in the rubble-strewn streets of Nam Dinh, his words echoed with sinister (words indistinct) of a true killer. And like the young Vietnamese woman I held in my arms clinging to me tightly—and I pressed my cheek against hers—I thought, this is a war against Vietnam perhaps, but the tragedy is America's.

One thing that I have learned beyond a shadow of a doubt since I've been in this country is that Nixon will never be able to break the spirit of these people; he'll never be able to turn Vietnam, north and south, into a neo-colony of the United States by bombing, by invading, by attacking in any way. One has only to go into the countryside and listen to the peasants describe the lives they led before the revolution to understand why every bomb that is dropped only strengthens their determination to resist.

. . .

But now, despite the bombs, despite the crimes being created—being committed against them by Richard Nixon, these people own their own land, build their own schools—the children learning, literacy—illiteracy is being wiped out, there is no more prostitution as there was during the time when it was a French colony. In other words, the people have taken power into their own hands, and they are controlling their own lives.

And after 4,000 years of struggling against nature and foreign invaders—and the last 25 years, prior to the revolution, of struggling against French colonialism—I don't think that the people of Vietnam are about to compromise in any way, shape or form about the freedom and independence of their country, and I think Richard Nixon would do well to read Vietnamese history, particularly their poetry, and particularly the poetry written by Ho Chi Minh.

SOURCE: U.S. Congress, House Committee on Internal Security, *Travel to Hostile Areas*, HR 16742, Sept. 19–25, 1972, p. 7671.

A REVIEWER'S ANALYSIS OF *COMING HOME* AS A STATEMENT ON THE OUTCOMES OF THE VIETNAM WAR

Coming Home
Seth Cagin

The first images we see of *Coming Home* are set in a Veteran's Administration hospital. Guys in wheelchairs watched by others confined to beds are playing pool when someone asks whether, given the chance, they'd return to fight in Vietnam. Voices are raised when one man in a wheelchair doubts another, equally crippled, who insists he would do it all over again. The year is 1968, passions run high, and opinion about the American involvement in Vietnam is bitterly divided.

. . .

Indeed, set among the living debris of war, the love between Sally and Luke is a potent regenerative force. Over the course of their relationship, Luke's bitter cynicism is tempered by Sally's love for him. He moves from the hospital to his own apartment and starts a difficult reentry into mainstream society. As for Sally, she is influenced by Luke into questioning the war. In her newfound independence, she lets her straight hair go curly, she buys a fast car, and she rents a house on the beach. Like the culture they're part of, both Luke and Sally undergo numerous changes in the space of a few short months.

. . .

Unfortunately, despite Bruce Dern's magic, anguished performance as a man who has lost everything, *Coming Home* fails to resolve the tensions that the first four-fifths of the film so successfully evoke. Incidents that lead up to the final confrontation between Sally, Luke, and Bob are contrived: for some obscure reason, the FBI informs Bob of his wife's infidelity. Worse still, where the rest of the film explores specifically how the times affected people, in Bob Hyde's case we are asked to assume that Vietnam drove him insane.

Coming Home was clearly a labor of love on the part of its collaborators who are among the most talented artists in Hollywood. Jane Fonda, for instance, not only stars in "Coming Home," but also instigated the project and coauthored the original story. The film's intensity of feeling attests to the fact that for Fonda, Jon Voight, Hal Ashby, and others, Vietnam and the attendant cultural tumult of the 60s had consequences that reach easily into the present. . . .

The big question now may be whether movie audiences are ready for a full confrontation with anguish only recently relegated to history. It will be a shame if people stay away from *Coming Home*, for, though the film never shies away from the depressing destruction that came of Vietnam, at its heart there beats a dramatic, tonic love story. The note that resounds throughout *Coming Home* is as much a hopeful one proclaiming the power of love as it is a cry of pain.

. . .

At times, it all seems too much, as if there was an overabundance of talent at work. *Coming Home* ambitiously stretches—past a comfortable reach—striving to be a definitive chronicle of the waste and subsequent renewal America underwent in the 60s. Though the film is less than that, it is considerably more than a simple story of a love triangle. Despite its flaws, *Coming Home* is a jolting meditation on the harrowing compromises, loud debate, and deep pain that characterized the Vietnam years.

SOURCE: Seth Cagin, "Coming Home," n.d., ca. 1978, Wisconsin Historical Society, *Coming Home* Clipping File.

Public Opinion Poll
Louis Harris and Associates

A particularly significant aspect of public and Vietnam-era veterans' attitudes toward the war in Vietnam is revealed by their reaction to two projective statements included in this study:

"The trouble in Vietnam was that our troops were asked to fight in a war we could never win."

"The trouble in Vietnam was that our troops were asked to fight in a war which our political leaders in Washington would not let them win."

While only 38 percent of the public strongly agree with the first statement (a proportion identical to that found in our 1971 survey of public attitudes toward Vietnam-era veterans), fully 47 percent agree strongly with the second. Vietnam-era veterans are even more firmly convinced that American troops lost this war not because of a failure of arms, but rather because of a failure of the country's leadership to exercise the necessary political will. Thus, while only 37 percent of all Vietnam-era veterans strongly agree that "the trouble in Vietnam was that our troops were asked to fight in a war we could never win," fully 72 percent strongly agrees that "the trouble in Vietnam was that our troops were asked to fight in a war which our political leaders in Washington would not let them win." And, while 37 percent of veterans who saw heavy combat in Vietnam agree strongly that we could never have won the war in Vietnam, fully 82 percent agree strongly that the war was lost because the nation's political leadership would not let these troops win that conflict. Among the public as a whole, those with prior military experience are those most persuaded (64 percent) that America's failure in Vietnam was a failure of the will of the country's political leadership.

The disillusionment of Vietnam veterans with the country's political leaders is further elaborated by their responses to two parallel statements. Only 37 percent of Vietnam veterans agree that "senior military commanders in Vietnam deliberately misled our political leaders in Washington about the way the war in Vietnam was going." By contrast, 76 percent of Vietnam veterans agree that "our political leaders in Washington deliberately misled the American people about the way the war in Vietnam was going."

. . .

The assessment of both the public and Vietnam-era veterans is that the impact of the war in Vietnam on the United States and American society has been overwhelmingly negative.

In the advance telephone survey of 1,200 adult Americans conducted for the Veterans Administration by Louis Harris and Associates in September 1979, we find that when asked, "What would you say have been the two or three most important effects of the war in Vietnam on the United States and American society?" most Americans find little reason to remember American involvement in the Vietnam conflict with pride. Two main themes appear in the public's response:

34 percent mention the deterioration of the nation's confidence in its institutions, especially the government;

33 percent cite the harm done to the veterans who served in Vietnam, especially the fatalities.

Other responses volunteered by the public are also overwhelmingly negative. These include 22 percent of the public who mention negative international effects (in terms of either national prestige or refugee problems), 18 percent who cite the harm done to the economy (either through inflation or the misallocation of resources), 14 percent who say the war caused social divisiveness (between factions, generations or races) and 7 percent who cite increased drug use. The only positive effect mentioned by a substantial number (14 percent) is that the peace movement and the popular opposition to the war might help keep the nation out of other conflicted, halfhearted involvements in the future. In addition, a scant 2 percent say that the war stimulated the economy. Overall, the public's verdict is that the war was not merely a mistake, but a costly one.

The most striking of the public's volunteered statements about the effects of the war in Vietnam focus on the price paid by the veterans of that war. It has often been noted that the war in Vietnam occasioned a loss of public confidence in the country's major institutions, and it is not surprising to have this confirmed by the public in this study. Less often noted is the public's concern for the effects of the war on the veteran. The data indicate that these two effects of the war are of equal salience to the general public. There is a high level of concern among the public for the personal price paid by the veteran, in terms of both direct effects (death and disability) and indirect effects (being badly treated by the rest of society and having employment, psychological and family problems).

The members of the Vietnam Generation (those 25–34 years of age) cite most effects more often than do other age groups, reflecting the impact that war in Vietnam had on them. They place special emphasis on the effects on veterans (42 percent) and loss of public confidence in institutions (40 percent).

. . .

On the basis of the findings from the advance survey, the Harris firm further explored attitudes toward the impacts of the war.

Here, our strategy was to present the public, veterans of the Vietnam era, educators and employers with a list of problems volunteered by the public in the advance survey, and, for each, to inquire among all four groups as to whether they felt that the Vietnam war caused the problem, contributed heavily to the problem, contributed slightly to it, or had, in their opinion, nothing at all to do with the problem.

Not surprisingly, the problem that all four groups most directly attribute to the war is the plight of the Vietnamese refugees who have become known as "boat people."

Aside from these predictable findings, the problem that the public believes to be most related to the impact of the war on the United States is "young people's hostility toward the government," cited by 57 percent of the public as being caused, or heavily contributed to, by that war. Vietnam-era veterans (63

percent) are even more persuaded of this than is the public as a whole.

Better than half of the public and 70 percent of Vietnam-era veterans cite the "loss of U.S. prestige and influence in other countries" as a major effect of the Vietnam war on America. An even 50 percent of the public and 60 percent of the Vietnam veterans cite "people's lack of trust in government to do what's right" as one of the war's consequences.

. . .

The extent to which Vietnam-era veterans see these problems as being caused or contributed heavily to by the war is strongly associated with the degree to which they are alienated from the American political and social system. For example, while 47 percent of the "low alienation" group believe the war is to have been a major causative factor in "young people's hostility toward the government," among "high alienation" Vietnam-era veterans that proportion is fully 68 percent.

White veterans of the Vietnam era are more likely to blame the war for perceived "loss of U.S. prestige and influence in other countries" than are black Vietnam-era veterans (72 percent to 61 percent), but these black veterans are more likely than whites to see the war as the major cause of the country's current problems with drug abuse (65 percent to 52 percent), alcohol abuse (40 percent to 32 percent), and the current high rate of inflation (44 percent to 30 percent).

Expectedly, Vietnam-era veterans who believe our involvement in that conflict was a mistake or who actively resisted or demonstrated against the war are more likely than other Vietnam-era veterans to see the war as a major cause of all these problems.

The American public takes a very positive view of the Vietnam-era veteran, and especially of those veterans who served in Vietnam itself. This is further confirmation of the public's separation of the Vietnam war from soldiers who fought in it. The public feels the war was a mistake but does not hold these warriors responsible for either the war or its consequences.

. . .

Thus, despite the increased feeling that "veterans who served in Vietnam are part of a war that went bad" (54 percent strongly agree today versus 37 percent in 1971), the public does not equate their participation in that ill-fated effort with personal complicity. Rather, what we detect is a growing feeling of sympathy for veterans of the Vietnam War. Thus, since 1971, the proportion of the public agreeing "veterans of the Vietnam War were made suckers, having to risk their lives in the wrong war in the wrong place at the wrong time" has increased from 49 percent to fully 64 percent.

SOURCE: Louis Harris and Associates, Public Opinion Poll, ca. 1979, in A. D. Horne, ed., *The Wounded Generation: America After Vietnam* (Englewood Cliffs, N.J.: Prentice-Hall, 1981, 81–90.

GENERAL NORMAN SCHWARTZKOPF ASSESSES VIETNAM'S IMPACT ON THE ARMY

Impact Assessment
General Norman Schwartzkopf

"The public seems to have lost faith in the military because of the war in Vietnam," Schwartzkopf continued. "After all, we're only an arm of policy of the United States government. We're public servants. If the public no longer has confidence in us, then what good are we? I think right now in the officer corps there are an awful lot of people who feel confused about the public's attitude. I came into the army because I wanted to serve my country. I took an oath saying that I'd protect this country from all enemies foreign and domestic—I didn't say I'd determine who the enemies were! I said I'd merely protect the country after somebody else made that determination. So this war comes around in Vietnam; the duly elected government officials send us, the Army, to fight the war. We go to Vietnam and fight the best way we know how—not needlessly wasting lives for the most part. We did the best we could, and it dragged on and on and on. Many of us were sent back a second time, a lot of young officers have been sent back a third time. I'm talking about the kid who went over first as a platoon leader, returned as a captain and commanded an infantry company and then, a third time, went over as a major. Three times he's gone off not knowing whether he was going to come back alive. He's got ten years in the service and in that ten years has been separated from his wife and family for three of them. He didn't go off to Vietnam because he wanted to. He was sent by his country. Now, suddenly, public opinion is violently antimilitary as though it had all been the kid's idea! So here he is, a young Army major with ten years' service and he's going to sit down and think. 'All of a sudden I'm being blamed for all this,' and he hurts. He's hurt! He doesn't understand why he's bearing the brunt of this animosity."

. . .

". . . My feeling now is that we should get out. What we're gaining by being over there is no longer significant, and of course, we are getting out. We're withdrawing much faster than I ever thought we could. But I think this is an important point: the government sends you off to fight its war—again, it's not *your* war, it's the government's war. You go off and fight not only once, but twice, okay? And suddenly a decision is made. 'Well, look, you guys were all wrong. You're a bunch of dirty bastards. You never should have been there!' Now this is going to make me think long and hard before I go off to war again. This is me, Norm Schwartzkopf, personally. I don't think there will ever be another major confrontation where huge armies line up on both sides. If that happens, it's inevitably going to be nuclear weapons and the whole thing. So I think all wars of the future are going to be—and again, God forbid, I hope we don't have any. War is a profanity. . . .

. . . but if we do have a war, I think it's going to be similar in nature to Vietnam and Korea. Limited in scope. And when they get ready to send me again, I'm going to have to stop and ask myself, 'Is it worth it?' That's a very dangerous place for the nation to be when your own army is going to stop and question." . . .

. . . "I *hate* what Vietnam has done to our country! I *hate* what Vietnam has done to our Army! . . ."

SOURCE: D. D. B. Bryan, *Friendly Fire* (New York: G. P. Putnam's Sons, 1976), 304–305.

CYNICISM IN THE POST-VIETNAM GENERATION

The Post-Vietnam Generation
Nicholas Lemann

I was born in 1954, which makes me about 10 years younger than the other contributors in this book and, I suppose, a member of the post-Vietnam generation. Here is how the war directly touched my life: I registered for the draft when I turned 18, and the following year I was given the lottery number of six. I remember summoning forth in myself at the time some mixture of panic and self-pity, but given the capacities of a 19-year-old in that department it was pretty halfhearted. It was 1973, and I knew in my heart that I wasn't going to be called. I filed a perfunctory request with my draft board for conscientious objector status because that was what one did, and was turned down. As I recall it, the draft board said that my application seemed to be born out of convenience. That was perfectly true; I didn't object; and a few weeks later the draft was ended. That's my experience with the Vietnam War.

. . .

Mostly because of Vietnam, I grew up regarding every American president in my lifetime as a pathological war criminal. Eisenhower was a general—what further proof was needed? Kennedy got us to Vietnam. Johnson started the escalation and bombing. Nixon said he had a secret plan to end the war and then kept it going for five years after his election. Naturally this attitude on my part logically extended itself, so that I also believed, as did my friends, that America could do nothing right; that it was force of evil in the world; that, therefore, the country's leadership was also stupid and venal (hadn't it produced all those evil presidents?); and that the whole idea of order and authority was probably wrong too. I can remember two political events in college that caused people to go out in the streets on warm nights, whooping and yelling with joy: the resignation of President Nixon and the fall of the government of South Vietnam to the Communists. Underneath everything is different. We have no center. Our parents did.

SOURCE: Nicholas Lemann, "The Post Vietnam Generation," Horne, 209–210.

Follow-Up Problems

1. What does the film's conclusion imply about the place of Vietnam veterans in American society in 1978? To what extent is the film an accurate historical snapshot of attitudes towards veterans? Is the film honest in its treatment of casualties? Explain.

2. In what way does this film, when viewed in combination with the documents, reveal the short- and long-term consequences of the war in Vietnam? What was the lasting, future significance of the Vietnam experience for American attitudes concerning overseas intervention, as well as the foreign policy of the United States?

3. What Vietnam War films of recent years are you familiar with? How do their portrayals of Vietnam and Vietnam veterans in the 1990s differ from the Hollywood films of the late 1970s? How would you account for the differences?

4. How did the war change Luke, Bob, and Sally, as depicted in the film? What does the evolution of their characters reveal about the political argument of the film?

5. How would you compare *Coming Home* and *All Quiet on the Western Front* as expressions of public sentiment on war in their respective generations?

Further Reading

Anderegg, Michael. *Inventing Vietnam: The War in Film and Television*. Philadelphia: Temple University Press, 1991.

Auster, Albert, and Leonard Quart. *How the War Was Remembered: Hollywood and Vietnam*. Westport, Ct.: Praeger, 1988.

Cook, David A. *Lost Illusions: American Cinema in the Shadow of Watergate and Vietnam, 1970–1979*. New York: Charles Scribner's Sons, 2000.

Dittmar, Linda, and Gene Michaud. *From Hanoi to Hollywood: The Vietnam War in American Film*. New Brunswick, N.J.: Rutgers University Press, 1991.

Muse, Eben J. *The Land of Nam: The Vietnam War in American Film*. Metuchen, N.J.: Scarecrow Press, 1995.

Toplin, Robert Brent, ed. *Oliver Stone's USA: Film, History, and Controversy*, Lawrence, Kans.: University Press of Kansas, 2000.

Walker, Mark. *Vietnam Veteran Films*. Metuchen, N.J.: Scarecrow Press, 1991.

Filmography

Apocalypse Now (Zoetrope, 1979).

The Boys in Company C (Golden Harvest/Columbia, 1978).

The Deer Hunter (EMI Films/Universal, 1978).

The Celluloid Document

Coming Home (MGM, 1978).

Chapter

Unfinished Business:
Do the Right Thing (1989) and
the Escalation of Social Tension

Ever since the production and premiere of *The Birth of a Nation* in 1915, the subject of African-American history and the representation of blacks on the screen had been controversial and sometimes divisive. While a rich body of all-black "race films" presented strong African-American characters in control of their destinies, mainstream Hollywood productions typically confined black actors to limited subordinate roles during the 1920s and 1930s. In most cases, these films perpetuated long-held stereotypes different only in degree from those presented in the silent era. As we have seen, the release of *The Negro Soldier* during World War II, while done for propaganda purposes, did reflect an awareness among government officials and military leaders that many Americans still lived with gross misconceptions concerning black life and character.

Hollywood's new sensitivity to the problem of race relations and the African-American quest for social justice gave rise to a series of postwar message films, including *Home of the Brave* and *Pinky* in 1949. Not long after the Supreme Court's *Brown* decision declared segregated education unconstitutional, the young African-American actor Sidney Poitier appeared in *The Blackboard Jungle* (1955), launching a long career that was to make him the nation's leading black screen performer and a popular figure with both black and white audiences in the 1960s and 1970s. In the racially explosive 1960s, as the modern civil rights movement crested, Poitier reached his peak influence with such strong statements of racial dignity as *The Defiant Ones* (1958) and *In the Heat of the Night* (1967), edgy films that reflected changing times, including the rise of racial assertiveness in the black power and black nationalist movements. Poitier's strong but integrationist image reached a climax with *Guess Who's Coming to Dinner* (1967), a picture that expressed a liberal argument for racial healing at a time when the nation's cities were ablaze with what seemed the fires of disintegration. Because of its strong integrationist message, this film reached a broad audience with its call for racial accommodation. From the 1970s on, however, gradualism in social change seemed dated. More to the point were serious questions about the future of interracial cooperation, many of which surfaced in Spike Lee's brutally frank treatment of urban racial tensions, *Do the Right Thing* (1989).

The Historical Background

Following the death of Martin Luther King Jr. in 1968, the time for nonviolent solutions to the racial problems of the cities ran out, and by the 1970s black America floundered without a unifying theme or captivating leader. By this time, diverse African-American voices had grown in intensity, including those that asserted black pride and called for black control of the black community. As modern scholarship has shown, Sidney Poitier's image, while reassuring to white liberal audiences, seemed strangely out of touch with hopelessness in the nation's urban African-American community. Not far behind the trends, Hollywood now turned to a series of "blaxploitation" films, most devoid of strong themes but satisfying to urban black audiences impatient with the pace of social change and economic improvement. These films featured sexually aggressive, larger-than-life, strong, and sometimes violent African-American figures who usually achieved their goals (which often involved meeting their personal needs). Typically operating within the confines of the black community, these black superheroes exploited an African-American audience seeking role models that reinforced black pride in a world that offered them relatively little real opportunity to succeed.

Against this background of drift, a new black artist emerged in the mid-1980s to revise these images and strengthen the African-American claim to a place in modern American society. Having come to maturity during the "blaxploitation" era, young filmmaker Spike Lee never drew inspiration from traditional cinematic art or artists. After completing film school at New York University, Lee set out to transform the black image on-screen by portraying African-Americans as real people with complex motives and lifestyles. He established an independent base for his production company, Forty Acres and a Mule Filmworks (a reference to the unfulfilled promise of post–Civil War Reconstruction), and proceeded to follow his own lights to explore the modern African-American experience. By locating his operation in Brooklyn, his home territory, Lee underscored his freedom from the restrictions imposed by the Hollywood system.[1] After two modest successes in *She's Gotta Have It* (1986) and *School Daze* (1988), he solidified his image as a proponent of social realism with a controversial exploration of urban racial tensions in a powerful study of urban race relations, *Do the Right Thing* (1989).

Set in Lee's own Bedford-Stuyvesant district of Brooklyn, *Do the Right Thing* is partly rooted in historical events, including the Howard Beach incident in which a young black man was killed as a result of a confrontation with Italian-American youths. Equally significant as part of the historical context for this film was the reality of racial tension in 1989, which had reached fever pitch as a result of the widely publicized Central Park rape of a white jogger by a group of African-American men. Within this historical setting, then, Lee's exploration of ethnic and racial conflict in Brooklyn burst upon the screen with intense force. While some black critics had expressed disappointment in his earlier work as lacking in revolutionary potential, mainstream observers now saw in *Do the Right Thing* a recipe for violence on a wide scale.

In this film, Lee created a rich portrait of an African-American neighborhood with all the nuances of youth, age, anger, accommodation, and varied personalities. While the conclusion is violent, on the way to this result the picture reveals the complexity of the many value systems present within the community. Because of its intensity and the controversial theme, some critics feared that *Do the Right Thing* would spark urban riots. Lee countered with the argument that he had merely exposed the reality of urban life in America, including a culture that "valued a white man's pizzeria over a black man's life."[2] There can be no doubt that the violent content of this picture touched a sensitive nerve within both the movie community and the audiences that were stunned by the directness of its argument.

Analyzing the Film

In his cinematic study of urban America, Lee focuses on the ethnic and racial hatreds expressed by the neighborhood youths who patronize Sal's Famous Pizzeria, an Italian-American business establishment operating in the heart of Brooklyn's Bedford-Stuyvesant neighborhood. While Sal seems the racial moderate, he and his sons, Pino and Vito, are unable to compromise with his African-American customers over the simple issue of including photographs of black athletes in the gallery of sports heroes on the walls of a business establishment supported by a largely black clientele. To the intense beat of "Fight the Power" (Public Enemy), the militant "Buggin' Out" and brooding but proud "Radio Raheem" force the issue and provoke a confrontation with Sal, which ends in police intervention. While the black delivery man, Mookie (played by Spike Lee), is a crossover figure who communicates with both white employer and African-American friends and neighbors, even he is forced to take sides after the death of Radio Raheem as a result of police brutality. Symbolically taking up arms in the racial struggle, he heaves a garbage can through the pizzeria window, an act followed by the torching of the building by angry neighborhood youths. As the beat goes on, the flames give way to sharply contrasting commentaries on violence by Martin Luther King Jr. and Malcolm X.[3] Viewers are left to choose the right thing; but what is the right path?

The film gives no definitive answer to this central question, but the issue raised was meaningful to urban African-American youth in the late 1980s. Without a doubt, the filmmaker wants to communicate a socially relevant message; at the same time, he is fully aware of the socioeconomic context in which his work is to be received and perceived. Lee's film was intended to both entertain and teach audiences, both white and black, who were themselves sharply aware of the interracial conflict that underlay the surface of civility in the United States at the dawn of the 1990s. While the story is told from an essentially black viewpoint, the diverse target audience is challenged to answer Lee's leading question as the film rolls on to its white-hot conclusion. In a nation soon to witness further urban police brutality as well as the divisive Los Angles riot of 1992, his query was, in a deadly serious sense, America's question.

As you study *Do the Right Thing,* be sure to take into consideration the historical context, especially the controversial use of excessive force by urban police. Be aware of the realities of neighborhood policing and sometimes tense police-community relations, especially in urban centers like New York. The first question to pose, therefore, involves the connection between the themes in Lee's film and the facts of everyday life in the cities of the United States. How is the New York Police Department portrayed in the film? Do you believe Lee has painted a truthful picture? How would you account for the film's solid box office performance as well as the largely favorable critical response?

As you turn to textual analysis, note that each of the film's characters is a symbolic figure and that, in some way, each is flawed. Identify both their strengths and weaknesses, and notice how each fits into the wider fabric of the local community. Overall, Lee provides viewers with a portrait of a neighborhood with major problems and a severely damaged population. Consider, for example, the place and meaning of work in this community. Examine and evaluate the various solutions advanced for the neighborhood's problems, and relate them to the actual realities of urban black life in the 1980s and 1990s. As you consider Lee's description of the community's people, think of them in comparison with the images of African-Americans you have seen in *The Birth of a Nation* and *The Negro Soldier*.

As you explore these issues, focus on the social problems that further contribute to the racial explosion at the end of the film. Try to separate individual character flaws from socially constructed dilemmas. Notice the presence of black rage, cynicism, and hopelessness, depending on the characters involved, and explore the explanations for those responses to ghetto life. Consider the relevance (or irrelevance) of the traditional civil rights argument to the problems of modern urban youth. How are generational differences revealed in the film? Locate the characters, if any, who seem to represent the long-standing vision of equal opportunity and assess their place in this modern tragedy.

As you think about the bearers of Lee's political perspective in this narrative, concentrate on Mookie, who is a complicated and conflicted man. While he seeks self-improvement, there is also a complacent side to his behavior. Ask what message his striving and mediating communicates to the viewing audience. Moreover, observe Mookie's actions between the killing of Radio Raheem and the burning of Sal's Famous Pizzeria, with an eye to the social outcomes of his behavior. How does he channel his anger, and indirectly that of the mob, away from violence against persons to an attack on property and property rights?

As you think about the trashing of Sal's white outpost in the African-American community, turn your attention to the community Lee describes. Although his Bedford-Stuyvesant neighborhood is a teeming seedbed of constant racial tension among whites, Hispanics, Koreans, and the African-American majority, there are other aspects of city life strangely absent from Lee's community. Evaluate the film's version of the urban ghetto and the relative calm that prevails in Lee's account of street life in Bedford-Stuyvesant, giving particular attention to social problems that fail to appear. What realities of urban life are missing in this film? How would you explain the filmmaker's apparent inattention to these hazards of life in urban America?

In Lee's Bedford-Stuyvesant, some hard realities of urban life are replaced by a sense of community and a block culture that has its own internal logic, rules, and relationships. This informal community is presided over by "da Mayor" (Ossie Davis), who urges Mookie to "do the right thing," without ever telling him what that thing is. It appears that "da Mayor," who is uncertain about what should be done by or for his community, represents the paralysis of old civil rights advocates confronted with urban social and economic challenges that defy easy solutions. Think about the phrase "the right thing." Do you think Mookie has followed "da Mayor's advice by the film's conclusion?

In one more way, the picture's outcome tests your analytic powers. Not only has Lee left the definition of "the right thing" unclear, but he has also fired a parting shot at the audience with the riddle posed by the statements of King and Malcolm X. You must compare the two comments and determine, if possible, which message is consistent with the filmmaker's perspective on the right solution to the African-American dilemma in urban America.[4] As the recent debate over the long-term impact of the *Brown* decision of 1954 reveals, the promise of the civil rights movement has not yet been realized. What was once a constitutional and legislative issue has become a class problem in modern America. The final puzzle in *Do the Right Thing* lies in Spike Lee's challenge to find a workable solution to a thorny problem that will at once defuse the racial powder keg and bring stability to the explosive inner cities of our time.

Thinking About Primary Sources

Your analysis of *Do the Right Thing* will be enriched by an effort to understand the racial climate and historical circumstances that form the setting for the film's narrative. You might begin this process with a careful reading of the report of the National Advisory Commission on Civil Disorders, which recorded the conditions of urban life and the state of American race relations in 1968. Once you have considered the problems identified in this document, look ahead to the 1990s and determine how much the urban environment had actually changed since the great riots of the late 1960s. Note that just three years after this film appeared, the nation witnessed yet another urban disaster when the Los Angeles ghetto was once again set ablaze in the violence following the announcement of the verdicts in the Rodney King case. Similar events continued to occur at the dawn of a new century in places like Cincinnati, New York, Los Angeles, and other urban centers where ghetto life and police-community relations had not changed much since the sixties. As you think about the ways in which the film's story line was rooted in the realities of ghetto life, as described in the primary sources, reflect upon the implications of Lee's scenario for the future.

Against this background, consider the available responses to the social and economic repression that was the life experience of many ghetto dwellers as the twentieth century moved towards its conclusion. Think about the periodic outbreaks of violence that plagued urban America as one possible reaction to the conditions that prevailed in many of the nation's largest cities. As you try to understand this self-destructive activity, use the words of Spike Lee as a source to gain some insight into urban violence. Assess his argument concerning the potential impact of his film on audience behavior. Under what conditions does Lee believe that violence can seem rational? How do you react to his conclusions?

As you review Lee's comments, search for an indication of the filmmaker's intent in shaping the film. Do the documents shed light on Lee's objectives? If so, try to determine whether he has achieved his goals in this film. As you follow the narrative, work to uncover the message communicated in *Do the Right Thing*. Observe the reviewer's reaction to the picture. Do you think Lee succeeded in stimulating the debate he had hoped for? As you consider Roger Ebert's analysis, be aware of the controversy surrounding the film and the debate over the definition of "the right thing."

Finally, consider the techniques employed by the filmmaker in his attempt to make his point in the strongest possible way. In what way are words used to set the tone for the narrative? How do the music lyrics from Public Enemy's "Fight the Power" contribute to the gradual buildup of tension that is to end in violence? Observe the combination of music, words, dance, and inflammatory interpersonal rhetoric that leads steadily towards an outburst of emotion and hostility as the film reaches its shocking conclusion. As you absorb the comments of Dr. King and Malcolm X while assessing the human and physical wreckage, ask which words offer the most useful guidance in understanding the film and plotting a direction in the future. Based on your knowledge of recent American history, to what extent have the questions Lee raised been resolved in your own time?

Historical Perspective

Do the Right Thing clearly established Spike Lee as a talented filmmaker with a message to communicate and the ability to successfully produce films loaded with topical political content. Given the status of racial tensions and police-community relations in New York and other urban centers in 1989 and subsequent years, his work has direct relevance as a meaningful historical document of its time. To the surprise of some observers, the film was a hit with both black and white audiences. As a result, it was a moderate box office success that confounded some of the doubters who saw it as unnecessarily provocative. *Do the Right Thing* did not set off a wave of race riots; what it did do was show in a dramatic way that Lee was capable of understanding the tangled web of interracial conflicts present in many of America's urban communities today. Though African-American critics sometimes attacked Lee for insufficient militancy, *Do the Right Thing* and several of his later productions demonstrated that he has found success without abandoning his outspoken rhetoric on the racial divide in modern America.

The critical reaction to this film was largely positive, despite the occasional warnings that violent themes would produce violent responses. Not only did most reviewers lavish praise on Lee's thought-provoking work, but the industry conferred on him a number of awards and honors, including Academy Award and Golden Globe nominations for Best Director and Best Screenplay, as well as Los Angeles Film Critics and Chicago Film Festival Awards for Best Picture and Best Director.

For students of history, the film stands as an important cultural marker that documents the power of a motion picture to force confrontation with the reality of racial tension in American society. The tinder box that is the urban ghetto is as old as the rioting of the 1960s and as new as the controversy over the Cincinnati beating of 2004. While *Do the Right Thing* offered no easy answers to undeniable and persistent social problems, it called attention to abuses that demand attention if some semblance of harmony is to be maintained in modern urban life. It is a useful primary source that directs your attention to those unresolved issues and raises social questions that have not yet been answered.

Endnotes

1. For background on Spike Lee's career development, see Cynthia Fuchs, ed., *Spike Lee Interviews* (Jackson, Miss.: University Press of Mississippi, 2002), vii–xix.
2. Fuchs, x.
3. The ambivalence of the film's conclusion is skillfully analyzed in Paula J. Massood, *Black City Cinema: African-American Urban Experiences in Film* (Philadelphia: Temple University Press, 2003), 138–139.
4. The film's social significance is discussed in Massood, 143.

THE PRIMARY SOURCES

The primary sources begin with an excerpt from the 1968 report of the National Advisory Commission on Civil Disorders, which outlined urban problems that contributed to a racially polarized America. In an interview with scholar Marlene Glicksman, Spike Lee responds to the charge that the film encouraged violence. Next, *Chicago Sun-Times* film critic Roger Ebert offers a critical analysis of Lee's work. The documents close with the abrasive lyrics of Public Enemy's "Fight the Power," which set the tone for the narrative that unfolds in *Do the Right Thing*.

THE NATIONAL ADVISORY COMMISSION ON CIVIL DISORDERS OUTLINES THE PROBLEMS OF URBAN AMERICA

Introduction
National Advisory Commission on Civil Disorders

The summer of 1967 again brought racial disorders to American cities, and with them shock, fear and bewilderment to the nation.

The worst came during a two-week period in July, first in Newark and then in Detroit. Each set off a chain reaction in neighboring communities.

On July 28, 1967, the President of the United States established this Commission and directed us to answer three basic questions:

What happened?

Why did it happen?

What can be done to prevent it from happening again?

To respond to these questions, we have undertaken a broad range of studies and investigations. We have visited riot cities; we have heard many witnesses; we have sought the counsel of experts across the country.

This is our basic conclusion: Our nation is moving toward two societies, one black, one white—separate and unequal.

Reaction to last summer's disorders has quickened the movement and deepened the division. Discrimination and segregation have long permeated much of American life; they now threaten the future of every American.

This deepening racial division is not inevitable. The movement apart can be reversed. Choice is still possible. Our principal task is to define that choice and to press for a national resolution.

To pursue our present course will involve the continuing polarization of the American community and, ultimately, the destruction of basic democratic values.

The alternative is not blind repression or capitulation to lawlessness. It is the realization of common opportunities for all within a single society.

The alternative will require a commitment to national action—compassionate, massive and sustained, backed by the resources of the most powerful and the richest nation on this earth. From every American it will require new attitudes, new understanding, and, above all, new will.

The vital needs of the nation must be met; hard choices must be made, and if necessary, new taxes enacted.

Violence cannot build a better society. Disruption and disorder nourish repression, not justice. They strike at the freedom of every citizen. The community cannot—it will not—tolerate coercion and mob rule.

Violence and destruction must be ended—in the streets of the ghetto and in the lives of people.

Segregation and poverty have created in the racial ghetto a destructive environment totally unknown to most white Americans.

What white Americans have never fully understood—but what the Negro can never forget—is that white society is deeply implicated in the ghetto. White institutions created it, white institutions maintain it, and white society condones it.

It is time now to turn with all the purpose at our command to the major unfinished business of this nation. It is time to adopt strategies for action that will produce quick and visible progress. It is time to make good the promises of American democracy to all citizens—urban and rural, white and black, Spanish-surname, American Indian, and every minority group.

SOURCE: "Introduction," *Report of the National Advisory Commission on Civil Disorders*, March 1968, in Stephen F. Lawson and Charles Payne, *Debating the Civil Rights Movement, 1945–1968* (Lanham, Md.: Rowman and Littlefield, 1998), 95–96.

SPIKE LEE EXPLAINS VIOLENCE IN HIS FILM
Interview with Spike Lee
Marlene Glicksman

MG: *How did* Do the Right Thing *come about?*

SL: It started because of the whole Howard Beach incident. I wanted to do something to address that and racism. It's been reported several places that this film is the retelling of Howard Beach. This is a completely *fictional* thing. We took four things from it: the baseball bat, a black man gets killed, the pizzeria, and the conflict between blacks and Italian-Americans.

MG: *How did the ideas develop for the film, and how were they influenced by logistics? It's hot material.*

SL: I wanted it to be one twenty-four-hour period, the hottest day of the summer. I wanted the film to take place on one block in Bedford-Stuyvesant. So that's all the stuff I needed to work with, to start with. From there I could just go ahead and do what I had to do.

The script doesn't come to life till you shoot it. The finished film's always going to be different. I'm always true to what I'm saying, but the most important thing is to do what's right. If I write something, and it comes out in rehearsals that something else is better, we change it.

Every time I do a film, people ask me, 'Did you have full artistic control?' I mean, *She's Gotta Have It, School Daze* and *Do the Right Thing*—we made the films we wanted to make.

. . .

MG: *The end of the film is very powerful, and yet, somewhat ambiguous. How do you reconcile the two quotes, one from Dr. King and the other from Malcolm X?*

SL: Well, I don't think it's ambiguous. I think you really have to concentrate on what the final coda of the film is: the Malcolm X quote, not the Martin Luther King quote.

MG: *Malcolm X said, "I am not against using violence in self-defense. I don't even call it violence . . . I call it intelligence." Is the riot then, doing the right thing?*

SL: In that specific case it is, because Mookie and the people around him just get tired of blacks being killed by cops, just murdered by cops. And when the cops are brought to trial, they know nothing's going to happen. There's complete frustration and hopelessness.

They've seen it many times: Howard Beach, Michael Stewart, Tawana Brawley, Eleanor Bumpurs. Nothing happens. The eight cops that murdered Michael Stewart—that's where we got that Radio Raheem stuff. That is the Michael Stewart chokehold. Except we didn't have his eyeballs pop out of his head like Michael Stewart's did—[the police and medical examiner] greased his eyeballs and tried to stick them back in the sockets. There's a complete loss of faith in the judicial system. And so when you're frustrated and there's no outlet, it'll make you want to hurl the garbage can through the window.

MG: *If you read about an incident like the one in Central Park in the* Amsterdam News *and then compare it with* The New York Times *coverage there are two different perspectives.* . . .

SL: A couple of days later a black woman was found raped and murdered in a park. No mention of it—you didn't see nothing—no headlines in the *Post, Newsday, Time, New York Times,* or *New York Daily News.* That's a devaluation of black life. It's like black life doesn't mean anything, doesn't count for anything.

As long as they see, well, it's niggers killing niggers, they're animals anyway, it's no news. But if a young woman—a young *white* woman, on top of that, from Wall Street—is raped in Central Park, you might as well spit in the face of Jesus or something, because, you know, a great atrocity has happened.

This [black] woman was raped four or five days after the incident in Central Park. *Raped and murdered!* Nobody said nothing. Didn't see no outcry. I didn't see Donald Trump taking any fucking ads out behind that shit.

. . .

MG: *Why provoke the fight in a seemingly safe civil arena, a gathering place, rather than on the street?*

SL: Well. That's where a fight like that would start. In the public eye. Buggin' Out's character is a direct reference to a couple days after the Howard Beach incident. Some black leaders got together and wanted all the black people in New York City to boycott pizza for a day. It was one of the most ridiculous things I ever heard in my life. It was stupid.

I mean Buggin' Out had the right idea. But what's going to be the value of having one black photo up on Sal's wall of fame? Is that going to do anybody any good? But on the other hand, he also has a point, because let's turn it around and say, 'Look, Sal, you make all your money off black people, why don't you have enough sensitivity to have at least one photo up on the wall?' So that's the way the film is to me. Everybody has a point.

MG: *And are you advocating the riot at the end?*

SL: I'm not advocating anything. These are just characters, and this is how they act. This is how *they* acted. And if we turn that around again, I think Sal

has a point, too: When you black people get together and have your own businesses, you can do what you want to do.

I don't think that blacks are going to see this film and just go out in the streets and start rioting. I mean, black people don't need this movie to riot. They've been doing it already. Just look at what happened in Miami the week before the Super Bowl, when those cops killed people. Now some people be killed in New York City in summer by the cops, and this movie's not going to help. But it's going to be tense here in New York anyway, with this whole mayoral election coming up. And it's going to be hot, you know. That was the whole premise of this film, that in 95 degrees people lose it anyway.

. . .

MG: *White people fear that you are advocating violence.*

SL: Look, all they have to do is read the last quote of the movie. I'm not advocating violence. Self-defense is not violence. We call it intelligence. People are full of shit. Israel could go out and bomb anybody, nobody says nothing. But when black people go out and protect themselves, then we're militants, or we're advocating violence.

MG: *It seems you almost glossed over the death of Radio Raheem. When Mookie goes to see Sal at the end, he just says, "Radio Raheem is dead."*

SL: Yeah, but that's Mookie's character. What happened that night was tragic, but Mookie's whole character is not going to change overnight. And the reason why he's there that morning is because he wants to get paid. He's been saying that the whole movie, you know, get paid, get paid.

No, I don't think I glossed over it. What's the last thing that Love Daddy says? "The next record goes out for Radio Raheem. We love you, brother."

MG: *When Mookie breaks the window, it's his decision to get off the sidelines, take a stand and really explode the situation.* . . . *Is that you?*

SL: We've always tried to take a stand no matter what. All creative filming does. I don't think that we're going to change anything. This is just a more explosive, volatile subject matter.

MG: *Is Mookie symbolic of art taking a stand?*

SL: Of art? No. I leave that up to you journalists.

MG: *After the riot, the only people who lose out at the end of the film are the people who live in the neighborhood.*

SL: That always happens. Look at the riots in '67, '68. Anytime there's a riot, the National Guard, police—whatever—they always make sure they contain that riot to the ghetto. And so the buildings they burn down will never be built back. When there were riots in New York City, they were never on Fifth Avenue. There's never been looting in Lord & Taylor's or Saks. It was on 125th street. So, in a way, we do lose out. But people don't *feel* they lose out, because they feel they lost already. People have nothing to lose.

MG: *Before the riot they had the pizzeria, whatever that meant. But now, the street's the same except it's filled with debris and they don't have a pizzeria anymore.*

SL: They felt better about it, though. They felt that for once in their lives, they'd taken a stand. And they felt they had some kind of say. They felt powerful.

MG: *It's brought up several times in the film that "it's a free country." Your character brings it up at one point;*

Clifton, the yuppie who moves into Bed-Stuy, brings it up. It's a very ironic statement.

SL: Well, yeah. *That* was no accident.

MG: *The street in the film—that was the cleanest street I've ever seen in New York.*

SL: I made that choice because any time you hear people say Bed-Stuy, right away they think of rapes, murders, drugs. There's no need to show garbage piled up high and all that other stuff, because not every single block in Bed-Stuy is like that.

It would be a fallacy to say that lower-income people always live in burned-out buildings. These are hard-working people, and they take pride in their stuff just like everybody else. So there's no need for the set to look like Charlotte Street in the South Bronx.

Another thing people ask: "Where are the drugs?" Drugs is such a massive subject, it just can't be dealt with effectively as a subplot. You have to do an entire film on drugs. This film was not about that. This film was about *racism*.

SOURCE: Marlene Glicksman, Interview with Spike Lee, in Cynthia Fuchs, *Spike Lee Interviews* (Jackson, Miss.: University Press of Mississippi, 2002), 16–21.

ROGER EBERT'S ANALYSIS OF *DO THE RIGHT THING*
Analysis
Roger Ebert

Spike Lee's "Do the Right Thing" is the most controversial film of the year, and it only opens today. Thousands of people already have seen it at preview screenings, and everywhere I go, people are discussing it. Some of them are bothered by it; they think it will cause trouble. Others feel the message is confused. Some find it too militant, others find it the work of a middle-class director who is trying to play street-smart. All of those reactions, I think, simply are different ways of avoiding the central fact of this film, which is that it comes closer to reflecting the current state of race relations in America than any other movie of our time.

Of course it is confused. Of course it waivers between middle-class values and street values. Of course it is not sure whether it believes in liberal pieties or militancy. Of course some of the characters are sympathetic and others are hateful. And of course some of the likable characters do bad things. Isn't that the way it is in America today? Anyone who walks into this film expecting answers is a dreamer or a fool. But anyone who leaves the movie with more intolerance than they walked in with wasn't paying attention.

The movie takes place during one long, hot day in the Bedford-Stuyvesant neighborhood of Brooklyn.

But this is not the typical urban cityscape we've seen in countless action movies about violence and guns and drugs. People live here. It's a neighborhood like those city neighborhoods in the urban movies of the Depression: People know one another and accept one another, and although there are problems, there also is a sense of community.

. . .

This looks like a good enough neighborhood—like the kind of urban stage the proletarian dramas of the 1930s liked to start with. And for a long time during "Do the Right Thing," Lee treats it like a backdrop for a Saroyanesque slice of life. But things are happening under the surface. Tensions are building. Old hurts are being remembered. And finally the movie explodes in racial violence.

. . .

Since Lee does not tell you what to think about it, and deliberately provides surprising twists for some of the characters, this movie is more open-ended than most. It requires you to decide what you think about it.

"Do the Right Thing" is not filled with brotherly love, but it is not filled with hate, either. It comes out of a weary, urban cynicism that has settled down around us in recent years. The good feelings and many of the hopes of the 1960s have evaporated, and today it no longer would be accurate to make a movie about how the races in America are all going to love one another. I wish we could see such love, but instead we have deepening class divisions in which the middle classes of all races flee from what's hap-

pening in the inner city, while a series of national administrations provides no hope for the poor. "Do the Right Thing" tells an honest, unsentimental story about those who are left behind.

It is a very well-made film, beautifully photographed by Ernest Dickerson and well-acted by an ensemble cast. Aiello has the pivotal role, as Sal, and he suggests all of the difficult nuances of his situation. In the movie's final scene, Sal's conversation with Mookie holds out little hope, but it holds out at least the possibility that something has been learned from the tragedy, and the way Aiello plays this scene is quietly brilliant. Lee's writing and direction are masterful throughout the movie; he knows exactly where he is taking us, and how to get there, but he holds his cards close to his heart, and so the movie is hard to predict, hard to anticipate. After we get to the end, however, we understand how, and why, everything has happened.

Some of the advance articles about this movie suggested that it is an incitement to racial violence. Those articles say more about their authors than about the movie. I believe that any good-hearted person, white or black, will come out of this movie with sympathy for all of the characters. Lee does not ask us to forgive them, or even to understand everything they do, but he wants us to identify with their fears and frustrations. "Do the Right Thing" doesn't ask its audiences to choose sides; it is scrupulously fair to both sides, in a story where it is our society itself that is not fair.

SOURCE: Roger Ebert, "Do The Right Thing," *Chicago Sun-Times*, June 30, 1989.

LEE USES THE LYRICS OF PUBLIC ENEMY'S RECORDING
"FIGHT THE POWER" TO SET A TONE FOR THE VIOLENCE TO COME

"Fight the Power"
Public Enemy

FIGHT THE POWER

We got to fight the powers that be

As the rhythm's designed to bounce
What counts is the rhyme

Designed to fill your mind
Now that you've realized the pride's arrived
We got to pump the stuff to make us tough
From the heart
It's a start, a work of art

To revolutionize, make change, nothin' strange
People, people, we are the same
No we're not the same
'Cause we don't know the game
What we need is awareness, we can't get careless
You say what is this?
My beloved, let's get down to business
Mental self-defensive fitness
(Yo) Bum rush the show
You gotta go for what you know

To make everybody see, in order to fight the
  powers that be
Lemme hear you say

FIGHT THE POWER

We've got to fight the powers that be

Public Enemy

SOURCE: Public Enemy, "Fight the Power"

Follow-Up Problems

1. In what way does this film present an accurate depiction of the racial tensions present in urban America in 1989? Can you connect these problems with the social pathology evident in modern ghetto neighborhoods?

2. Did Mookie "do the right thing"? What did "da Mayor" mean when he advised Mookie to "always do the right thing"?

3. What were the philosophical differences between Martin Luther King Jr. and Malcolm X, as developed in this film? How are the photographs and quotations used in this film important to an understanding of Spike Lee's intent? Why does Lee place them side by side at the end of the film? What viewpoint do you think Lee has adopted in this film?

4. What is the relationship between Sal and Mookie's sister? Why does this relationship anger Mookie?

5. What was the impact of the police unit's arrival on the scene to quell the violence at Sal's? What is the connection between this sequence and the realities of modern African-American life?

6. What images has Hollywood historically applied to African-Americans? How do those longstanding impressions compare with those you observe in *Do The Right Thing*? Think about these images in comparison with those you observed in *The Birth of a Nation* and *The Negro Soldier*.

7. Some critics insisted that *Do the Right Thing* was an open incitement to violence. What is your reaction to this argument?

Further Reading

Bogle, Donald. *Toms, Coons, Mulattoes, Mammies, and Bucks: An Interpretive History of Blacks in American Films*. 3rd ed. New York: Continuum, 1994.

Cripps, Thomas. *Making Movies Black: The Hollywood Message Movies from World War I to the Civil Rights Era*. New York: Oxford University Press, 1992.

Fuchs, Cynthia, ed. *Spike Lee Interviews*. Jackson, Miss.: University Press of Mississippi, 2002.

Goudsouzian, Aram. "The Rise and Fall of Sidney Poitier." In Steven Mintz and Randy Roberts, eds. *Hollywood's America: United States History Through Its Films*. 2nd ed. St. James, N.Y.: Brandywine Press, 2001, 323–332.

Guerrero, Edward. *Framing Blackness: The African American Image in Film*. Philadelphia: Temple University Press, 1993.

Massood, Paula J. *Black City Cinema: African-American Urban Experiences in Film*. Philadelphia: Temple University Press, 2003.

Reid, Mark A. *Redefining Black Film*. Berkeley, Calif.: University of California Press, 1991.

Rosenbaum, Jonathan. *Movies as Politics*. Berkeley, Calif.: University of California Press, 1997.

Filmography

Bamboozled (Forty Acres and a Mule Productions, 2000).

Malcolm X (Forty Acres and a Mule Productions, 1992).

The Celluloid Document

Do the Right Thing (Forty Acres and a Mule Productions, 1989).

Chapter 16

Suburban Anxiety in Modern America:
American Beauty (1999)
and the Pitfalls of Prosperity

Starting with the dramatic postwar housing boom of the late 1940s, the suburban communities of the United States have been both the goal towards which middle-class citizens aspired and the social nightmare most feared by the American intelligentsia, of which Hollywood was a part. As early as the 1950s, social scientists like William Whyte and David Riesman decried the depersonalization that came as Americans entered corporate organizations and became part of "the lonely crowd." As Americans entered the explosive 1960s, filmmakers began to ridicule suburban life in such films as *The Graduate*. While alienated youth were at the forefront of the early attack on social conformity, by the 1980s the critique of middle-class values and the quest for financial well-being had become a staple of the liberal intellectuals who watched with disapproval the rampant pursuit of wealth in Ronald Reagan's America. Given this distaste for the conservative values that swept the United States in the 1980s, it is not surprising that before long, the motion picture industry would respond with films that questioned the concept of community embraced by suburbanites in the race to prosperity.[1] Among the most penetrating criticisms of suburban life, *American Beauty* (1999) launched a broad assault against the value system that held sway in modern America at the dawn of the twenty-first century.

The Historical Background

By 1980, the liberal idealism that dominated social and economic reform in the 1960s and resulted in the drive to create President Lyndon B. Johnson's Great Society had collapsed in disarray. Wary of efforts to reduce inequalities in the distribution of wealth and power in the United States and burdened by the vague uneasiness that hung like a shroud over Jimmy Carter's America, the public yearned for the energy and optimism that had been missing since the affluent 1950. Into this environment came the leader of a conservative revolution, President Ronald Reagan, who promised a renewal of the American spirit so badly damaged in the era of Watergate and Vietnam.

Part and parcel of the new order was the unashamed pursuit of wealth in the competitive arena by whatever means necessary. Freed from the watchful eye of governmental regulators and flush with the financial resources provided by a program of tax relief that benefited the comfortable, entrepreneurs engaged in an intense scramble for the spoils of the new economic freedom. Not surprisingly, the motion picture industry soon moved to depict the prevailing business ethos and the value system that accompanied it.

Perhaps the clearest cinematic critique of the modern corporate value system came with the production of maverick director Oliver Stone's brutally frank account of stock market trading and scheming, *Wall Street* (1987). In this morality tale of self-destruction in the pursuit of self-interest, Stone exposes some of the shady security industry practices that could be observed in the world of finance. The heart of the story and the central message in the film are contained in trader Gordon (Michael Douglas) Gekko's memorable summation: "Greed, for lack of a better word, is good." While criticized for its lack of balance and excessive emphasis on money lust, the film touched upon an economic reality that helps explain its substantial cultural impact. Despite the movie's mixed reviews and a lackluster box office performance,[2] *Wall Street*'s depiction of insider trading and hostile takeovers driven by greed addressed an important aspect of American values in the 1980s.

The rampant pursuit of wealth that was the central feature of *Wall Street,* while not unique to the 1980s, was certainly evident in the relentless striving that characterized suburban life in the late twentieth century. While improvements in mass transportation made the suburban lifestyle possible, it was rising wages and expanded economic opportunity that meant families could live in private enclaves outside the city. The price was an ever-escalating struggle to enhance family economic status, which was a recipe for anxiety. Beyond the constant economic competition, the suburbs brought environmental destruction, loosened family ties, a smothering sameness, racial exclusiveness, artificial relationships, and the loss of privacy; but despite the negative side of suburban life, it remained the ideal towards which middle-class Americans aspired as the twentieth century came to an end.

As we have seen, suburban life and the anxieties that accompanied it had long been the target of filmmakers who consistently found suburbia morally and socially deficient. The critique begun in the 1960s resurfaced in the 1990s with a series of films highlighting the shortcomings of middle-class life on the suburban fringe. From the eccentric neighbors in *The Burbs* (1989) to the emptiness and sterility of *Pleasantville* (1998), Hollywood's suburbia continued to be the home of dysfunctional people and fragmented families. Even more devastating was the biting satire in the widely acclaimed *American Beauty* (1999), in which the hollowness of family life and the loneliness of the stranded individual exposed the dark side of the "American dream." Close analysis of this film will reveal some of the cultural dilemmas of our own time.

Analyzing the Film

From the opening shots in *American Beauty*, the orderly tree-lined streets of a typical suburban town project an image of sameness and conformism that was the fate of its unfortunate inhabitants. While Lester Burnham (Kevin Spacey) and his family seem to be living out the American dream, their lives are in reality empty and shallow imitations of the middle-class ideal. In fact, Lester is a shadow of a man, hounded by an employer preparing to cut him loose and tormented by a materialistic, success-driven wife and hopelessly self-ish daughter, both of whom regard him as a loser. Faced by these obstacles, he determines to alter his miserable existence by quitting his job, aligning himself with his neighbor's drug-dealing son (who has become infatuated with his daughter, Jane), and fantasizing about a sexual relationship with Jane's flirtatious classmate, Angela. The result is Lester's illusion of a new freedom experienced as he breaks all the rules governing his humdrum middle-class world. Yet the new freedom comes with a high price tag, and he finally pays the ultimate debt when the latent homosexual, Colonel Fitts, ends his life, thus shattering the remnants of an already distorted American dream.

The film may be analyzed on several levels. First, concentrate your attention on the evolution of the American family, as represented by the dysfunctional Burnhams and the equally peculiar neighboring family headed by a sexually tormented ex-Marine. In what way do you think this film reflects the social dilemmas facing the home in modern American society? How does the treatment of the family unit in *American Beauty* compare with the images of family life projected in *Dancing Mothers* and *The Grapes of Wrath*? How would you account for these differences?

Closely related to the film's exploration of family life is the way in which the film deals with women's place in postmodern American society. Since the 1950s, social critics had debated the impact of women's incorporation into the consumer culture as potential competitors with the men with whom they were allied by marriage or love. As you think about women's relationships with men in this film, observe the behavior displayed by Lester's wife, his daughter, and the youthful object of his romantic obsession. How would you account for the sometimes manipulative and often vicious aspects[3] of their interaction with the men in their lives? Can you connect the film's representation of women with any changes evident in American society and culture since the 1970s?

Since women and female behavior are central to the narrative, it follows that issues related to sex and sexual relationships are not neglected. Indeed, *American Beauty* focuses on such matters as infidelity, voyeurism, homosexuality, and pedophilia in ways that make sex the driving force behind human action. As you explore the tangled relationships among the film's major characters, consider the connection between these entanglements and the sweeping social changes that had revolutionized sexual behavior and moral values since the 1960s. In what way do the interpersonal relationships depicted in this film reflect prevailing moral standards in modern American society? As you think about this issue, emphasize the way in which homosexuality is presented in this film. Compare the Burnhams' "friendly" neighbors with the repressed homosexual with fascist tendencies. In what way does the representation of gay men in *American Beauty* shed light on the evolving American value system?

The film's obsession with sex opens it to the charge that it is little more than a sophisticated "soap opera." Of course, by definition, the American soap opera does in fact deal with the trials, conflicts, and dilemmas often faced by ordinary people. As you think about the relationships depicted in the film, decide whether they were typical or ordinary. By what standards? What characteristics do you attribute to the soap opera? To what extent are they present in *American Beauty*? Does the social analysis in the film go deeper than the soap opera standard? If so, in what ways?

In many respects, *American Beauty* opens the frustrations and anxieties of American suburban life to harsh scrutiny. It is perhaps most brutal in its treatment of the relentless economic competition and powerful success drive that propels Lester's wife, Carolyn (Annette Bening), towards greater and greater sales results. Equally significant is Lester's decision to abandon the economic expectations typical of the suburban tribal culture. How do screenwriter Alan Ball and director Sam Mendes succeed in exposing the negative consequences of engagement in the never-ending search for greater financial rewards? Compare *American Beauty* with *The Graduate* as critiques of the crass materialism that penetrated middle-class culture. To what extent had the value system of 1960s Americans changed by the 1990s?

In many ways *American Beauty* held up a mirror to the world inhabited by the upwardly mobile middle class of our own time. The reflection was not always flattering. You may use this film as a document of the acquisitive 1990s and the social issues created by the ongoing pursuit of financial success. By employing this motion picture as primary source, you will open discussion of some of the most complex and unsolved problems resulting from the achievement of the elusive American dream. As you reflect on these issues, you will identify many of the cultural challenges of our time.

Thinking About Primary Sources

As you ponder the deeper social questions raised by this film, you will find the primary sources especially valuable in uncovering the goals of director Sam Mendes. As you examine his comments, try to understand the impact of modern American social trends on the director's thinking. Compare his ideas with the views of critic Charles Jarvis as you attempt to place the subtext in *American Beauty* within the context of changing values in the United States at the dawn of a new century. What factors lie behind the arguments presented by each commentator?

Turn again to the words of Sam Mendes, watching for the broader social criticism the director hoped to introduce with this film. What do his recollections about the script's potential reveal about the way in which he believed he could make a statement concerning some of the anxieties present in suburban life, as well as the interpersonal tensions associated with the middle-class lifestyle found in the communities beyond America's urban centers? From his perspective, what were the flaws in the unrealized American dream? What dilemmas had the pursuit of the dream created for the men and women caught up in the chase?

As you consider the film's critique of suburbia, locate *American Beauty* in the spectrum of Hollywood's concern over this aspect of American life. Think about Richard Schickel's pointed remarks related to the movie industry's historical fascination with the suburbs and predictability in dealing with the shortcomings of suburban life. What is Schickel saying about the Hollywood product since 1950? Evaluate this film against the background of such films as *The Graduate* and other movie critiques of suburban materialism. In what way does *American Beauty* contribute to the ongoing discussion of suburban anxieties? What makes this film unique? What new insight into modern American social behavior does it offer? What does it tell us about the way in which financial competition and the search for economic security have come to influence social aspirations and personal relationships?

Since *American Beauty* was a smashing critical and financial success, we must ask why this film touched the public and impressed the critics as it did. Reexamine the two reviews and the director's comments for an explanation of the film's remarkable record. In what way did the picture speak to the contemporary audience about problems experienced in their lives? How did the film address social pathologies that complicated family and personal relationships? Was it merely a good story or did it provide deeper insight into the society in which it was produced and viewed? Use the documents to formulate an explanation for the largely positive response to a film that went to the heart of popular concern over an unrealized dream.

Historical Perspective

There can be little doubt about the reaction to this film. *American Beauty* was a huge financial success, as Dreamworks skillfully marketed the picture to both adults and teenagers. Within two months a film budgeted at $15 million had grossed $66 million in the United States alone,[4] this well before the critical accolades that resulted in multiple Academy Awards, including Oscars for Best Film, Best Director, Best Original Screenplay, and Best Actor. Widely praised by reviewers and critics as well, the film was regarded as one of the most important pictures of the year. *American Beauty* had clearly touched a nerve in the audience, the film community, and the wider world. Part of the explanation for this result lies in the skill with which Mendes, Ball, Spacey, and the entire production team addressed problems confronted by the millions of Americans trapped in the race to succeed. Equally significant was their effective, if not entirely original, critique of an empty dream of suburban contentment. In so doing, the filmmakers trod a familiar Hollywood path, though updated with emphasis on a moral code in transition and a willingness to treat sexuality more openly than once was true. The social response to these changes in our time has been mixed at best and poisonous at worst. The film's frontal attack on materialism, intolerance, and conformity touches on the social confusion and climate of doubt experienced by Americans not quite sure that the good life has brought personal satisfaction. In focusing on this reality, *American Beauty* documents the central dilemma of modern American life.

Endnotes

1. Hollywood's treatment of suburbia is fully discussed in Peter C. Rollins, ed., *The Columbia Companion to American History on Film: How the Movies Portrayed the American Past* (New York: Columbia University Press, 2003), especially 485.
2. Martin S. Fridson, "Wall Street," in Robert Toplin, ed., *Oliver Stone's USA: Film, History and Controversy*, 121–124.
3. See Gary Hentzl, "American Beauty," *Film Quarterly* 54 (winter 2001): 46–50.
4. Casey McKittrick, " 'I Laughed and Cringed at the Same Time': Shaping Pedophilic Discourse Around *American Beauty* and *Happiness*," *The Velvet Light Trap: Review of Cinema* 47 (spring 2001): 5.

PRIMARY SOURCES

The primary sources enable students to gain deeper insight into the intentions of the filmmakers as well as the critical response to *American Beauty*. In his introduction to the published version of the script, director Sam Mendes outlines his initial reaction to Alan Ball's screenplay. The two remaining documents offer conflicting critical reactions to the film. In *Time*, film critic Richard Schickel outlines the strengths in the film, while self-described "entrepreneur" and "action tank" scholar Charles W. Jarvis provides a contrary view, published in the conservative journal *Human Events*.

<u>DIRECTOR SAM MENDES DESCRIBES HIS FIRST REACTION TO THE SCRIPT</u>

American Beauty: The Shooting Script
Sam Mendes

I first read *American Beauty* sitting on a plane traveling between Los Angeles and New York. I finished it and read it again. I arrived in New York, called my agent, Beth, and told her that I wanted to make the movie. Then I read it again. Normally it was a trial for me to get through a script once, and I'd read this one three times back to back. I wanted to know why this was. So I read it again.

The strange thing was that at each reading the script seemed to be something else. It was a highly innovative black comedy. It was a mystery story with a genuine final twist. It was a kaleidoscopic journey through American suburbia, and a hugely visually articulate one at that. It was a series of love stories. It was about imprisonment in the cages that we all make for ourselves and our hoped-for escape. It was about loneliness. It was about beauty. It was funny. It was angry, very angry sometimes. It was sad. One thing I was certain of, the script, like its characters, wasn't at all what it first appeared.

Our relationship with the characters shifted and changed. What was this man Lester doing? Acting like a spoiled child or raging against the dying of the light? His wife Carolyn? Furious and frigid, yet vulnerable and lost. Jane? Impassive, unreadable, but with a well of tenderness barely visible to the naked eye. And Ricky. His camera emotionlessly recording its subject or reaching out to touch it? In the end my feelings about the finished movie and script are indivisible. I love it (I'm biased, of course), but I still don't know how it *works*. With me, and also I suspect with Alan, instinct was my strongest and only guide.

One thing I did know on those initial readings, however, was that the writer wasn't scared to leave the characters alone with themselves; he seemed to know them well enough to allow them that privilege. Indeed, many of my favourite passages from the finished movie involve these moments of solitariness, caught by the camera's impassive and uninflected gaze. Carolyn in the empty sale house, putting herself back together again; Jane studying her reflection in the mirror after her mother has hit her; Ricky similarly alone in his room cleaning the blood from his face; Angela sitting on the stairs crying, with the rain outside; And of course Lester gazing at the image of his family, seeing it all clearly as it were, at the moment before his own death. Indeed, the voice that hovers over the movie seems to be the ultimate spiritual extension of that: Lester at once alone and at peace with himself, yet missing, genuinely missing, his 'little life'.

The movie was, of course, to repeat the old adage, extensively reshaped in the cutting room. A framework involving Ricky and Jane being tried and convicted of Lester's murder seemed clever but a mite cynical and at odds with Lester's spirit taking wing. This was excised along with any indications of the Colonel's ambivalent sexual feelings and other signposts that softened the movie's unexpected plot twists and changes of tone. Other changes were not so considered. The scene with Ricky and Jane walking home down the avenue of trees, for example, was written at the last minute to save us money and time, and turned out better than the scene it replaced. But it would be wrong to suggest that the film was ever in need of major surgery: Alan wrote it from the heart as well as the head, and it made it on to the screen with remarkably little interference from outside forces, other than the constant and unstinting support of producers Dan Jinks and Bruce Cohen, its torch bearers from the very beginning.

. . .

But in the end, without Alan's work on the original script, none of these people, myself included, would have taken this particular journey. And as I sit writing this in the dry, odourless L.A. sunshine, contemplating my twelve months working on the movie and looking forward to going home, I can only reflect on the power of the written word to change our little lives.

SOURCE: Sam Mendes, "Introduction," *American Beauty: The Shooting Script* (New York: Newmarket Press, 1999): xi–xiii.

TWO CONFLICTING CRITICAL REACTIONS TO THE FILM
Dark Side of the American Dream
Richard Schickel

Lester Burnham (Kevin Spacey) hates his job and the cubicle to which it confines him. He has also come to despise his tense and frigid wife Carolyn (Annette Bening), to mourn the sullen silence that has descended between him and his teenage daughter Jane (Thora Birch), to loathe the sterile suburbia where they all try to make emotional ends meet. Lester masturbates a lot, especially when he gets to thinking about his daughter's friend Angela (Mena Suvari), the *American Beauty* of the title.

Oh, God, not that again. Not another midlife crisis, with its subcurrents of suppressed violence and repressed sexual longing. Not another tale in which we wait patiently or impatiently—depending on our tolerance for cultural clichés—for the cathartic, concluding burst of morally instructive gunfire.

But wait. Sometimes there is salvation in parentheses, especially when they surround the name of Kevin Spacey, giving a truly great performance. He's cynical. He's funny. He's rueful. He's a mean truth teller and sometimes a curiously tender one. Best of all, he makes the transitions between these and a dozen other emotions heedlessly, without warning or visible preparation. You never know where he's coming from, or where he's going to end up in a scene. Yet boldly challenging our sympathies, he somehow wins them because, to borrow a phrase, he's a man in full.

He also has a dark and problematic double, the weird, smart boy next door. His name is Ricky (Wes Bentley). He deals drugs underneath the crazy nose of his abusive father (Chris Cooper), a retired Marine colonel of the neo-fascist persuasion, and creepily stalks Lester's daughter with his everpresent camcorder, eventually winning her because of the purity of his subversive nature. He is, perhaps, everything Lester might have been, if he had not long ago compromised himself. This also, perhaps, explains why Jane falls in love with him.

Ricky is a disturbing presence. Prior to Littleton, he might have been dismissed as an improbable one. But that tragedy—created by kids held in contempt by their peers and able to conduct a criminal life free of parental interference—gives him a peculiar, if entirely coincidental, resonance. He is not, in the end, tragedy's primary victim, but he is its precipitator, and the instructor of the complacency that it is the business of this movie to shatter.

Shatter stylishly, one must add. The writing by Alan Ball, whose first produced screenplay this is, consistently surprises—not so much in what it says, but in how it says it. He even risks having his story narrated by Lester from beyond the grave and makes Billy Wilder's old trick seem fresh. And the stage's Sam Mendes, also making his first film, dares a touch of expressionism, which we happily indulge, partly because he knows when to stop, mostly because the energy and conviction he and his cast bring to this movie do not permit second thoughts—at least until you are outside the theater, trying to shake off its mysterious spell.

Source: Richard Schickel, "Dark Side of the American Dream," *Time* 154 (Sept. 20, 1999): 79–80.

American Beauty is an American Horror
Charles W. Jarvis

My prediction is that the Academy Awards worship service on March 26 will involve many blessings and anointings of the film *American Beauty*. Already this film has won the top awards at The Directors Guild of America and The Writers Guild of America. The glitterati and literati are in glossolalic euphoria about it. The New Religion judges, or "critics" as they're called, are running up and down the aisles lifting the name of *American Beauty* on high.

What is it about this film that causes tears of joy to flow in liberals with otherwise cauterized consciences? Why are at-your-throat competitors in the media singing Ave *Beauty* in unison?

Perhaps it's the shock value of the film's subcurrent of pedophilia or Loilta fixation. Or is it the politically correct presentation of the two homosexual neighbors as the only normal people in the film? Showing the two young teenage girls topless? Is it the orgasm-is-liberation theme of Carolyn, played by Annette Bening, committing adultery with a rival realtor?

Perhaps it's the Marine Colonel (Chris Cooper) as a violent, moralistic, gun totin', Nazi memorabilia collectin', closet queen who murders. Is it the daughter, Jane (Thora Birch), musing with the neighbor boy (Wes Bentley) about killing her father, the central character Lester (played by Kevin Spacey)? It could be the Al Gore theme embedded in the film that suburban sprawl is the most threatening place to live in America (not Detroit or South Central LA). Or it just might be the pop-Buddhism that permeates the whole film.

Yes, *American Beauty* will be worshiped for all those reasons, but primarily because it depicts the American nuclear family as a cauldron of curses and lies. "There's nothing worse in life than being normal," one character intones. I'll take C. S. Lewis's insight any day; Heaven is where the inhabitants say to God, "Thy will be done" and hell is where God says, "Thy will be done."

SOURCE: Charles W. Jarvis, "*American Beauty* Is an American Horror," *Human Events* 56 (March 24, 2000): 14.

Follow-Up Problems

1. In what way does *American Beauty* document changing moral values and attitudes concerning sexuality in modern America? How does the film's treatment of these issues shed light on the social dilemmas faced by American citizens in the twenty-first century?

2. What does this film reveal about the economic and financial concerns of the upwardly mobile middle class in American society? How does the film address these concerns? How does *American Beauty* compare with *The Graduate* in its handling of these issues?

3. One reviewer refers to this film as "dark comedy." What is meant by this phrase? Compare this film with *Dr. Strangelove* as efforts to employ humor to deal with serious issues.

4. Many reviewers and film scholars have noted that the attack on suburbia is an old Hollywood convention. In what ways do you think that *American Beauty* updates or adds to the critique of suburban values and life?

5. As you reflect on the problems, anxieties, and social pathologies explored in this film, how do you relate the film's concerns to issues in your own life? Look down the road twenty years and ask yourself what your personal situation will be like. How do the dilemmas facing the Burnham family relate to your own expectations?

6. In what way do the issues confronted by the characters populating the film's suburban community reflect the personal objectives of the director and screenwriter? How do the narrative and action connect with private agendas? How do these goals relate to the society of which the filmmakers are a part?

Further Reading

Fishman, Robert. *Bourgeois Utopias: The Rise and Fall of Suburbia*. New York: Basic Books, 1987.

Jackson, Kenneth T. *Crabgrass Frontier: The Suburbanization of the United States*. New York: Oxford University Press, 1985.

Rothman, William. "Hollywood and the Rise of the Suburbs." *East-West Film Journal* 3 (1989): 96–105.

Silverstone Roger, ed. *Visions of Suburbia*. London: Routledge, 1997.

Wilt, David E. "Suburbia." In Peter C. Rollins, ed., *The Columbia Companion to American History on Film: How the Movies Have Portrayed the American Past*. New York: Columbia University Press, 2003, 480–487.

Filmography

Pleasantville (New Line, 1998).

The Stepford Wives (Dreamworks, 2004).

The Celluloid Document

American Beauty (Dreamworks, 1999).

Epilogue

Thinking About Your Movies

We have now traversed a full century of United States history, using feature films to high-light the key themes in the American social and cultural experience. Throughout the twentieth century, motion pictures have addressed many of the critical issues facing the nation in ways that often mirrored the concerns and beliefs of the audience. Moreover, at times the movies have influenced public attitudes on a wide range of social, economic, and political issues confronting the nation. A review of the topics dealt with in *Screening America* will reveal a number of recurring issues that have drawn the attention of film-makers and viewing audiences alike.

One of the critical problems to surface repeatedly on the screen and in real life was the issue of race as a factor in American society. From the negative stereotypes of *The Birth of a Nation*, through the propaganda in *The Negro Soldier*, to the sharp images of con-flict in *Do the Right Thing*, filmmakers have concentrated on the volatility of race relations as one of the central themes in modern American history. And not to be ignored is the way in which Hispanic-Americans have forced their own civil rights to the forefront, as evidenced in the bold statement made by *Salt of the Earth*. These celluloid documents tell us that the dilemma of race has been at the heart of the twentieth-century cultural expe-rience. Moreover, in a society in which the white population will soon be a minority, these on-screen images force us to recognize that race will continue to be the key social issue of our time.

Equally significant as a subject for moviemakers has been the ongoing debate over the place of women in American society, which may be traced in celluloid from the silent era onward. Variously represented as child-women, flirtatious flappers, compliant wives, crafty showgirls, wartime family heads, committed labor activists, independent feminists, or castrating shrews, women have occupied a central role in the Hollywood narrative. At the dawn of a new century, the familial disruption and social confusion identified as early as the 1920s continued to appear as an important issue on the silver screen. These con-flicts assumed new forms in the many "women's films" that appeared in the last decade of the twentieth century. As we have seen, women's place in American society remains a contested question, and the product of Hollywood has mirrored the unresolved dilemma of gender relations in the modern era.

Closely tied to the issues of race and gender is the still controversial problem of class relations and economic equity in the American historical experience. The presence of economic disparities and class differences in United States history, while often minimized by the Hollywood dream machine, has reappeared on the screen periodically as socially concerned filmmakers have elected to expose those inequities. From the sharp social commentary of *The Grapes of Wrath* and the working-class activism of Sally Field in *Norma Rae* to the raw conflict of *Do the Right Thing*, the motion picture industry has periodically displayed the unmet needs of the underclass for the consideration of a national audience. As the United States increasingly veers towards a two-class society, the movies have reminded us that class differences constitute important unfinished business in our own time.

While race, class, and gender have consistently been addressed in film for the past century, the motion picture has also been a barometer of political sentiment in a variety of situations. For example, while the antiwar sentiment of *All Quiet on the Western Front* reflected the foreign-policy views of most Americans in 1930, the open interventionism of *Foreign Correspondent* marked an important change taking place in American opinion as World War II threatened to engulf all nations. Equally significant were the political statements made by *Alice's Restaurant* and *Coming Home* as attitudes toward overseas intervention changed once more. And while Michael Moore can hardly be seen as part of the Hollywood system, his controversial work continues to generate fierce debate, most recently with the sharp criticism of President George W. Bush in *Fahrenheit 9/11*. In short, a review of Hollywood's effort to deal with divisive political issues reveals that while a time lag often delays their consideration, these problems eventually reach the screen.

No matter how difficult the issue may have been, the movies have extended debate to a large national audience. Many of the problems addressed by Hollywood focus and refocus our attention on recurring questions that each generation must resolve for itself. Just as the generation of the 1920s was forced to reconstruct a value system to replace the dated Victorian moral structure, so the current generation will grapple with the reality of alienation and moral ambiguity, as explored in *The Graduate* and *American Beauty*. Contemporary anxieties are today's version of social uncertainties experienced in other forms by men and women of earlier generations. For you, as was true for them, the motion picture industry and the movies are central features in modern American culture. These celluloid documents grapple with the many cultural issues that you, as a consumer and citizen, must resolve for yourself.

As you reflect upon the social meaning of film in both the present and past, rethink the distance you have come and the insight you have gained on the importance of film as a social signifier. Modern Americans have continued their love affair with the movies, though the audience demographics have shifted towards younger moviegoers than those who made up the viewing public in the golden age of the 1930s and 1940s. In our own time, difficult social and political issues continue to be explored on the screen as filmmakers record the history of the modern era. Since the 1980s, a variety of problems have been the subject of scrutiny by the now more independent filmmakers of a new movie age. From the searing critique of Reagan era corporate financial values in *Wall Street* (1987) to the Vietnam revisionism in *We Were Soldiers* (2002), Hollywood frames and reframes our understanding of the most important problems of our time. The culturally attuned student will recognize that contemporary films document the most troublesome problems confronting American society, and that the box office response still records the extent of public preoccupation with those questions. In short, we are now witnessing the creation of the celluloid documents of the future.

Conscious of the motion picture's value as a social indicator, thoughtful observers will mine modern films for their meaning and develop the habit of critical analysis in the process. At no time in our history has it been more important for viewers to apply their analytical skills to media images, which are unavoidable products of information distribution in an age of mass culture. Bombarded by visual images on a daily basis through movies, television, videotape, and now the Internet, students must learn to accept and reject ideas based upon the evidence available for analysis. As they confront this media barrage, the ability to think critically (and historically) will become a valuable survival skill in the world of ideas they now inhabit.

In view of these new realities, the analysis of motion pictures as documentary evidence can serve the modern consumer of visual images in many ways. Not only will the motion picture continue to shed light on historical events in the making, but analysis of these current documents will encourage us to ask meaningful questions about our times, our leaders, and the most controversial social issues of the modern era. Just as *Wall Street* exposed the moral emptiness of yuppie culture in the 1980s and the power of corporate capitalism to subordinate the individual and control the lives of those caught up in the system, so the work of Oliver Stone reveals the deep skepticism of the 1990s in such controversial films as *Natural Born Killers* (1994), which explores the penetrating violence that has become part of American life. Whatever films are the subject of analysis, one thing is certain: critical viewing of the Hollywood product will better enable American students to understand their culture and society.

Readers of this volume will be acutely aware of the value of the motion picture as a window into the past. By this time, you are aware of the moving image as much more than a simple transmitter for a pleasant dramatic story line. Rather, it is clear that, more than other media, movies (and television) have reacted to the constantly changing interests, fears, concerns, and hopes of the viewing audience. It is this responsiveness that makes film such a valuable historical resource. There is no universally accepted list of films that scholars will agree on as the line of inquiry for historical analysis. As the filmographies in this text indicate, alternative choices for each chapter might responsibly have been made, and students are encouraged to explore these sources on their own.

While you consider the many older films that might serve as alternative documents, you will also want to sharpen your analysis of the motion pictures you choose to explore in your own leisure time. When you laugh at the humor in *American Pie 2*, ask yourself what this film tells you about your own world and social experience. Connect the issues raised by this film with the cultural problems facing Benjamin Braddock and Elayne in *The Graduate*. Is there past-present linkage between their world and yours? In what way do the cultural dilemmas that fill *American Beauty* raise questions about your private life and the situation you envision 20 years down the road? When you view Michael Moore's provocative *Fahrenheit 9/11*, what does the film reveal to you about the history of your own time? As you proceed with your lifelong exploration of history through film, be sure to employ the analytical tools that support sound historical thinking. And when you enter the darkened theater for your personal entertainment experience, always remember to look behind the film to ask searching questions that place it in the context of the historical moment. That moving image is, in the final analysis, a cultural marker of your own times.

Credits

Allen, Frederick L. *From Since Yesterday: The 1930s in America* by Frederick L. Allen. Copyright © 1939, 1940 by Frederick Lewis Allen. Copyright renewed © 1968 by Agnes Rogers Allen. Reprinted by permission of HarperCollins Publishers Inc.

Amalgamated Clothing and Textile Workers Union (ACTWU). "The *real* 'Norma Rae' was fighting J. P. Stevens" prepared by ACTWU, March 1980. Reprinted by permission of UNITE HERE.

Bendiner, Robert. *Just Around the Corner: A Highly Selective History of the Thirties* (New York: E. P. Dutton, 1967). Reprinted by permission of the author.

Benson, Edward and Strom, Sharon Hartman. "Crystal Lee Jordan, Norma Rae, and All Their Sisters," by Edward Benson with Sharon Hartman Strom from the *Film Library Quarterly* XII (1979). Reprinted by permission of the authors.

Cagin, Seth. From a review of *Coming Home* by Seth Cagin (1978). Reprinted by permission of the author.

Canby, Vincent. "Review of *Alice's Restaurant*" by Vincent Canby from *The New York Times*, January 1, 1969. Copyright © 1969 by The New York Times Co. Reprinted with permission.

Committee for a SANE Nuclear Policy, New York Times, November 15, 1957. Reprinted by permission of Peace Action.

Crowther, Bosely. "Review of *Dr. Strangelove*," by Bosley Crowther from *The New York Times*, January 31, 1964. Copyright © 1964 by The New York Times Co. Reprinted with permission.

Ebert, Roger. Taken from the "Roger Ebert" column by Roger Ebert © 1989. Distributed by Universal Press Syndicate. Reprinted with permission. All rights reserved.

Erickson, Clarence. Clarence Erickson, Vice-President and Treasurer, Walter Wanger Productions, "Memo for Mr. Wanger," January 25, 1941, Reprinted by permission.

Glicksman, Marlene. From "Spike Lee's Bed-Stuy BBQ" Spike Lee interviewed by Marlene Glicksman. From *Film Comment*, July/August 1989. Copyright © 1989 by the Film Society of Lincoln Center. All rights reserved. Reprinted with permission.

Guthrie, Woody. From Woody Guthrie column, *Peoples' World*, 1940, in *Woody Sez* (New York: 1961). Courtesy of the Reference Center for Marxist Studies.

Harris, Louis and Associates, Inc. Public opinion poll from *Myths and Realities: A Study of Attitudes Toward Vietnam-Era Veterans*, July 1980, Louis Harris and Associates, Inc. Conducted for The Veterans Administration. Reprinted by permission

of Harris Interactive Inc., 2004. All rights reserved.

Hollywood War Activities Committee. Letter from the War Activities Committee, Dated April 4, 1944 Regarding "The Negro Soldier." Reprinted by permission.

Hurst, Fannie. "A New Marriage Style Discussed" by Fannie Hurst from *The New York Times*, December 12, 1923. Copyright © 1923 by The New York Times Co. Reprinted with permission.

Jarrico, Paul. "*Salt of the Earth*—Chronology," by Paul Jarrico, May 9, 1955. Reprinted by permission.

Jarvis, Charles W. "American Beauty is an American Horror," by Charles W. Jarvis. *Human Events* 56 (March 24, 2000). Reprinted with permission.

Lemann Nicholas. "The Post Vietnam Generation" by Nicholas Lemann. Reprinted by permission of the author.

Library of Congress, Prints & Photographs Division, FSA/OWI Collection, [reproduction number, e.g., LC-USF34-9058-C]

Mendes, Sam. "Introduction" in *American Beauty: The Shooting Script*. Published by Newmarket Press, 1999. Reprinted by permission.

Montgomery, Robert H., Jr. Letter to Arthur Penn and Hillard Elkins, August 19, 1968. Reprinted by permission.

Motion Picture Association of America. "The Motion Picture Production Code," Second Section, 1930. Reprinted by permission of the Motion Picture Association of America.

New York Times. "Reviewer Acknowledges Lewis Milestone's Achievements" from *The New York Times*, April 30, 1930. Copyright © 1930 by The New York Times Co. Reprinted with permission.

Public Enemy. "Fight the Power" written by Carlton Ridehour, Hank Shocklee, and Eric Sadler. Copyright © 1990 Terrordome Music Publishing, administered by Reach Global Songs (BMI) and Songs of Universal, Inc. Used by permission. International Copyright Secured. All rights reserved.

Remarque, Erich Maria. *All Quiet on The Western Front* by Erich Maria Remarque. "Im Westen Nichts Neues," copyright 1928 by Ullstein A. G.; Copyright renewed © 1956 by Erich Maria Remarque. "All Quiet On The Western Front", copyright 1929, 1930 by Little, Brown and Company; Copyright renewed © 1957, 1958 by Erich Maria Remarque. All rights reserved. Reprinted with permission of the Estate of Paulette Goddard Remarque.

Rosenfeld, Megan. "Through the Mill with Crystal Lee and 'Norma Rae' "; Through the Mill: The Labors of Crystal Lee Sutton from *The Washington Post*. By line by Megan Rosenfeld. June 11, 1980. Copyright © 1980, The Washington Post. Reprinted with permission.

Schickel, Richard. *Second Sight: Notes on Some Movies, 1965–1970* by Richard Schickel. Reprinted with the permission of Simon & Schuster Adult Publishing Group. Copyright © 1972 by Richard Schickel.

Schickel, Richard. "Dark Side of the Dream," by Richard Schickel from *Time*, September 20, 1999. Copyright © 1999 Time, Inc. Reprinted by permission.

Schwarzkopf, Norman. From *Friendly Fire* by C. D. B. Bryan, copyright © 1976 by Courtland Dixon Barnes Bryan. Used by permission of G. P. Putnam's Sons, a division of Penguin Group (USA) Ltd.

Siceloff, Bruce. "Moviegoers Get View of Textile Mill Organizing," by Bruce Siceloff" from *The Raleigh News and Observer*, March 18, 1979. Copyright © The News and Observer. Reprinted with permission.

Southern, Terry. Terry Southern Recalls the Origins of *Dr. Strangelove*. From: "Strangelove Outtake: Notes from the War Room," Memoir, by Terry Southern from Grand Street published by Jean Stein. Reprinted by permission of the Estate of Terry Southern.

Steinbeck, John. From *The Grapes of Wrath* by John Steinbeck, copyright © 1939, renewed © 1967 by John Steinbeck. Used by permission of Viking Penguin, a division of Penguin Group (USA) Inc.

Stone, I. F. From *I. F. Stone's Weekly*, Vol. 10, No. 40 (November 5, 1962).

Terkel, Studs. *Hard Times: An Oral History of the Great Depression* by Studs Terkel, published by Pantheon. Copyright © 1970 by Studs Terkel. Reprinted by permission of Donadio & Olson, Inc.

Time magazine. "A Wartime Analysis of Selznick's Work" from *Time*, July 17, 1944. Copyright © 1944 Time, Inc. reprinted by permission.

Wanger, Walter F. "Questions for Mr. Wanger," in Walter Wanger, "The Social Significance of the American Film," Speech, University of Southern California, April 1, 1940. Reprinted by permission.

Wanger, Walter F. "An Open Letter to Franklin D. Roosevelt, President of the United States (A Broadcast by Walter F. Wanger under the Auspices of the Committee to Defend America)," August 2, 1941. Reprinted by permission.

Wanger, letter to Gardner Cowles, Jr., Office of War Information, July 30, 1942. Reprinted by permission.

Zimmerman, Paul D. "Review of *Alice's Restaurant*" by Paul D. Zimmerman from *Newsweek*, September 29, 1969. Copyright © 1999 Newsweek Inc. All rights reserved. Reprinted by permission.

Index